NEW SAT® ESSAY

✓

ADVANCED
PRACTICE SERIES

◇ For the Redesigned SAT

◇ 25 Practice Essays

◇ Over 100 Essay Writing Terms & Concepts

ies TEST PREP

Authors
Khalid Khashoggi, CEO IES
Arianna Astuni, President IES

Editorial
Patrick Kennedy, Executive Editor
Christopher Carbonell, Editorial Director
Rajvi Patel, Senior Editor

Contributors
Arianna Astuni
Danielle Barkley
Larry Bernstein
Raphael Cael
Christopher Carbonell
Sheila Choade
Crystal Eastman
Matthew Gaertner
Cynthia Helzner
Chris Holliday
Jonathan Holt
Patrick Kennedy
Khalid Khashoggi

Philip Kowalski
Gabrielle Lenhard
Joy McGillian
Derrick McQueen
Tallis Moore
Rajvi Patel
Nelson Randall
Mariel Zachs

Published by IES Publications

www.IESpublications.com

© IES Publications, 2017

ON BEHALF OF

Integrated Educational Services, Inc.

355 Main Street

Metuchen, NJ 08840

www.iestestprep.com

We would like to thank the IES Publications team as well as the teachers and students at IES Test Prep who have contributed to the creation of this book. We would also like to thank our Chief Marketing Officer, Sonia Choi, for her invaluable input.

The SAT* is a registered trademark of the College Board, which was not involved in the production of, and does not endorse, this product.

ISBN-10: 1545238286

ISBN-13: 978-1545238288

QUESTIONS OR COMMENTS? Visit us at iestestprep.com

TABLE OF CONTENTS

Introduction

Welcome 4

How to Use This Book 5

Chapter 1: Familiarize Yourself with the New SAT Essay 7

Chapter 2: Logos, Pathos, and Ethos 13

Chapter 3: Annotating 21

Chapter 4: Master of Quotation Usage 27

Chapter 5: Essay Introduction 41

Chapter 6: Logos Body Paragraph 45

Chapter 6: Logos Glossary and Exercises 51

Chapter 7: Pathos Body Paragraph 65

Chapter 7: Pathos Glossary and Exercises 71

Chapter 8: Ethos Body Paragraph 95

Chapter 8: Ethos Glossary and Exercises 101

Chapter 9: Conclusion 113

SAT Essay Vocabulary: Diversifying and Enhancing 120

Grammar and Style Mastery: Refining the SAT Essay 126

Practice Essays 1-25 141

Practice Essays: Main Idea Reference 342

Student Response: Examples and Analyses 358

Dear student,

Every day that I spend at IES is a day immersed in the world of writing. Whenever I visit one of our campuses, I encounter editors and copywriters hard at work on our next book, and students hard at work on their college application essays. But I also encounter students who are busy preparing for an SAT section that gives students a first-of-its-kind opportunity to show their skills: the SAT Essay. These students don't simply have the benefits of the methods and strategies that we have developed at IES, valuable as those are. They, moreover, have the benefit of a community of writers, editors, and instructors who can comment incisively because—for us at IES—writing is inextricable from daily life.

While this book cannot physically transport you to an IES classroom, it can impart to you many of the same advantages that enrolled IES students experience. Our SAT Essay Book is the product of much teaching, much reflection, and numerous meetings between instructors and editors. The aim was to create a volume that would be easy-to-use yet ultimately comprehensive in its approach, your one-stop resource for SAT Essay knowledge. The result is a collection of exercises, sample essays, templates, and terms—a resource that has helped our on-site students succeed, and that will lead you to similar success.

Traditionally, standardized test essays have been used to separate extraordinary students from the mass of test-takers. As it is now designed, the SAT Essay is not mandatory—but it is a must-take part of the test, if you are aiming for the best college placement possible. It is, after all, reflective of the kind of writing assignments that occur at the university level. This is an essay that you can compose with great intelligence and insight, and such aptitude will pay off both when it comes time to file your applications and when you walk into your first college class. Essay writing is second nature to us at IES; with this book to guide you, you will achieve the same comfort, the same mastery, of the written word.

Wishing you the best in your test-taking endeavors.

-Arianna Astuni, President IES

How to Use This Book

IES has reverse-engineered the Redesigned SAT Essay into three distinct areas of priority: logos, pathos, and ethos. Do not worry! These three areas will be discussed in depth as you use this workbook.

Reading and Analysis

Reading and correctly annotating the essay passage are foundational skills that are absolutely necessary for writing an impressive essay response. With this workbook, you will learn a precise and efficient technique that will guide you to both quickly and rigorously analyze the essay passage.

Then, with the same technique, you will learn how to transfer your annotations into the powerful and detailed body paragraphs that are needed to demonstrate an extensive analysis and understanding of the essay passage.

Writing

After you have mastered how to write an outstanding body paragraph, you will learn how to write an introductory paragraph that will grab the reader's attention and pen an impressive conclusion that will leave the reader wanting more.

Practice

You will find several SAT Essay passages that can be used to practice the skills in this book, a list of main ideas for each essay prompt for guidance, and student response samples and analyses.

CHAPTER ONE
FAMILIARIZE YOURSELF WITH THE NEW SAT ESSAY

ESSAY COURSE PLACEMENT

(for current IES students only | if interested in private tutoring, please visit iestestprep.com)

For the essay course, we place students based on **how much** and **what quality** ANALYSIS they did in their diagnostic essays, which in turn is based on their READING & UNDERSTANDING of the passage. This does not mean students who score high overall are placed with other students who score high overall. To call a class an "advanced" class or another "lower-level" would be a misnomer. Our goal is to provide the best instruction we can to our students, and the best way we can do that is to place students with other students who need to focus on the same skill sets. Only then can a class run smoothly; the pace and what is covered will only then be tailored to the students in that class. It is not our job to place students based on who is friends with whom, or because a student demands to be placed in a certain class. All our teachers are highly qualified and can work with a range of students, but it's a more efficient use of class time if like students are placed together. That's the only way we can come close to giving individualized attention in a classroom setting, and that means more bang for your buck!

SAT ESSAY SCORING

The SAT Essay will be scored based on the three following content dimensions:

READING: how well you understood the passage
ANALYSIS: how well you evaluated the effectiveness of the argument in the passage
WRITING: how well you conveyed your reading and analysis of the passage

Each content dimension above will be based on a score range of **1 through 4** with a composite score of **4** through **12** for your entire essay response. Two graders will grade your essay, giving you a total score out of **24**. For an in depth understanding of each score range, please consult the rubric table provided by the official College Board Blue Book.

UNDERSTANDING THE IES GRADING RUBRIC

READING (1 point each | total 4)

Does the student...

A. State the author's central idea? (found in introduction)

_____ (.5 points) Yes, the student states the correct central idea.

_____ (.5 points) Yes, the student states it clearly in one sentence.

B. Provide important details that support the central idea? (found in body paragraphs)

_____ (.5 points) Yes, the student provides a multitude of relevant details that support the author's central claim.

_____ (.5 points) Yes, the student connects the details back to the author's central claim.

C. Provide text evidence (quotations, structural location of evidence, etc...) that supports the details mentioned? (found in body paragraphs)

_____ (.5 points) Yes, the student provides enough (more than 5 instances of quote usage) text evidence to support the previously mentioned details.

_____ (.5 points) Yes, the student does not misinterpret the meaning of the quotes.

D. Refrain from personal opinion/ personal interpretation? (throughout the whole essay)

_____ (.5 points) Yes, the student does not mention personal opinions or assumptions.

_____ (.5 points) Yes, the student analyzes ONLY the information in the passage without bringing in outside information.

ANALYSIS (1 and 3 points, respectively | total 4)

Does the student...

E. Analyze the author's use of evidence? (found in body paragraphs)

_____ (1 point) Yes, the student states the evidence that the author uses.

F. Analyze the author's use of reasoning? (found in body paragraphs)

_____ (1 point) Yes, the student shows the logic that the author uses.

_____ (1 point) Yes, the student shows the effectiveness of the logical structure that the author uses.

_____ (1 point) Yes, the student shows how the evidence functions in the logic of the passage (i.e. supports argument, disproves opposition, shows opposition lacks merit/ logic, establishes context, helps supply a counterargument, etc.)

WRITING (1 point each | total 4)

Does the response have…

G. A precise thesis that explains the author's central claim? (found in introduction)

_____ (.5 points) Yes, the student wrote a precise thesis that satisfies the assignment (to show HOW the author persuaded his/her audience of his/her central claim)

_____ (.5 points) Yes, the student's thesis is precise and anticipates (and follows) the developmental structure of the essay.

H. A skillful introduction and conclusion?

_____ (.5 points) Yes, the student has a well-organized introduction.

_____ (.5 points) Yes, the student has an effective conclusion that is also not redundant.

I. A logical progression of ideas explaining how the author proves the central claim? (found in body paragraphs)

_____ (.5 points) Yes, the student has a logical progression from paragraph to paragraph.

_____ (.5 points) Yes, the student has a logical progression from sentence to sentence (idea to idea).

J. A variety in sentence structure, word choice (both free of error) and a formal/objective tone? (throughout the whole essay)

_____ (.25 points) Yes, the student has a variety in sentence structure and avoids sentence structure errors.

_____ (.25 points) Yes, the student has no errors in word choice.

_____ (.25 points) Yes, the student maintains a formal/objective tone.

_____ (.25 points) Yes, the student does not make any major spelling errors.

Final Score = Total x 2:

DO's AND DO NOT's ON THE SAT ESSAY

◊ DO analyze what you are reading and delve into the author's meaning and examples

◊ DO annotate as you read (extract the author's main idea, logos, pathos, and ethos)

◊ DO vary sentence structure

◊ DO vary word choice and use appropriate vocabulary (example: nefarious vs. harmful)

◊ DO agree with the author's point of view

◊ DO use textual evidence

◊ DO aim for a 5-paragraph essay (since these are the ones that receive the highest scores!)

◊ DO aim to fill all the space allotted with writing

◊ DO **NOT** give any personal opinions (they are irrelevant)

◊ DO **NOT** use outside knowledge or material (everything in your essay should be from the text)

◊ DO **NOT** rush reading through the passage (reading, understanding, and analyzing the passage is just as important as what you write)

1

TURN TO NEXT PAGE FOR CHAPTER 2

CHAPTER TWO
LOGOS, PATHOS, & ETHOS

LOGOS

Logos is the first of the major persuasive or rhetorical methods that you will need to consider. In some ways, logos is an accessible concept: the word "logos" itself can be readily translated as "logic." Indeed, logos should be understood primarily as logic or reasoning. Without a firm basis in logos, an essay will often be fundamentally unconvincing or incoherent.

However, logos can occur in several different forms. Concrete examples, cause-and-effect analysis, cost-benefit analysis, statistics, specialized terminology, and clarifying analogies are but a few types of logos that you will encounter in studying the SAT Essay.

← ex of how authors use logos

You will undoubtedly come across paragraphs and excerpts that are heavy on the versions of logos listed above. Yet logos plays a further role in many SAT Essay passages: it is the rhetorical device that often structures an essay AS A WHOLE. The authors chosen by the College Board tend to build toward their conclusions gradually and logically, so if you see logos guiding the total structure of an essay, keep this fact in mind when you go to write your analysis.

QUICK TIP: It is possible that some essays may not use perfect logic by your own standards. If this is the case, read for logos by finding the MOST effective logos examples, or by trying to understand why the essay is logical from the author's perspective. Remember, do not undermine the essay task by arguing against the author.

SAMPLE LOGOS EXCERPTS

1) *At present, raising interests rates—or even suggesting that interest rates will be raised—is liable to send shockwaves through the economy. Federal Reserve Chair Jan Yellen suggested last Thursday that a slight rate hike would be coming; major stock indexes declined immediately, with the Nasdaq posting a loss of 2.39 percent and the Dow Jones Industrial Average posting a loss of 1.87 percent. But on Monday, when Yellen reversed course and suggested that rates would stay the same for the foreseeable future, the markets breathed a sigh of relief and reversed course. Both the Nasdaq and the Dow climbed by at least 1.50 percent.*

2) *Statistics show that even our basic human relationships are migrating online. In 2014, over half of Americans were using websites as their primary means of finding new friendships and relationships: a new paper from the Georgetown Department of Sociology indicates that this figure will increase to four out of every five Americans by 2020. Unfortunately, this online mentality has led to a mentality of paranoia and distrust that has been termed "connected disconnect": a feeling that you have a large number of ever-present yet fundamentally meaningless relationships.*

CHAPTER TWO
LOGOS, PATHOS, & ETHOS

3) *The idea that Grosvenor Lake was a hotbed of pre-historic life was resoundingly validated in 1995. That year, an adventurous fifth-grader named Rennie Stewart found three fossils that, in his words, looked "a bit like centipedes and a bit like horseshoe crabs." He showed these fossils to his father, who consulted a local museum: it turned out that the fossils were left by trilobites, marine arthropods that had gone extinct hundreds of millions of years ago. A subsequent expedition by graduate students from nearby Trennor University unearthed yet more trilobite fossils.*

PATHOS

Pathos involves appealing to an audience's emotions; the point of this tactic is to guide or manipulate how the audience feels about a specific topic, mostly in order to make the author's ideas more appealing. Pride, sadness, anger, and optimism are but a few of the emotions that an author with a strong command of pathos will know how to conjure. Even humor—which tends to serve few purposes other than winning a reader over or making a writer's personality more vivid—can become a potent form of pathos on the SAT.

Although uses of pathos can be striking, the most successful instances tend to be carefully engineered. A skilled author will know how to engineer a story, example, or instance of personal testimony to convey an extremely specific emotion. While completing the SAT Essay, you may see an entire paragraph, or an entire extended anecdote, that is designed to make the author's audience feel a certain way or (in a highly emotional manner) to sympathize with a certain side. These are strong uses of pathos that are BUILT INTO an author's evidence.

Pathos also operates on the level of style and word choice. Dramatic vocabulary, sensory imagery, humor, and repetition for emphasis do not really serve any logical purpose in an essay. They DO appeal to a reader's emotions. If you see any of these devices, classify them readily as instances of pathos.

SAMPLE PATHOS EXCERPTS

1) *Envision this: you wake up, startled out of your sleep by an unfamiliar crackling noise. You look around, and see the homes nearby engulfed in vicious orange flames. You cry out for help, but your family is nowhere in sight; they have fled, a motley mix of distant neighbors and complete strangers throngs past, and merciless clouds of smoke choke your lungs and bring tears of hopelessness to your eyes. We humans only know scenes such as this from our worst wars. Yet for today's orangutans, whose homes are rapidly falling to deforestation, such scenes are a common, almost everyday part of life.*

2) *The truth hit me like a freight train: What had I been doing with my life, with the one precious existence I had been given on this great earth? I'd spent years reading about heroic figures—Greek gods, Roman generals, Renaissance aristocrats—but here I was plunking away in a library, watching my eyesight go bad and my muscles turn to goo. This paralysis had lasted too much, too long. I needed to turn everything around. I would get out and reclaim my dignity as a human being; I would show the world that my lifetime of reading had inspired me to live boldly, daringly, fearlessly. At the very least, I'd start going to the gym.*

3) *So I looked, and what did I see? Out there, gathered in that high school gymnasium, were parents, grandparents, aunts, uncles, brothers, sisters, close friends, distant relatives—all of them waiting. Their community had been battered, buffeted back and forth like a small boat in a stormy sea. But they were undaunted. The glimmers of their eyes told me that they were ready to look past the sorrows of yesterday and build, effort by effort, piece by piece, the edifice of a brighter tomorrow.*

ETHOS

Ethos is the appeal to an audience that involves an author's credibility. Naturally, an author would want to appear trustworthy and personally appealing—whether by providing qualifications and other proofs of expertise, by taking a proactive and confidence-inspiring approach, or by professing strong moral standards. Indeed, word "ethos" is linked to the English term "ethics."

On the SAT, locating ethos can sometimes be quite easy. Sentences that begin with "As a specialist in . . . ", "During my time in . . .", or some comparable phrase signal the author's background and credibility in a rather obvious manner. Annotate them immediately and prepare to analyze them in terms of ethos.

However, an author's uses of ethos may not always be so obvious; if you do NOT find easy verbal cues of the type noted above, you will need to think about the more subtle, between-the-lines forms of ethos that an author is employing. For instance, if an author constantly provides highly technical terms or highly specialized information WITHOUT providing his or her credentials, the author is still using strong ethos by demonstrating his or her comfort with specialized material. Similarly, if an author appeals to a strong set of moral principles—even without referring to his or her life—then that author is using a powerful form of ethos

SAMPLE ETHOS EXCERPTS

1) *Since 1997, I have served as a consultant to startups in a variety of industries that rely not on services but on the production of tangible goods, from aspiring pet food brands to makers of artisanal candles. To my dismay, too many of the entrepreneurs behind these budding companies do not understand their own supply chains. Commodity prices, international sales, even basic cash flow—these concepts are beyond them. As the founder of one small leather goods company recently told me, "I know how to make gloves and how to advertise my gloves. The rest is Greek to me."*

2) *I am going to say what, frankly, nobody else in this labor union has the courage to say: nothing, from here on out, is going to be easy. And yet, I embrace the struggle that is ahead, because as history has proven time and time again, only struggle can ensure progress of the kind that we have dedicated ourselves to. Compared to what we have been through together in the past two decades, the next few years may seem infinitely more taxing. Yet to accept this burden is to do right by everything we believe.*

3) *What most people call "sea cucumbers" are more scientifically known as echinoderms, members of the class Holothuroidea. Often, we marine zoologists study them alongside somewhat better-known echinoderms such as starfish and sea urchins, although the process of studying these animals is not entirely similar. Sea cucumbers are much more fragile than their fellow echinoderms, so that they cannot be handled easily, and can also react much more poorly to changes in the temperature and salinity (or salt concentration) of the water in their storage tanks.*

author setting himself apart from "most people"

classifies himself as marine zoologist

EXERCISE

Directions: **Label** *each paragraph as Pathos, Logos, or Ethos.*
Briefly explain **why**.

1) _Logos_

If the student does not improve her vocabulary, she will continue to get almost all of the highest level (level 4 and 5) questions wrong in sentence completion (as these utilize the hardest vocabulary and most complicated logic). This will translate to her critical reading score in that she will not likely break 650, or even 600, since it will mean she will get a minimum of about 2 to 3 wrong in every sentence completion section due solely to an inadequate vocabulary. (There are 3 critical reading sections on every test.) Remember, this is only an estimate of how many she may get wrong in sentence completion only; she may also get some wrong in the reading comprehension passages that follow the sentence completions in every section, further reducing her chance of reaching 600. She must improve her vocabulary skills in order to reach her goal score; there's no way around it.

EXPLAIN: A logic, sequential excerpt is shown. The author explains the need for an improved vocabulary & explains the effects if one doesn't attain a vocabulary mastery in a logical manner.

2) _Pathos_

Fear and anxiety are this test's greatest allies. However, you cannot cower and tremble before it. Accepting that you feel fear and anxiety is not the same as expecting that you'll feel fear and anxiety. Your acceptation of those feelings will more than likely reduce their ferocity. But your expectation of feeling these things will increase their intensity and give these feelings more power than they deserve. Take back that power! And learn to control the test so that, on test day, you're the boss, not these feelings that are swirling around in your head, causing your hands to sweat and your knees to shake. I know, as well as you, that this test is far from trivial, but it also doesn't determine who you are, who you're going to be, and what you can (and will) accomplish in life. It is just a test, albeit a somewhat important one.

EXPLAIN: Appeals to readers emotions through use of 2and person pos & dramatic vocabulary to emphasize overall message

3) Ethos

I'm not going to ask you to believe me or even trust me. I don't need to. All I need to do is tell you that I've been doing this for almost a decade and that I have a long list of students who will testify to my abilities. I've learned not only every nuance and twist this test has but also how to maneuver through these. I've learned these tricks so well that I can even mimic them. I promise, you don't have to be a genius or even a straight-A student to master this test. All you need is a reasonable degree of competency in reading comprehension, which you will bring with you to class, and familiarity with the subtleties of the test, which you will leave this class with. Beyond that, it's just a matter of execution.

EXPLAIN: establishes credibility by stating "ive been doing this for a decade". continues to state that he/she has mastered/understood every part of the job due to their time & experience in it.

TURN TO NEXT PAGE FOR CHAPTER 3

CHAPTER THREE
ANNOTATING

EXTRACTING THE MAIN IDEA

As you read the passage below, consider how the author uses

◇ evidence, such as facts or examples, to support claims.
◇ reasoning to develop ideas and connect claims and evidence.
◇ stylistic or persuasive elements, such as word choice or appeals to emotion, to add power to the ideas expressed.

Adapted from Gabrielle Lenhard's "An America Hungry for Change." Lenhard is an urban sociologist.

1 Imagine a child arriving home for dinner to find a tub of Kentucky Fried Chicken on the table, rather than a home cooked meal with plenty of fruits and vegetables. And this occurs three times a week on average. Imagine living in a community where a raw cantaloupe could be considered exotic for its scarcity. For many geographic areas in the United States with limited access to fresh and nutritious food, the fried chicken phenomenon is a reality. Yet even the biggest fans of KFC need a balanced diet.

2 The USA Department of Agriculture has termed areas such as these "food deserts." More than 29.7 million Americans currently live in neighborhoods that qualify as food deserts, where fast food restaurants and convenience stores are the nearest, and primary, options for nourishment. My consulting and research company, Mari Gallagher, labels these as "fringe retailers." Resulting diets are high in sugar, fat, and salt—the calling card of processed comestibles. Community and health organizations, like mine, are searching for ways to improve the diets of America's food deserts in an effort to eliminate the high levels of obesity and chronic diseases that they foster.

3 The circumstances hindering the residents of food deserts are unique in each community. The distance of a mile or two in an urban area that relies heavily upon public transportation is more comparable to the distance of 10 miles in a rural community. While an overwhelming number of qualifying sites are low income, factors such as education, ethnicity, and dietary restrictions must also be taken into account. Thus, proposing broad solutions to the problem of inadequate nutrition is quite complex and challenging.

4 The 2011 presidential budget requested over 400 million dollars for a Healthy Food Financing Initiative (HFFI) to be launched. This program aims to open supermarkets and wholesome food retailers in food deserts across the nation. In addition to providing fresh food to nutritionally starved areas, the program purports that supermarkets can stimulate the economy of a disadvantaged area by creating jobs, fostering surrounding retail, and making the area more attractive to investors. In 2010, the neighborhood supermarket shut its doors in Highland Falls, New York. The town supported a weekly bus service to the nearest equivalent merchant 11 miles away as an alternative to the discontinued resource and fringe retailers. With financing from HFFI, a local couple was able to re-open the abandoned store, with

16,000 square feet of new or improved produce vending space—creating 27 jobs. Highland Falls is just one example of the many success stories that this government initiative boasts since its inception.

5 Yet, research does not firmly suggest that establishing a new grocery store in a food desert will change the diets of those people living in it. A study conducted by population health professor, Steven Cummins, observed the population of a food desert in Philadelphia after a new supermarket was opened. The study showed no changes in BMI's (body mass index) or the consumption levels of produce, and participants did not switch to better provisions. Rather, the community perception of access to food was changed; inhabitants had the sense that their area had improved.

6 There is limited data analyzing the effectiveness of implementing new retailers in food deserts, and Professor Cummins' study only examined one Philadelphia location for a period of 6 months. Meanwhile, an abundance of information links chronic conditions and a nutritionally challenged diet to those living in food deserts. It's possible that policy makers jumped to address a very real problem with a solution ill-tested for success. But one thing is clear. People have heavily ingrained eating and food shopping habits, and more than one measure will be needed to initiate change.

7 Citizens seeking to initiate their own change may help fill the gaps between fresh food availability and affordability. Community farms and gardens provide one method of augmenting diets in disadvantaged, urban areas with the nutrients that fringe retailers do not. The Shawnee area of Louisville, Kentucky has hosted The People's Garden since 2011, an outpost of the local non-profit Louisville Grows. The organization has produced more than 3,000 pounds of produce to be circulated amongst local markets since 2012. Farms like these viscerally connect individuals to the foods that they are eating, inviting them to be active, educated participants in the process of food arriving on the dinner table.

8 With hope, homegrown initiatives can supplement government programs, satisfying a need for community specific solutions and helping to alleviate America's hankering for healthy options.

Write an essay in which you explain how the author builds an argument to persuade the audience that government health assisted programs are insufficient in providing quality nutrition. In your essay, analyze how the author uses one or more of the features listed in the box above (or features of your own choice) to strengthen the logic and persuasiveness of his argument. Be sure that your essay focuses on the most relevant features of the passage.

Your essay should not explain whether you agree with the author's claims, but rather explain how the author builds an argument to persuade the audience.

The **Main Idea** is found in the first sentence of the 2nd box. It always follows the words, *"builds an argument to persuade [his/her] audience that..."*

Take note of this **Main Idea** either by circling or underlining it.

It's helpful to know the **Main Idea** BEFORE you begin reading the passage so that you will know what to look for while annotating.

TIME TO ANNOTATE

Note: Annotating is a crucial step and should NOT be taken lightly. An annotated essay is generally more organized and ensures that you will not miss key points in the text.

When you are annotating, you are focusing on HOW the author proved his or her argument. Take note of the STRUCTURE of the argument.

Ask yourself these questions as you are annotate:

For **LOGOS:**

◊ How does the author set up the context of his or her argument?
◊ Does the author use facts/statistics? AND for what purpose? (i.e. to establish a problem, to discredit the opposition, etc.)
◊ Does the author provide a solution? AND does the author give drawbacks to certain solutions?
◊ Does the author address any counterarguments? How?
◊ How does the author ultimately conclude his/her argument? What is the final push?

For **PATHOS:**

◊ What rhetorical devices does the author use? (i.e. anecdotes, repetition, parallel structure, hyperbole, etc.)
◊ Does the author use specific word choice to strengthen his/her argument? (i.e. negatively charged words for certain concepts and/or positively charged words for certain concepts)

For **ETHOS:**

◊ What does the author do to establish his or her credibility?

 Remember: You are annotating **once over** for **all three**: Logos, Pathos, & Ethos.

 QUICK TIP: Annotate for **LOGOS** so that you can understand the **primary structure** of the argument, and as you come across PATHOS and ETHOS, take note. This approach will ensure that you *annotate efficiently and with purpose* since you do not have the time to go back and reread the passage.

③

OVERVIEW
THE ADVANCED STUDENT'S ANNOTATED ESSAY

Below is an example of what you are aiming to accomplish when reading and annotating the essay passage after extracting the main idea. As you can see, there are plenty of notes in the margins of the passage. The test provides plenty of margin space for you to write your notes while you annotate.

As you read the passage below, consider how the author uses

◇ evidence, such as facts or examples, to support claims.
◇ reasoning to develop ideas and connect claims and evidence.
◇ stylistic or persuasive elements, such as word choice or appeals to emotion, to add power to the ideas expressed.

Adapted from Gabrielle Lenhard's "An America Hungry for Change." Lenhard is an urban sociologist.

PATHOS — *presents hypothetical scenario to pull reader in*

1 Imagine a child arriving home for dinner to find a tub of Kentucky Fried Chicken on the table, rather than a home cooked meal with plenty of fruits and vegetables. And this occurs three times a week on average. Imagine living in a community where a raw cantaloupe could be considered exotic for its scarcity. For many geographic areas in the United States with limited access to fresh and nutritious food, the fried chicken phenomenon is a reality. Yet even the biggest fans of KFC need a balanced diet. *hook*

LOGOS — *gives a # that's hard to ignore*

2 The USA Department of Agriculture has termed areas such as these "food deserts." More than 29.7 million Americans currently live in neighborhoods that qualify as food deserts, where fast food restaurants and convenience stores are the nearest, and primary, options for nourishment. My consulting and research company, Mari Gallagher, labels these as "fringe retailers." Resulting diets are high in sugar, fat and salt—the calling card of processed comestibles. Community and health organizations, like mine, are searching for ways to improve the diets of America's food deserts in an effort to eliminate the high levels of obesity and chronic diseases that they foster. *Ethos*

referring terminology — **PATHOS** *definition* **ETHOS**

LOGOS — *shows the complexity of the problem*

3 The circumstances hindering the residents of food deserts are unique in each community. The distance of a mile or two in an urban area that relies heavily upon public transportation is more comparable to the distance of 10 miles in a rural community. While an overwhelming number of qualifying sites are low income, factors such as education, ethnicity, and dietary restrictions must also be taken into account. Thus, proposing broad solutions to the problem of inadequate nutrition is quite complex and challenging.

LOGOS — *one proposed solution* ↑ *benefits of solution*

4 The 2011 presidential budget requested over 400 million dollars for a Healthy Food Financing Initiative (HFFI) to be launched. This program aims to open supermarkets and wholesome food retailers in food deserts across the nation. In addition to providing fresh food to nutritionally starved areas, the program purports that supermarkets can stimulate the economy of a disadvantaged area by creating jobs, fostering surrounding retail, and making the area more attractive to investors. In 2010, the neighborhood supermarket shut its doors in Highland Falls, New York. The town supported a weekly bus service to the nearest equivalent merchant 11 miles away as an alternative to the discontinued resource and fringe retailers. With financing from HFFI, a local couple was able to re-open the abandoned store, with

2

16,000 square feet of new or improved produce vending space—creating 27 jobs. Highland Falls is just one example of the many success stories that this government initiative boasts since its inception.

5   Yet, research does not firmly suggest that establishing a new grocery store in a food desert will change the diets of those people living in it. A study conducted by population health professor, Steven Cummins, observed the population of a food desert in Philadelphia after a new supermarket was opened. The study showed no changes in BMI's (body mass index) or the consumption levels of produce, and participants did not switch to better provisions. Rather, the community perception of access to food was changed; inhabitants had the sense that their area had improved.

6   There is limited data analyzing the effectiveness of implementing new retailers in food deserts, and Professor Cummins' study only examined one Philadelphia location for a period of 6 months. Meanwhile, an abundance of information links chronic conditions and a nutritionally challenged diet to those living in food deserts. It's possible that policy makers jumped to address a very real problem with a solution ill-tested for success. But one thing is clear. People have heavily ingrained eating and food shopping habits, and more than one measure will be needed to initiate change.

7   Citizens seeking to initiate their own change may help fill the gaps between fresh food availability and affordability. Community farms and gardens provide one method of augmenting diets in disadvantaged, urban areas with the nutrients that fringe retailers do not. The Shawnee area of Louisville, Kentucky has hosted The People's Garden since 2011, an outpost of the local non-profit Louisville Grows. The organization has produced more than 3,000 pounds of produce to be circulated amongst local markets since 2012. Farms like these viscerally connect individuals to the foods that they are eating, inviting them to be active, educated participants in the process of food arriving on the dinner table.

8   With hope, homegrown initiatives can supplement government programs, satisfying a need for community specific solutions and helping to alleviate America's hankering for healthy options.

LOGOS *(handwritten margin annotation: "drawbacks of solution")*

(handwritten margin annotation: "why Sweson did not agree")

LOGOS *(handwritten margin annotation: "real solution")*

(handwritten margin annotation: "evidence of")

PATHOS *(handwritten margin annotation: "word choice")*

Write an essay in which you explain how the author builds an argument to persuade the audience that government health assisted programs are insufficient in providing quality nutrition. In your essay, analyze how the author uses one or more of the features listed in the box above (or features of your own choice) to strengthen the logic and persuasiveness of his argument. Be sure that your essay focuses on the most relevant features of the passage.

Your essay should not explain whether you agree with the author's claims, but rather explain how the author builds an argument to persuade the audience.

3

MAIN IDEA

3

TURN TO NEXT PAGE FOR CHAPTER 4

TURN TO NEXT PAGE FOR CHAPTER 4

CHAPTER FOUR
MASTERY OF QUOTATION USAGE

INCORPORATING PASSAGE QUOTATIONS

The SAT Essay will require you to consistently and at times aggressively quote the passage prompts. However, as you are doing so, you must avoid two dangers:

1) **Placing a quotation alone as a stand-alone sentence**

2) **Formatting a quotation as an incomplete sentence**

Fortunately, the **ways to avoid** these pitfalls are extremely simple and straightforward.

◊ You could use a complete sentence and a colon to introduce the quotation. Simply create a sentence that anticipates the quotation's content or significance in some form, end the sentence in a colon, and place the full quotation after.

 QUICK TIP: Do NOT assume that you can use a semicolon to introduce a full-sentence quotation. Semicolons and colons cannot be used interchangeably in this respect; employing a colon properly sets up the evidence.

> Example:
>
> *But she doesn't leave the reader hanging at this point; she provides an answer to the problem: "With hope, homegrown initiatives can supplement government programs."*

◊ You can use a **phrase** that sets up the content of the quotation, either by simply introducing the topic of the quotation or by briefly explaining its context. Separate this phrase from the quotation with a comma. Two different phrases of this sort will call for comma usage:

A) **Short introductory phrases** include "According to the author," "In the author's opinion," or "As the author explains." Place a comma immediately after a phrase of this sort, then immediately supply the quotation.

B) **Phrases ending in verbs** describes actions performed by the author in making a point or presenting an argument: "states," "explains," "argues," "posits," "muses," and other verbs that describe what the author does in the course of the passage are common in this case. If you use a structure of this sort to set up a quotation, place a comma immediately after the verb, then supply the quotation.

Example:

As Lenhard speculates early in her essay, "imagine living in a community where a raw cantaloupe could be considered exotic for its scarcity."

◊ You can make the quotation flow together with the rest of your sentence by using transitions. Simply follow the general advice for the previous rule, but use the word "that" to replace the comma that normally offsets the quotation. Perhaps you are writing a sentence about what the "author claims". You could use the phrase "the author claims," follow this phrase with a comma, and place the quotation right after. Or you could use the phrase "the author claims that" and lead right into the quotation without a comma.

Example:

Lenhard's purpose for delineating these factors is simple: it's to show that "proposing broad solutions to the problem" may not be the path to take.

◊ You can quote small yet important phrases from the passage and incorporate them into your own, longer sentence. Quotation marks are absolutely necessary for the content that you are quoting in such cases, even if each quotation is only a few words long. However, no other special punctuation (such as the special commas in the cases above) is needed. Simply punctuate the rest of the sentence as though all the words are your own.

Example:

Lenhard expands the imagery from something so specific as one home, to the whole "community."

USING AN ELLIPSIS

An ellipsis (plural: ellipses) is typically employed to show that you have omitted a portion of a quotation. Ellipses can be used for a **few different reasons**:

1) **To shorten a quotation for the sake of writing speed and efficiency**
2) **To pinpoint two distant yet related points in a longer quotation**
3) **To quickly eliminate long transitions or other inessential phrases**

However, do NOT under any circumstances treat an ellipsis as a way of modifying the author's meaning. You must still quote the author's opinion accurately; ellipses are designed ONLY to make content more manageable. You MUST maintain the integrity of the text.

Otherwise, an ellipsis can be used fairly flexibly. It can factor out the middle portions of one sentence, or factor out content that divides two sentences that are linked in a clear way. Yet however you choose to use ellipses, you MUST make sure that the content before and after the ellipsis reads like a single, seamless thought—in other words, like a coherent and grammatically correct sentence.

Example:

Lenhard concludes that because "people have heavily ingrained eating and food shopping habits...more than one measure will be needed to initiate change."

USING BRACKETS

1) Brackets are typically used to make minor yet necessary changes that involve formatting explanations of content. They explain essentials but NEVER change the meaning of a sentence. A set of brackets may contain a clarification of a point that would otherwise remain unclear or awkwardly worded in context.

> Example:
>
> *This shows that her company, herself included, is working "in an effort to eliminate the high levels of obesity and chronic diseases that [food deserts] foster."*

2) Brackets may also be used to establish stylistic consistency through changes to pronouns and verb tense. One common use is changing an author's direct testimony ("I" constructions) into a smooth third-person sentence.

> Example:
>
> *Lenhard states in her final paragraphs that "despite [her] many reservations, [she is] convinced that food reformers have no choice but to redouble their efforts."*

QUOTES PER PARAGRAPH: HOW MANY?

When writing your essay, you must incorporate quotes into your writing. This does not necessarily mean FULL QUOTES (in fact, it's better to break up the quotes and use bits and pieces seamlessly in your writing, as this approach shows a better command of quotation usage).

As you've read above, there are many ways to incorporate quotes. Remember, it is our job to equip you with every trick we know to get you the best possible score.

Here are the general guidelines:

Paragraph Instances of Quote Usage

Introduction	1 quote (the hook)
Logos Body Paragraph	3 to 4 quotes
Pathos Body Paragraph	2 to 3 quotes
Ethos Body Paragraph	1 to 2 quotes
Conclusion	1 to 2 quotes

As long as you have this many instances of QUOTE USAGE (which can mean just one or two words in quotes or whole phrases or sentences in quotes), you can count on getting the full points allotted for showing a mastery of quotation usage.

EXERCISES: QUOTATION MASTERY

EXERCISE 1:

DIRECTIONS: Circle the error in the sentence, and write the error type and the correct phrasing on the lines below.

Example

Early on in the essay, the author explains to all of his readers that—"nobody is perfect". ✗

TRANSITION INTO QUOTATION ERROR: *that "nobody* ✓

1) The essay's claims are based on a process that the author calls, symbiotic learning, and which is defined at length in the early paragraphs.

ERROR TYPE: _use of commas & need for " "_ CORRECT PHRASING: _author calls "symbiotic learning" &_

2) According to Clampitt: "it is undeniable that wind turbines are thought to be unsightly."

ERROR TYPE: _improper colon use_ CORRECT PHRASING: _According to clampitt, " ..._

3) In the final portions of the essay, Chris Holliday states that "Philip Larkin . . . ultimately an exceptional poet."

ERROR TYPE: _illogical use of ellipses_ CORRECT PHRASING: _more info/words needed_

4) Later, Littenberg explains "we have no reason for broad-based legal reforms."

ERROR TYPE: _comma use_ CORRECT PHRASING: _explains, "we have..."_

5) Here, the author states her contention clearly; "any use of performance-enhancing drugs, at all, is an insult to professional athletics."

ERROR TYPE: _improper use of semicolon_ CORRECT PHRASING: _clearly: "any use..."_

6) Dominic Henri claims, that "few people would be willing to let themselves be insulted so repeatedly."

ERROR TYPE: _Extra comma_ CORRECT PHRASING: _claims that_

7) The author introduces an idea called "close listening, which she contrasts with a second idea, distant listening.

ERROR TYPE: _need to close quote_ CORRECT PHRASING: _"close listening"_

8) In light of these factors, Spiegel explains; "there is no reason to distrust the FCC."

ERROR TYPE: _Extra semicolon (need only comma)_ CORRECT PHRASING: _Spiegel explains, "There..._

9) "[What are we meant to do in such cases?]" asks the author in a moment of desperation.

ERROR TYPE: _improper bracket use_ CORRECT PHRASING: _"what are we meant to do in such cases?"_

10) It is Romanovich's belief that: "government spending is not the true problem by any means."

ERROR TYPE: _no need for colon_ CORRECT PHRASING: _belief that "government..._

EXERCISE 2:

DIRECTIONS: Read each short excerpt, then use a quotation or multiple quotations from it in a sentence that fulfills the designated requirements. (If needed, simply refer to the author of each excerpt as "the author.")

Example

> EXCERPT: Nobody is perfect, not even today's self-made billionaires.
>
> REQUIREMENT: Introduce the quotation using "that."
>
> YOUR SENTENCE: The author sets out to convince his readers that "Nobody is perfect, not even today's self-made billionaires."

1) I simply cannot accept a position that goes against all of my principles as a woman.

Requirement: USE BRACKETS TO CHANGE TO THIRD PERSON.

YOUR SENTENCE: The author states "[she] simply cannot accept a position that goes against of [her] principles as a woman."

2) We need to do more to give children access to interactive math and science software.

Requirement: INTRODUCE A QUOTATION USING A COLON.

YOUR SENTENCE: The author continues arguing her point: "we need to do more to give children access to interactives math & science software."

3) As a result of the year I spent in Berlin, which was an enjoyable experience but one that I will probably never reproduce, I gained a better understanding of how youth hostels operate.

Requirement: USE AN ELLIPSIS.

YOUR SENTENCE: The author summarizes her experience abroad by stating "As a result of the yr I spent in Berlin, I gained a better understanding of how youth hostels operate."

4) There is no point in continuing an argument that has gone on unresolved for fifty-five years.

Requirement: OPEN WITH A SHORT EXPLANATORY PHRASE (NO VERB).

YOUR SENTENCE: According to the author, "There is no point in continuing an argument that has gone on unresolved for 50 yrs."

5) The world of corporate philanthropy is more efficient than most people believe.

Requirement: OPEN WITH A SHORT EXPLANATORY PHRASE (USING A VERB).

YOUR SENTENCE: As concluded by the author, "the world of corporate philanthropy is more efficient than most people believe."

6) Shape and color suddenly became important to artists once again.

Requirement: INTRODUCE A QUOTATION USING "THAT."

YOUR SENTENCE: The author claims that shape & color became important to artists once again.

7) It is evident that, unless we start holding federal judges to higher standards, our standards of legal discretion will only continue to suffer.

Requirement: USE AN ELLIPSIS.

YOUR SENTENCE: The author argues "It is evident ... our standards of legal discretion will only continue to suffer."

8) While I would define the former as an instance of empty theorizing, I would argue that the latter is an instance of meaningful theorizing and is therefore sociologically valid.

Requirement: PLACE SMALL QUOTATIONS WITHIN A SENTENCE OF YOUR OWN.

YOUR SENTENCE: The author strengthens his stance by stating "while I would define the former as... empty theorizing... I would argue that the latter is... meaningful theorizing ...therefore sociologically valid."

9) Could Japanese civilization have developed an entirely different writing technology?

Requirement: INTRODUCE A QUOTATION USING A COLON.

YOUR SENTENCE: The author ponders upon his idea by asking a rhetorical question: "could Japanes

10) Unless we come together, we will be unable to cure this plague on environmental policy.

Requirement: INTRODUCE A QUOTATION USING "THAT."

YOUR SENTENCE: The author concludes the passage by emphasizing that "unless we come together, we will be unable to cure this plague on environmental policy."

④ ANSWERS: QUOTATION MASTERY

EXERCISE 1: ANSWERS

1) The essay's claims are based on a process that the author **calls "symbiotic learning" and** which is defined at length in the early paragraphs.

ERROR TYPE: Punctuation for short quotations

2) According to **Clampitt, "it** is undeniable that wind turbines are thought to be unsightly."

ERROR TYPE: Transition into quotation

3) In the final portions of the essay, Chris Holliday states that "Philip Larkin **. . . is ultimately** an exceptional poet."

ERROR TYPE: Using an ellipsis

4) Later, Littenberg **explains, "we** have no reason for broad-based legal reforms."

ERROR TYPE: TRANSITION INTO QUOTATION

5) Here, the author states her contention **clearly: "any** use of performance-enhancing drugs, at all, is an insult to professional athletics."

ERROR TYPE: TRANSITION INTO QUOTATION

6) Dominic Henri **claims that "few** people would be willing to let themselves be insulted so repeatedly."

ERROR TYPE: TRANSITION INTO QUOTATION

7) The author introduces an idea called "**close listening," which** she contrasts with a second **idea, "distant listening."**

ERROR TYPE: PUNCTUATION FOR SHORT QUOTATIONS

8) In light of these factors, Spiegel **explains, "there** is no reason to distrust the FCC."

ERROR TYPE: TRANSITION INTO QUOTATION

9) **"What are we meant to do in such cases?" asks** the author in a moment of desperation.

ERROR TYPE: USE OF BRACKETS

10) It is Romanovich's belief **that "government** spending is not the true problem by any means."

Error Type: Transition into quotation

Exercise 2: Possible Answers

1) The author declares that "[she] simply cannot accept a position that goes against all of [her] principles as a woman."

2) Indeed, the author takes a strong stance on education: "We need to do more to give children access to interactive math and science software."

3) The author explains that "As a result of the year I spent in Berlin . . . I gained a better understanding of how youth hostels operate."

4) In the author's opinion, "There is no point in continuing an argument that has gone on unresolved for fifty-five years."

5) Thus, the author proclaims, "The world of corporate philanthropy is more efficient than most people believe."

6) The author clearly demonstrates that "Shape and color suddenly became important to artists once again."

7) As the author emphasizes, "It is evident that . . . our standards of legal discretion will only continue to suffer.

8) The author defines "the former as an instance of empty theorizing," yet is convinced "that the latter is an instance of meaningful theorizing" that the reader should understand as "sociologically valid."

9) This discussion concludes with a pointed question: "Could Japanese civilization have developed an entirely different writing technology?"

10) To combine the different strands of the argument, the author asserts that "Unless we come together, we will be unable to cure this plague on environmental policy."

4

TURN TO NEXT PAGE FOR CHAPTER 5

CHAPTER FIVE
ESSAY INTRODUCTION

THE HOOK

The hook is the first sentence of your essay. It should be a sentence that grabs the reader's attention. Coming up with a hook of your own can be tricky. In order to simplify the process, we have come up with a solution: pick a profound, interesting, funny, or engaging sentence right from the passage. This way, you're not using up precious minutes to come up with something on your own.

QUICK TIP: To save even more time, find your hook while you are annotating.

Example:

"Yet even the biggest fans of KFC need a balanced diet."

EXPLANATORY SENTENCE FOR HOOK & INTRODUCTION OF THE AUTHOR

The explanatory sentence for your hook is the sentence that will follow your hook. As the title suggests, it explains your hook. However, this sentence does double duty. It not only explains the relevance of the hook, but also introduces the author.

Example:

Here, Gabrielle Lenhard emphasizes the need for nutritious meals, no matter how much one may love the unhealthy alternative.

INTRODUCTION OF THE PASSAGE & AUTHOR'S ARGUMENT

The next sentence is the one in which you must introduce both the title of the passage and the main idea. This sentence is extremely important and must not be worded incorrectly. In order to avoid any misinterpretation, we suggest taking the main idea directly from the second prompt box, verbatim.

> **Example:**
>
> *In her essay, "An America Hungry for Change," Lenhard persuades her audience that government health assisted programs are insufficient in providing quality nutrition.*

THESIS

Now, it's time to finally write your thesis. This is the most important sentence of your essay, and must be written with care and precision. Your thesis is not what the author is proving; rather, it's **how** the author proves it. You must address Logos, Pathos, and Ethos in your thesis.

> **Example:**
>
> *She proves this by appealing to the audience through the use of facts and statistics, including the drawbacks to proposed solutions, and using purposeful language, all the while maintaining a credible account.*

Now, BRING IT ALL TOGETHER!

"Yet even the biggest fans of KFC need a balanced diet." Here, Gabrielle Lenhard emphasizes the need for nutritious meals, no matter how much one may love the unhealthy alternative. In her essay, "An America Hungry for Change," Lenhard persuades her audience that government health assisted programs are insufficient in providing quality nutrition. She proves this by appealing to the audience through the use of facts and statistics, including the drawbacks to proposed solutions, and using purposeful language, all the while maintaining a credible account.

⑤INTRODUCTION TEMPLATE

If you are still uncertain about how to write an introduction to the SAT Essay, we have included a simple template that you can follow. You just have to fill in the blanks! This template will work for MOST passages; even if you find that you need to modify it, do not change the overall structure and order of the sentences, as this is the most logical and effective organization for the introduction.

Note: please be mindful of the author's gender which is specified in the 2nd prompt box.

INTRODUCTION

[HOOK QUOTATION_____] Here, [AUTHOR] emphasizes the need for [THEME OF ESSAY_____], no matter how much one may [ALTERNATIVE TO THEME_____]. In [his or her] essay, "[TITLE OF ESSAY]," [AUTHOR OF ESSAY] persuades [his or her] audience that [THESIS OF ESSAY_____]. [He or She] proves this by appealing to the audience through the use of compelling facts and information, including [TYPE OF LOGOS_____], and using [TYPE OF PATHOS_____], all the while maintaining a credible account.

CHAPTER SIX
LOGOS BODY PARAGRAPH

6
LOGOS BODY PARAGRAPH
TOPIC SENTENCE

A coherent topic sentence for the logos paragraph is necessary for a good score. Luckily, it's not complicated to write one. Since logos is premised on logic and reason, we're going to incorporate those concepts in our topic sentence.

Quite simply, the purpose of the logos paragraph topic sentence is to state that the author proves his or her claim by building a logical argument through a variety of ways, which will be explained later in this chapter.

Remember: Be mindful of what the author uses to prove his/her claim when you are annotating.

> Example:
>
> *Lenhard builds a convincing, logical argument through the use of facts and statistics.*

LOGOS BODY PARAGRAPH
SUPPORT AND ANALYSIS

The logos body paragraph is one of the longest and most important paragraphs of your essay, so it is crucial for your support and analysis to be precise and, more importantly, logical.

When you are writing the logos body paragraph, follow the structure of the passage; do not jump around in the passage. This approach will ensure that the logic of your paragraph follows the logic of the passage.

Furthermore, do not forget that 1/3 of your score comes from your analysis of the argument in the passage. Such analysis should be woven into your essay seamlessly.

The simple format to follow is:
◊ introduce a point about the author's argument
◊ then, give a quote that exemplifies that point
◊ following the quote, provide an analysis of the quote; what is the SIGNIFICANCE of the quote in the grand scheme of the argument (i.e. The author provides such statistics to establish context by showing that the problem of food deserts pervades society.)

Example:

She writes in the second paragraph, "more than 29.7 million Americans currently live in neighborhoods…where fast food restaurants and convenience stores are the nearest, and primary, options for nourishment." Lenhard utilizes this fact (about what she tells us are called "food deserts") because a number as big as "29.7 million" is hard to ignore; it's a number that reflects just how prevalent the problem of food deserts really is. She tells us that there are other factors that exacerbate this problem, "such as education, ethnicity, and dietary restrictions," which are all in addition to the most common factor, "low income." Her purpose for delineating these factors is simple: it's to show that "proposing broad solutions to the problem" may not be the path to take since this problem is "quite complex

> *and challenging." Lenhard does give us one solution that was tried, "The 2011 presidential budget requested over $400 million for a Healthy Food Financing Initiative (HFFI) to be launched [which] aims to open… wholesome food retailers in food deserts." She then gives an example of a local supermarket in Highland Falls, NY that was affected by this initiative, writing, "Highland Falls is just one example of the many success stories that this government initiative boasts since its inception." But then in paragraph 5, she tells us that the "research does not firmly suggest that establishing a new grocery store in a food desert will change the diets of those people living in it." Moreover, she writes, "It's possible that policy makers jumped to address a very real problem with a solution ill-tested for success."*

LOGOS BODY PARAGRAPH
CLOSING SENTENCE

The closing sentence of the logos body paragraph is also important and should not be forgotten. By the time you have gotten to the end of the logos body paragraph, you should have established the author's argument in full, so your closing sentence will reflect this.

 Remember: You should not end with a quote!

Example:

All of this information is used to bring us to the climax of her argument: that government initiatives may not be the one and only solution to food deserts.

Now, BRING IT ALL TOGETHER!

Lenhard builds a convincing, logical argument through the use of facts and statistics. She writes in the second paragraph, "more than 29.7 million Americans currently live in neighborhoods…where fast food restaurants and convenience stores are the nearest, and primary, options for nourishment." The result of Lenhard's utilization of this fact is potent: a number as big as "29.7 million" is hard to ignore. This number reflects just how prevalent the problem of food deserts really is. She tells us that there are other factors that exacerbate this problem, "such as education, ethnicity, and dietary restrictions," which are all in addition to the most common factor, "low income." Lenhard's delineation of these factors shows that "proposing broad solutions to the problem" may not be the path to take since this problem is "quite complex and challenging." Lenhard does give us one solution that was tried, "The 2011 presidential budget requested over $400 million for a Healthy Food Financing Initiative (HFFI) to be launched [which] aims to open…wholesome food retailers in food deserts." She then gives an example of a local supermarket in Highland Falls, NY that was affected by this initiative, writing, "Highland Falls is just one example of the many success stories that this government initiative boasts since its inception." But then in paragraph 5, she tells us that the "research does not firmly suggest that establishing a new grocery store in a food desert will change the diets of those people living in it." Moreover, she writes, "It's possible that policy makers jumped to address a very real problem with a solution ill-tested for success." All of this information is used to bring us to the climax of her argument: that government initiatives may not be the one and only solution to food deserts.

WRITING TIP:

Words that are often used in logos body paragraphs are terms such as the following:

◊ Categorizes
◊ Demonstrates
◊ States
◊ Outlines
◊ Delineates
◊ Structures
◊ Exemplifies

6

LOGOS BODY PARAGRAPH TEMPLATE

If you are still uncertain about how to write a logos body paragraph, we have included a simple template that you can follow. You just have to fill in the blanks. This template will work for MOST passages, but if you find that you need to modify it, do not change the overall structure and order of the sentences, as this is the most logical and effective organization for the logos body paragraph.

LOGOS BODY PARAGRAPH

[AUTHOR] builds a convincing, logical argument through the use of

[_____]. [He or She] writes in the [_____] paragraph, [FIRST

QUOTATION_____]. [AUTHOR] utilizes

this fact about [WHAT THE QUOTE IS ABOUT_____] because [WHY

THE QUOTE IS IMPORTANT_____]; indeed,

[ADDITIONAL REASON WHY THE QUOTE IS IMPORTANT]. [He or She] tells us

that there are other factors that relate to this issue, explaining that [SECOND

QUOTATION_____]. [His or Her] purpose

in providing this information is simple, yet potent: it's to show [WHY DOES THE

AUTHOR PROVIDE THIS INFORMATION?_____].

[AUTHOR] does, however, give us one further line of reasoning that enriches

[his or her] argument: [THIRD QUOTATION_____]. [He or

She] then gives an example of [EXAMPLE HERE], writing, [ADDITIONAL

QUOTATION_____]. Together, these excerpts use

[WRITING DEVICES_____] to clearly and decisively indicate that [WHAT DO THEY

INDICATE?_____]. All of this information is used

to bring us to the climax of [his or her] argument: [RE-STATE THE MAIN POINT OF THE

AUTHOR'S ARGUMENT USING DIFFERENT WORDING].

LOGOS: ESSAY GLOSSARY

ANALOGY

To clearly explain the nature or significance of a situation, writers will often create analogies. This strategy uses comparison to clarify problems for a reader. However, analogy can take a few forms:

> **What we are seeing with the recent destruction of the sea cucumber population recalls the 1999 decimation of a sea sponge population off the coast of New England. In both cases, we lost an ecosystem that nobody—not conservationists, not the government—can replace.**

In this first excerpt, the analogy clarifies or explains a problem, and its severity, by comparing it to a similar case. Now consider another analogy usage.

> **It may seem that these recent free speech protests are a valuable addition to a political discussion, but in reality, the participants are little better than spoiled children, crying over spilled milk.**

This second excerpt also involves an analogy, but functions differently: here, the author explains content by comparing a potentially complex debate to a simpler scenario ("spilled milk") that the reader will grasp quickly.

ABSURDITY

Writers can create powerful counter-arguments by showing that how unfavorable perspectives are illogical, absurd, or ridiculous. This technique of reducing an opposing side to absurdity (known as *reductio ad absurdum*) play out in multiple ways:

> **If we continue to indulge consumers in this manner, what will happen next? Today, free iPads—tomorrow, free cars, free ponies, free houses? Free everything?**

Here, the author argues that the CONSEQUENCES of an idea are ripe with absurdity. Yet there are other ways to critique absurd reasoning on the SAT Essay.

> **The only way we can accept Hornby's position is if we accept the idea that charging $1700 for a simple high blood pressure pill is a good idea. That means that, for Hornby, a single small dose of a single medication is worth as much as eight months of car payments, or two months of rent. Let that settle in.**

This second excerpt shows how the PRINCIPLES behind an author's ideas reduce themselves to similarly high absurdity. It is possible, indeed, to attack absurd situations from any one of a few different angles.

BROAD TREND

Often, authors will build strong cases by showing how large bodies of data, or large masses of examples, all contribute to the same point. The use of such broad trends on the SAT Essay can, for instance, back up a single main argument.

> **This movement towards increased openness to new ideas in college English departments manifested itself in the 1970s, as women's studies, African-American studies, and studies of indigenous cultures all simultaneously became subjects of heightened inquiry.**

Note that a broad trend, however, does not need to be a COMPLETE trend. The information cited simply needs to be overwhelming enough to be CONVINCING, as in the following example.

> **What we have found is that, of the 127 studies performed in the past year, 108 support our claims about infant cognition. The others, for the most part, returned ambiguous results.**

Although there may be some room for skepticism when addressing a broad trend, there should be no reason to FUNDAMENTALLY doubt what the author is saying. If anything, citing a large body of examples shows that an author can thoughtfully and confidently synthesize a large amount of information.

CAUSE AND EFFECT

In an SAT Essay passage, an author will often build his or her case by showing how certain conditions, logically, will lead to certain results. Cause-and-effect relationships can convince a reader that a desired outcome is possible, as in the example below.

> **By increasing the number of homes with solar panels on their roofs, a community can decrease its total electricity expenditures by almost 35%.**

It is clear that a well-advised measure will lead to a positive effect in the example above. But other types of cause-and-effect scenarios can be employed.

> **The introduction of invasive species such as the Nile Crocodile, though accidental, has led to loss of biodiversity and even to loss of human life.**

In this case, a negative "accidental" cause leads to highly negative effects. As a rule of thumb with cause-and-effect relationships, positive causes lead to positive effects, and negative causes lead to negative effects.

Cost and Benefit

One powerful logical tool is comparison of the costs and benefits of a course of action: logically, the advisability of any course of action depends on how exactly the costs and benefits line up. For instance, in the example below, a small cost leads to enormous benefits.

> **Yes, investing in consumer discretionary stocks may result in short-term financial pain. But over the long term, these same stocks can return profits of over 700%—within just a ten-year period.**

In contrast, it is possible that costs may be much greater than any possible benefits that could be gleaned, as in the next example.

> **So it was that the Metropolitan Museum of Art spent four years and $136 million acquiring—what exactly? A small medieval icon that maybe half a dozen experts in the entire world can identify by name, and that is of no conceivable interest to even the most educated museum-goer.**

The costs here are clearly out of proportion to the value of the results. Because it relies on such strong positives and negatives, cost-benefit analysis of this sort can be a lucid and cogent method of arguing for the advisability (or inadvisability) of specific decisions.

Concrete Example

In order to build their larger arguments, authors will often focus on specific, single examples. The details contained in such concrete examples help readers to relate to and more easily remember broad points. Consider the following instances:

> **One woman who has been profoundly affected by such housing trends is Martha Hoynes, a 34-year-old single mother of three.**

> **This is exactly what happened in 2004, when an entire catfish population mysteriously disappeared from Hemlock Lake.**

> **For proof, look no further than Slidell Services, which until a few years ago was the most powerful waste management company operating in five different Rocky Mountain states.**

The authors of these excerpts all gesture towards larger arguments, but clearly tie those arguments to specific people, events, or organizations in order to show how specific ideas have played out in—and are validated by—real life.

DEDUCTIVE REASONING

The process known as "deductive reasoning" typically begins with a broad and accepted logical rule, then shows how that rule explains or justifies more specific cases. For such reasoning, the foundational principles must be credible; if they are, logical cases and consequences can proceed naturally and easily.

> **This innate human tendency to fear the unknown explains why science fiction aliens—even aliens that look part-human—are a source of terror.**

Here, the author moves convincingly from a general principle ("fear" of the unknown) to a more specific case ("science fiction"). Deductive reasoning can also help to set up a specific example.

> **Indeed, economic self-interest was what motivated Dr. Tso to continue operating his family's long-lived printmaking business and abandon his fanciful dreams of becoming a sculptor.**

In this case, a broad principle ("economic self-interest") is the motivating factor behind how a single individual decided on a course of action.

DEFINITION OF TERMS

By defining specific terms, authors can show that their arguments are based on stable and logical ideas; moreover, definitions can give clarity to complex ideas and allow readers to easily grasp these ideas when they reappear. An author, for instance, may define a term from a specialized discipline.

> **This form of drama is known today as "metatheater"—a type of dramatic writing that uses the actions and gestures of characters themselves to comment on theatrical motifs, commonplaces, and history.**

However, authors may also define terms of their own invention.

> **What we are seeing on social media is a broad-based but undiscriminating mode of interaction that I call "conspicuous conversation": people have vast networks with which they interact regularly, but do not really interact in depth with anyone.**

In both cases, the author designates a specific term for definition, and explains that term in a way that makes it logically accessible to any reader.

ELIMINATION OF DOUBTS

It is possible that a reader may not be entirely convinced of an argument upon its initial presentation, or based on its own merits. In such a case, an author can anticipate, address, and logically eliminate any doubts that the reader may have. Consider the following example.

Although reinstating fracking in such communities may strike some as a fearsome safety hazard, a group of new industrial technologies make fracking safer than ever. Deaths related to fracking are currently seventeen times less common than deaths related to shark attacks, and those are already mercifully rare.

The author, thus, both acknowledges doubts head-on and eliminates those doubts using logical and concrete evidence. Pay careful attention to the wording, too: logos that involves elimination of doubts will commonly refer to a different perspective (the "some" above) that may seem valid but is ultimately erroneous.

FAILURE VERSUS SUCCESS

One especially powerful appeal to logos involves the contrast between strongly positive and strongly negative results. The readers, in such cases, can see for themselves that one course of action is logically supported by good outcomes, while another is logically invalidated by poor outcomes. One example of such a failure versus success situation is the following.

The Democrats' inability to successfully embrace modern "attack" politics can explain the party's catastrophic presidential campaign losses in 2000 and 2004. Conversely, their embrace of such attack politics decided the 2008 and 2012 elections in the Democrats' favor.

Here, a single factor (embracing "attack politics") can be linked to two different outcomes, depending on how that factor was approached. Failure versus success is a common logos tactic both in such social and historical cases and in accounts of studies and experiments, such as that below.

While a small addition of chocolate to the daily diet of the mice resulted in more robust muscle growth, a large addition of chocolate resulted in less robust muscle growth and, in some cases, led to rapid heart failure.

In this case, outcomes at different levels of desirability occur, once more, in connection with a single factor. The important point in success versus failure examples is not necessarily why different outcomes arise, but that strong positives and strong negatives are clearly linked to specific causes.

HYPOTHETICAL EXAMPLE

Instead of explaining what HAS happened in specific conditions, some writers build logical arguments explain what COULD happen under conditions that are just as specific. Such hypothetical examples are powerful instances of logos, if used correctly, since they help readers to imagine plausible outcomes and clear logical consequences.

If a student were to submit an essay laden only with false statistics, that student

would surely be caught. In fact, avoiding statistics of any sort—false, true, half-remembered—would earn a student a better grade than making up statistics on this type of assignment.

It is not clear that any students actually HAVE made up statistics on the essay described. Yet the author uses a hypothetical example to explain, in an extremely reasonable way, what WOULD happen in such a case. The power of hypothetical examples is that they enable authors to quickly and effectively work through general cases—since the example could, hypothetically, apply to a fairly broad group of people—and to predict likely, logical events.

PATTERNS

At times, the same logic will be at work in somewhat different cases. By calling attention to patterns of behavior, an author can make a strong case for specific logical principles: after all, a pattern that unifies different examples can be hard to dispute, as in the excerpt below.

> **These drastic declines in stork populations on one continent, finch populations on another, and bustard populations on yet a third all point to the same truth. Fluctuations in global temperature are undermining the ecosystems in which birds once thrived, almost regardless, of species.**

Here, the author calls attention to a negative reality by bringing in three different cases and noticing a similarity or pattern. The evidence may seem disparate (and the author acknowledges as much by calling attention to geographical differences), but is even MORE powerful because it all clusters around a single truth.

Keep in mind that, in calling attention to patterns, SAT Essay authors will typically NOT cluster meaningless details (such as letters, numbers, or weird coincidences) in order to make their points. This kind of thinking is more appropriate to conspiracy theories than to the strong argumentative essays that you can expect on the SAT.

PRECEDENTS AND PAST RESULTS

One way to make a strong logical case for a particular position or course of action is to point out similar (or almost identical) positions or courses of action that have yielded positive results. By emphasizing a strong precedent, an author can demonstrate why a particular measure or idea is appealing.

> **In the 1930s and again in the 1950s, government expenditure ensured prosperity all across America. The same prosperity can be ours once again if we remember that an actively-spending government can be active for supreme good.**

The author's assumption is both clear and logical: "government expenditure" was once an extremely potent strategy and could have comparable success today. Keep in mind, though, that negative precedents and past results are also useful in argumentative essays

> **They made three, four, five attempts to sell their almond milk in major supermarkets. Attempt six is currently underway, and will most likely be one more entry in a record of complete futility.**

Again, the assumption is easy to see and logically valid: it is reasonable to conclude that a product and a strategy that have not been successful in the past will continue to be unsuccessful if replicated in the future.

PROBLEM AND SOLUTION

By highlighting specific problems, and then offering solutions, authors enhance the logical power of their arguments in a few ways. A solution is an effective way to logically indicate the sense of strong, lucid purpose behind a chain of reasoning that is somewhat involved, and will win over readers by convincing them that even negative statements serve a constructive purpose, as in the example below.

> **Years of investigation brought these scandals to light, but also revealed a way forward that even a small business such as ours could implement. Hired on a part-time basis, an ethics and compliance consultant would save us time, money, and headache.**

Solutions will commonly (but not always) be introduced in the final stages of SAT Essays. This placement indicates another reason that solutions are an effective logical tool: they indicate that an author's arguments are unified, orderly, and informed by a strong overall rationale.

REASONABLE CONJECTURE

In some cases, even a logical and convincing author may not be able to offer completely undeniable conclusions. Yet authors can still achieve logical rigor by working with sound principles and methods to arrive at estimates, guesses, or conjectures, as in the case below.

> **Scientists believe that this distant planet is roughly twice as large (in diameter) as Earth, and are firmly convinced that its orbit, unusually enough, is somewhat more elliptical.**

The above statement does not present certitudes; it does, however, present logical ideas that have been formulated by scientists studying a distant planet. In fact, reasonable conjectures are valuable because they show both rigor and skepticism. Consider a second example in this regard.

> **By drawing on Childress's theories, I was able to accurately predict how the mice would respond in 63 of the 70 cases under my observation.**

The author's predictions are not completely correct, but they are impressively accurate. Just as importantly, the author is arriving at a reasonably valid conclusion by using reasoning (the method of an apparent authority) that is fundamentally sound.

REASONABLE COURSE OF ACTION

Once a problem has been identified and a critique has been performed, an author can begin to make a practical recommendation. As a logical tool, such a reasonable course of action is potent in a few different ways. It can lend a clear negative-to-positive structure to a logical chain of reasoning, and can show that an author's arguments were undertaken with the meaningful end goal of ensuring some sort of productive change. Consider the following excerpt.

> **We are caught between two alternatives: neither ideal, yet one necessary. But if we embrace violence at this late stage, once the moral high ground is ours, we risk compromising all that we have built through steady, long-suffering, nonviolent effort.**

Note that the course of action promoted by the author is not "ideal". Indeed, in endorsing a reasonable course of action, an author can further demonstrate strong logic by continuing to point out strengths and weaknesses. What makes a course of action "reasonable" is not that it is perfect, but that it is preferable to other alternatives and likely to yield the most desirable results that are within the realm of possibility.

REASONABLE GENERALIZATION

Once an author has accumulated a sufficient amount of meaningful evidence, he or she can synthesize this evidence to draw meaningful and fairly large conclusions. The use of such reasonable generalizations can structure individual paragraphs, or an essay as a whole. After all, an essay's final paragraphs will often synthesize evidence to deliver overarching statements or messages of some sort.

> **It is becoming clear that we live in a country that has still not extended opportunity to long-underprivileged urban communities. In providing viable after-school programs and healthy lunches, we continue to fail. As of now, the old idea that an underprivileged urban child will get a better education watching *Sesame Street* than listening to some of his teachers continues to hold true.**

The author is delivering a few assertions here that would seem grand or presumptuous were they NOT backed by clear evidence. Yet the rest of the author's argument, if coordinated effectively, should provide a strong and specific basis for supporting even an "old idea" such as that which appears in the last sentence of the excerpt.

Keep in mind that, in essay writing, UNREASONABLE generalizations such as stereotypes and platitudes absolutely are possible. However, SAT Essays are chosen on the basis of their strong logical coherence, and will tend not to present generalizations that are logically suspect in major ways.

Rebuttal

The rhetorical device known as "rebuttal" involves quickly raising and efficiently defeating an opposing argument. This is an especially powerful form of logos, since it both demonstrates an author's awareness of different perspectives and indicates that an author's ideas are strong enough to withstand logical criticism. Consider the example below.

> **It is widely believed that the studies were too heavily weighted towards rural respondents, yet rural respondents were among the few citizens to be truly aware of the workings of the modern dairy industry.**

This example takes a possible objection ("too heavily weighted") and shows that this objection can be logically eliminated by a point in favor of the methodology of the "studies". For rebuttals, expect wordings that signal strong contrasts. In this respect, consider a second example.

> **Although some commentators dismiss complaints about the debates as inconsequential, the truth is that televised debates shape voter preferences in profound ways, and at times with dire consequences.**

Here, the author refers to a prevailing opinion ("some commentators") but is confident enough in the reasoning at work for his or her own opposing argument to deliver a clear, effective logical statement.

Representative Cases

One especially potent type of example that an author can use is a representative case: a person, group, or occurrence indicative of a broadly applicable idea or conclusion. Consider the usefulness of the following example.

> **What Mrs. Donovan observed, as she navigated a hostile and confusing healthcare market, is similar to what people all across America must struggle through on a monthly, if not weekly basis.**

Here, the author is presenting strong negatives about the "healthcare market" but is only really considering a single example, "Mrs. Donovan." Nonetheless, because Mrs. Donovan is DEFINED as representative of what happens on a broader scale, she becomes an effectively logical stand-in for OTHER people who face similar troubles.

In cases such as these, pay careful attention to the wording. The most evident virtue of representative cases is that they allow the author to achieve a high level of specificity and attention to detail through a relatively narrow focus. On a somewhat less evident level, they introduce phrases and analysis ("similar to what") that firmly indicate that what applies in one instance applies in many others.

STATISTICS

An author can use statistics to demonstrate that a specific idea or conclusion is not simply supported by emotions, anecdotes, or impressions; instead, information of the most empirical and authoritative sort provides validation. Consider the following short excerpts.

> In fact, the study found that a porcupine has only a 25% chance of surviving an open-ground encounter with an adult weasel.

> Hirsh's results were stunning: of the 2307 individuals interviewed, only 14 had any idea what Amazon's core business really is.

> It is a well-known fact that any wage increase, once the threshold of $75,000 per year has been reached, will not correlate to an increase in an individual's personal happiness.

All of these examples present numerical figures that can be used to support specific points. When discussing statistics, be sure to clarify what kind of statistics the author favors (percentages, headcount numbers, financial quantities) and be sure to explain EXACTLY what point the statistics are being used to validate.

EXERCISES: Logos Terms

DIRECTIONS: Briefly identify the type of logos employed in each excerpt.

ANSWER BANK, QUESTIONS 1-5

Deductive Reasoning	Concrete Example	Statistics
Precedents and Past Results	Rebuttal	

1) As much as some professors of media studies argue that the newspaper industry is in decline, the exact opposite, the idea that the industry is flourishing, is closer to the truth.

TYPE: _____

2) The failure of these governments can be explained by the fundamental supply-and-demand problems that accompany any communistic system.

TYPE: _____

3) Such a scarcity of obscure vocabulary on past versions of the test makes it unlikely that the words on this list will ever be included in the future.

TYPE: _____

4) In one recent poll, 122 Pittsburgh residents—roughly 63% of the total respondents—stated that they were satisfied with the casual dining options available in their city.

TYPE: _____

5) One instance of such professional luck is offered by the career of Larry Fisk, an asset manager who, indeed, was in the right place at the right time.

TYPE: _____

ANSWER BANK, QUESTIONS 6-10

Failure versus Success	Reasonable Conjecture	Hypothetical Example
Representative Cases	Absurdity	

6) Although this software initially created poor matches between students and appropriate colleges, a well-considered update led to more effective matches—and to positive reviews from participating institutions.

Type: _____

7) All of the fundamental conditions that I have observed indicate that the manatee population will continue to grow, despite short-term ecological problems.

Type: _____

8) The only way to accept these findings is to accept the unfounded and, frankly, inane premise that a crustacean can exhibit the same wealth of emotion as an artist or a philosopher.

Type: _____

9) Imagine, if you will, a patient from a poor and isolated town walking into a clinic for the first time without insurance.

Type: _____

10) There is little difference between Dr. Fells and hundreds of other young men who have worked their way up from poor households to become some of this century's most respected scholars.

Type: _____

ANSWER BANK, QUESTIONS 11-15

Broad Trend	Elimination of Doubts	Analogy
Reasonable Generalization	Reasonable Course of Action	

11) On the basis of polls, personal testimonies, and anecdotal evidence, we can conclude that Australians simply do not see race relations as one of the primary issues that their government needs to address.

Type: _____

12) These psychiatric methods are the modern equivalent of the sham medicine of the Middle Ages—and the forms of meaningless mumbo-jumbo that accompany both are just as bad.

Type: _____

13) All across America, parents are demanding after-school programs that combine rigorous exercise with educational activities that are practical, interactive, and fun.

TYPE: _____

14) Such contracts may not be ideal, but they are the only way to bring affordable computers and printers to smaller colleges.

TYPE: _____

15) Although Professor Genovese is fairly young, there is no reason to question her authority: she has been investigating hot-button nutritional issues for the better part of twelve years, and is a fixture on the "Young Influencers" lists of well-respected science magazines.

TYPE: _____

ANSWER BANK, QUESTIONS 16-20

Problem and Solution	Cause and Effect	Definition of Terms
Patterns	Cost and Benefit	

16) In certain parts of contemporary Europe, we are seeing a resurgence of the same fear of change that afflicted the late Roman Empire, Victorian England, and early twentieth-century Japan.

TYPE: _____

17) Operating a cafe requires you to sacrifice peace of mind (since the restaurant business has always been volatile) in the interest of long-term gain (since a successful cafe gives you the opportunity to create a profitable franchise after several years of development).

TYPE: _____

18) Its name derived from the title of Joseph Heller's famous novel, a "catch-22," is a situation that is paradoxical, irresolvable, and often darkly ironic.

TYPE: _____

19) It would be easier to keep these butterflies healthy by isolating them from zoo visitors—*not* by keeping them with the more common species that are best served by life in the butterfly tent.

TYPE: _____

20) These scandals have led to a decrease in the public prestige of investment banking, and to stock-market losses among the largest investment banking firms.

TYPE: _____

ANSWERS: Logos Terms

1) Type: Rebuttal

2) Type: Deductive Reasoning

3) Type: Precedents and Past Results

4) Type: Statistics

5) Type: Concrete Example

6) Type: Failure versus Success

7) Type: Reasonable Conjecture

8) Type: Absurdity

9) Type: Hypothetical Example

10) Type: Representative Cases

11) Type: Reasonable Generalization

12) Type: Analogy

13) Type: Broad Trend

14) Type: Reasonable Course of Acton

15) Type: Elimination of Doubts

16) Type: Patterns

17) Type: Cost and Benefit

18) Type: Definition of Terms

19) Type: Problem and Solution

20) Type: Cause and Effect

CHAPTER SEVEN
PATHOS BODY PARAGRAPH

PATHOS BODY PARAGRAPH
TOPIC SENTENCE

The pathos body paragraph topic sentence is extremely important. After all, this paragraph will more than likely be your second-longest paragraph. Since pathos is about emotional appeal, which is usually conveyed through word choice or literary devices like metaphors and hyperbole, we are going to incorporate such appeal to emotion into the topic sentence.

Remember: Pathos is **any** instance of emotional appeal. Thus, pathos will include vivid imagery and detailed anecdotes that are meant to make the reader "imagine" and "feel."

Example:

The purposeful language Lenhard uses also helps persuade the audience of her argument.

PATHOS BODY PARAGRAPH
SUPPORT AND ANALYSIS

You must always keep in mind the PURPOSE of your paragraphs. While the logos body paragraph is concerned with showing the logical layout of the argument in the passage, the pathos body paragraph is concerned with showing how the words or literary devices that the author uses ultimately manipulate the reader into feeling specific emotions.

 Remember: This clever manipulation may be done subtly or overtly. In order to make sure that you don't miss it when you are annotating, pay close attention to the type of words the author uses when talking about concepts he/she is for and the type of words that the author uses when talking about concepts he/she is against. Also, take note of any literary devices the author uses.

Example:

She skillfully begins the essay by presenting an imaginary scenario that immediately pulls the reader into the problem, from the very first sentence. She opens with, "Imagine a child arriving home for dinner to find a tub of KFC on the table, rather than a home cooked meal with plenty of fruits and vegetables." This imagery is something most readers can picture and many readers have experienced: it's relatable because we can all imagine coming home to a meal waiting for us at the dinner table. She is alluding to a universal image of dinnertime. Then she takes us further into this imaginary tale, "Imagine living in a community where a raw cantaloupe could be considered exotic for its scarcity." She expands the imagery from something so specific as one home, to the whole "community." When the reader gets to the community perspective, he or she is taken from something relatable, to something that he or she may find shocking, and even a little sad. This emotional response is evoked purposefully and creates a sense of care in the reader and possibly even a sense of responsibility. Even simply repeatedly using the terminology, "food deserts," conjures up a sobering image of the severity of this problem, of vast numbers of people lacking access to nutritional food.

PATHOS BODY PARAGRAPH
CLOSING SENTENCE

The pathos body paragraph closing sentence is as important as the topic sentence. By the time you have come to the end of your pathos body paragraph, you should have shown that the word choice the author uses is meant to have an effect on the reader (including what effect(s) the words could potentially have). Your closing sentence will reflect the effectiveness of using certain words to convince the reader by manipulating his/her emotions.

Remember: You should not end with a quote!

Example:

Tugging at the heartstrings of the reader and choosing phrasing meant to jar or sober the reader is a clever way that Lenhard pulls the reader onto her side.

Now, BRING IT ALL TOGETHER!

The purposeful language Lenhard uses also helps persuade the audience of her argument. She skillfully begins the essay by presenting an imaginary scenario that immediately pulls the reader into the problem, from the very first sentence. She opens with, "Imagine a child arriving home for dinner to find a tub of KFC on the table, rather than a home cooked meal with plenty of fruits and vegetables." This imagery is something most readers can picture and many readers have experienced: it's relatable because we can all imagine coming home to a meal waiting for us at the dinner table. She is alluding to a universal image of dinnertime. Then she takes us further into this imaginary tale, "Imagine living in a community where a raw cantaloupe could be considered exotic for its scarcity." She expands the imagery from something so specific as one home, to the whole "community." When the reader gets to the community perspective, he or she is taken from something relatable, to something that he or she may find shocking, and even a little sad. This emotional response is evoked purposefully and may create a sense of care in the reader and possibly even a sense of responsibility. Even simply repeatedly using the terminology, "food deserts," conjures up a sobering image of the severity of this problem, of vast numbers of people lacking access to nutritional food. Tugging at the heartstrings of the reader and choosing phrasing meant to jar or sober the reader are clever ways that Lenhard pulls the reader onto her side.

WRITING TIP:

Words and phrases that are often used in pathos body paragraphs:

- ◊ "the author appeals to the reader's emotions with…"
- ◊ wins over the audience
- ◊ provides a personal account
- ◊ utilizes the extended metaphor of
- ◊ stories
- ◊ aesthetic
- ◊ vivid imagery

PATHOS BODY PARAGRAPH TEMPLATE

If you are still uncertain about how to write a pathos body paragraph, we have included a simple template that you can follow. You just have to fill in the blanks. This template will work for MOST passages, but if you find that you need to modify it, do not change the overall structure and order of the sentences, as this is the most logical and effective organization for the pathos body paragraph.

PATHOS BODY PARAGRAPH

The [TYPE OF PATHOS that AUTHOR] uses also helps persuade the audience of [his or her] argument. [He or She] skillfully begins the essay with [AN EARLY USE OF PATHOS] that immediately pulls the reader into the problem, right from the outset, without any reservations. [He or She] begins with, [FIRST QUOTATION THAT INVOLVES PATHOS_____ _____]. [He or She] uses [TYPE OF PATHOS] because [WHY THE PATHOS BEING USED: EMPHASIZE WHY THE PATHOS IS SIGNIFICANT, CITE A QUOTATION OR DETAIL_____]. Then [he or she] takes us further into the emotional subtleties and intricacies of [his or her] argument, [SECOND QUOTATION THAT INVOLVES PATHOS_____].
From there, [he or she] deepens the emotional appeal of [his or her] argument, stating that [THIRD QUOTATION THAT INVOLVES PATHOS_____]. This emotional response is evoked purposefully and creates a sense of [PARTICULAR EMOTION] in the reader and possibly even a sense of [PARTICULAR EMOTION]. Even simply repeatedly using the phrase "[SPECIFIC PHRASE]" conjures up [WHAT REACTION DOES THE PHRASE INVOLVE?_____]. Activating the innate, human pathos of the reader and choosing phrasing meant to [THE INTENTION OF THE PHRASING] is a clever way that [AUTHOR] pulls the reader onto [his or her] side.

Pathos: Essay Glossary
Part I, Style Terms

Alliteration

Alliteration is the use of repeated letter sounds to call attention to a specific portion of a text. The purpose is to create points of drama or high emotion, or to single out specific ideas for emphasis and consideration. The most obvious and, often, the most effective uses will involve series of words that share a first letter, as in the examples below.

After a time, his acute annoyance with alliteration attained its apogee.

Shall we sit in silence as the bombs burst, blowing to bits the world to which we once dedicated our most determined diligence?

Note that alliteration can involve either vowel sounds (as in the first example) or consonant sounds (as in the second). Technically, vowel-based alliteration is known as "assonance" while consonant-based alliteration is known as "consonance": this distinction is helpful, but the use of the broader term "alliteration" is perfectly acceptable for the SAT.

Anaphora

Anaphora is a device that involves repeating the same word, or the same cluster of words, within a relatively small space. Often, authors will use anaphora in order to create special points of stress and drama within a long text, or to call attention to linked and urgent ideas, as in the example below.

I refuse to give in. I refuse to stand idly by and watch as our society embraces policies that I know to be disastrous in every other context. And I refuse to pretend that the results, in this country, will be any different.

Here, the use of anaphora is designed to heighten the emotion present in the author's discussion. Anaphora can also be used to place especially strong emphasis on a single topic, as a second example demonstrates.

Of course Berringer was qualified: qualified to discuss macroeconomics at great length, qualified to speak to fellow businessmen in any of the three languages he knew, qualified to teach a college seminar on the fall of mercantilism. Qualified, in fact, to sit in a self-constructed ivory tower and drive a perfectly good company into the ground.

The emphasis on the word "qualified" is established through anaphora, and the reader is easily led to see that being "qualified" (in various ways) is the main, essential trait of the man ("Berringer") being discussed.

COLLECTIVE VOICE

An author will typically signal collective voice by using the pronoun "we." Often, the motive for this stylistic tactic is to articulate a sense of concord and connection between the author and his or her audience, as in the example below.

> **We have come too far, and fought too long, to forsake our efforts right now, just as years of struggle—of uncertainty, of loss, of heartbreak—are so close to bearing their hard-cultivated fruit.**

In the excerpt above, the "we" clearly refers to the author's allies in a specific "struggle" and calls forth a sense of unity. But the use of collective voice can also be used to project an author's ideas onto an audience and simply ASSUME agreement, regardless of whether that audience is truly in concord with the author.

> **Of course, we all know what is going on. We have seen it in our communities, we have heard about it on our radios, we have read about it in the evening papers— and we will not let this menace go unchecked.**

Here, the use of a broad "we" may overstate the extent of the support for the author's stance. But the collective voice nonetheless construes the author as confident and suggests that, at some level, the author's position is broadly reasonable and acceptable—thus serving a valuable argumentative purpose.

CONVERSATIONAL TONE

To engage an audience and to create an air of straightforwardness and spontaneity, an author can use a conversational tone to deliver an argument. Such a tone is not, however, meant to seem sloppy or slangy. Instead, conversational tone is a way of making the author seem more approachable in the course of a rigorous argument.

> **Well, of course I couldn't resist. Who could? But the more I considered my actions, the more I began to wonder: had I *really* done the right thing? Not a chance: I had made a donation that made *me* feel good about myself, but didn't accomplish anything else at the end of the day.**

The author is considering an issue that could have broad importance (the psychology behind making a donation) but is doing so in a way that a reader would find accessible—as accessible, certainly, as a spontaneous conversation. Here, the sentences are mostly short and stark, the vocabulary is not overly complex, and the author uses readily-seen points of emphasis. All of these are conversational traits, and are translated into writing for the purpose of more energetic and straightforward communication.

Colloquial Expressions

A phrase or sentence that is "colloquial" is highly familiar from everyday speech or discourse. On the SAT, such phrases serve a dual purpose: they make a writer's ideas readily understood, and they allow the writer to seem more approachable to his or her audience. Here are a few examples of colloquial usages, with the colloquialisms underlined.

> **To make a long story short, Cartwright's theory really doesn't add anything to what we already know.**

> **An entire branch of professional sporting has been trying to <u>have its cake and eat it too</u>: matches are promoted, sometimes within the same advertisement, as displays of athletic intelligence and as pointless dumb fun.**

> **Some voters thought that Reagan was <u>the best thing since sliced bread</u>; others, that he was little more than an especially articulate <u>wolf in sheep's clothing</u>.**

These phrases are English commonplaces: a "wolf in sheep's clothing," for instance, is simply a description that is applied to somebody who looks deceptively moral or appealing. Such phrases, though, have the immense benefit of being immediately understandable to the many readers who have seen them before.

Digression

A digression is a portion of a passage that clearly moves away from the central topic. While a writer may use a digression to amuse or entertain a reader, the most effective digressions also reinforce a passage's main points in unexpected ways. Consider how the digression that occurs in the excerpt below functions.

> **But what about today's college students? I remember that my own college career was basically an endless gag reel: food fights, ill-advised all-nighters, pranks that somehow led to all sorts of farm animals running across campus. One time we even removed the tires of a (much-hated) professor's car and left them outside his office, as a sort of gift. If I could go back and do it all again, I would—just the same, in a heartbeat. Now, I ask you, how many of today's authority-fearing, pressure-burdened college students will look back and feel the same way?**

It may seem unclear at first what purpose the author's personal account serves. In context, however, this account builds up an important point: the author is very different from today's "authority-fearing, pressure-burdened" students in terms of basic college experience. Readers are thus immersed in an interesting new topic, but are then led to admire the author's cleverness in making a coherent point.

DIRECT ASSERTION

One of the most obvious and (when used properly) most potent uses of pathos is direct assertion of the author's specific emotions. Rather than leading readers to interpret their content at will, some authors will explain EXACTLY how a scene, fact, or idea is meant to work on emotional terms.

> **It was, quite simply, the most beautiful thing I had ever seen—a majesty of nature such as I may never witness again.**

In the except above, it is not even clear what exactly the author is describing: what IS clear is the author's strong positive tone of awe. By establishing clear emotions upfront, the author both establishes a tone of directness and inflects any later content (such as the description of the "beautiful thing") with a strong, specific emotion.

Keep in mind that such direct assertions of emotion can convey many forms of pathos, from positive (admiration, optimism, joy) to negative (fear, anger). Look for words that DIRECTLY relate to the emotions (including phrases as simple as "I admire" and "I fear") to see if a writer is using this technique.

DRAMATIC ADJECTIVES

An author can strengthen a point or intensify an emotion by deploying adjectives that are vivid and attention-grabbing. Often, such adjectives will be loaded with strong and clearly discernible emotions.

> **His voice was crackling, explosive; his hands swept forward in overpowering gestures; his words were searing, ferocious, flawless.**

The adjectives that are used to describe the "voice", "gestures", and "words" are clearly meant to indicate that the author is impressed. Notice also that the adjectives tend to be grouped in the above example; this enables points of emphasis to emerge. However, a single well-placed adjective can also lend drama to a passage.

> **After listening to both sides of the debate and weighing all that had been said, she cut through the nonsense and summed up all that she had heard with one scapel-sharp response.**

In this case, "scapel-sharp" is the only prominent adjective of any sort. Yet this adjective stands out from the rest of the writing and characterizes the "response" in a vivid fashion.

DRAMATIC VERBS

To channel specific, strong emotions, authors will use verbs that are especially powerful in effect. Many of these dramatic verbs describe actions, and thus create strong mental pictures that naturally resonate with readers.

So far the officials have lounged in obliviousness, watching as bombs and grenades pummel the city that is theirs to protect.

Here, verbs such as "lounged" and "pummel" call to mind dramatic physical actions. They are also more vivid than other reasonable alternatives: the author could have said "remained in obliviousness" instead, but would have lost dramatic effect in the process. Notice also that dramatic adjectives do not always describe actions literally. As in the following example, they can introduce a sense of metaphor and imagery into a sentence.

He was bruised by the conflict, but just as his spirits began to stumble, his faith in the future raised itself into glorious flight.

The author, indeed, could have used more commonplace positive and negative verbs. But words such as "bruised" and "stumble" are designed to resonate more and to more fully convey the dramatically negative emotions present in this excerpt.

Elevated Vocabulary

To make strong points—and to project confidence and mastery—authors frequently resort to vocabulary that may not be known to all readers, but that shows eloquence and expertise. Such sophisticated or advanced language can serve a few different strategic purposes: it can stir up emotions such as admiration, as in the following example.

Lulled into a languorous lethargy, they could do nothing, nothing at all, so susceptible had they become to the ramifications of his ruse.

The point in this sentence (that some people had let down their guard and fallen into a "ruse" or clever trap) is fairly simple, but the elevated language is designed to show that the author is erudite (an advanced word that itself means "extremely knowledgeable) in terms of English vocabulary.

Note that elevated vocabulary is NOT the same as technical terminology (which is, technically, closer to a logos or ethos tactic). The vocabulary in the above example is impressive; however, the words are impressive synonyms for simpler words ("lethargy" meaning "tiredness"; "susceptible" meaning "vulnerable"), NOT words taken from a specific scholarly or academic discipline.

Exclamations

An author may use exclamations to call attention to a specific point—or to quickly indicate passion, urgency, or honesty. Normally, an exclamation will be short and crisp, and will either build upon or qualify content that occurs immediately before, as in the example below.

And after delivering thirty-seven pages of complaints about the current education industry, the authors of the document concluded, somehow . . . that things could be worse. Unbelievable!

Here, the exclamation "Unbelievable!" clearly shows how the author interprets a piece of information and how, by implication, the reader is meant to understand it. Exclamations can serve other purposes, though: for instance, they are extremely effective at creating a bluntly conversational tone.

> **To you I say: wake up. Wake up! We have seen the ravages of this kind of ignorance before, and we will see it again unless we defeat it here, now. The future is knocking, ominously, at our door. Wake up. Wake up!**

Note that the second excerpt combines exclamations with longer sentences and with short though less intense sentences. This kind of variety keeps the reader from being overwhelmed by emotion or from being alienated by a monotonous tone—but still allows the author to deliver moments of stark emotion.

FORMAL AND CONTROLLED TONE

Although successful pathos often involves communicating strong and passionate emotion, sometimes a tone that is polished, low-key, and confident can persuade readers equally well. Such a formal tone can make an author seem calm and objective, and cleverly stir up strong emotions of admiration and approval in the reader.

> **Having considered all the evidence, I decided that it was in the best interests of the entire department to revise our curricula to bolster the funds directed to existing subjects—since diversification had been detrimental to other, comparable departments.**

The language here is designed to be clear and assertive, but in a way that incorporates the lack of overpowering emotion and the longer sentence structures that a sophisticated formal essayistic tone requires. A formal tone also has the added advantage of allowing logos and ethos devices to become especially prominent; if an essay is light on pathos of other types, try analyzing WHY a controlled yet elegant voice is in the author's best interests.

HYPERBOLE

"Hyperbole" is a pathos technique that can best be defined as "obvious or unmistakable overstatement." Such exaggeration can serve a few purposes: it can energize a formal essay by creating moments of comedy, or it can cause a position that the author dislikes to seem bizarre or ridiculous. Below is an example of hyperbole that accomplishes both.

> **The new aquarium will be the beginning of the end. Money will be diverted from other projects, the rest of the area will remain in a state of disrepair, infrastructure will crumble, earthquakes will hit, mutant sharks will break through their tanks and devour hapless schoolchildren. Or at least a good 16.5% of our tax revenue will go to waste.**

Some of the ideas ("mutant sharks", obviously) in this example of hyperbole are meant to seem outlandish. But the presence of such ideas colors the entire discussion; the author clearly sees the "new aquarium" as destructive and ridiculous, and uses hyperbolic references to convey those emotions in the most striking manner possible.

ITALICS FOR EMPHASIS

While some authors will use devices such as alliteration, anaphora, and exclamations to emphasize important points, other authors will use a tactic that can be even more direct: italics. Beyond creating points of importance and stress within an essay, italics can vary the author's tone, add to a conversational voice, or heighten an argument's intensity.

> **Examination after examination yielded the same results, that *nothing at all* was wrong with the mice.**

In this case, the author is stressing the importance of an idea. In other cases, an author may use italics for purposes that have less to do with a conclusion and more to do with stark emotion and personality.

> **But *of course*, I thought, there was something different about *these* artworks, even though they resembled paintings I had seen not so long before.**

Here, relatively minor words and phrases such as "of course" and "these" are given italics for emphasis. They do not get to the core of the author's argument, but they do help the author to mimic a "spoken" and approachable voice when given such emphasis.

JUXTAPOSITION

The tactic of posing starkly contrasting ideas or items against one another is known as juxtaposition. Often, the clearest juxtapositions involve unmistakable opposites (dark and light, good and bad, etc.). On SAT Essays, the juxtapositions may be more subtle but will nonetheless serve valuable purposes, such as comparing clear positives to clear negatives.

> **It was strange indeed to behold: just as the hybrid publishing industry saw its profit margins skyrocket, the traditional publishing industry begin registering steady declines in profit, revenue, and (if such a thing can be measured) basic reputation.**

In this case, the author poses hybrid publishing (positive) against traditional publishing (negative). This strong juxtaposition accentuates the positive and negative emotions at work in the passage, and urges the reader to disapprove of traditional publishing even in the absence of an extensive logical argument.

METAPHOR

One of the devices that can quickly add vividness and clarity to an author's ideas is metaphor. As classically defined, "metaphor" is a form of imaginative comparison that treats a parallel between two dissimilar items as literal. Unlike a simile, which uses "like" or "as" to spell out a comparison, a metaphor will often use some form of "to be" to pair off two items, as in the examples below.

Our nation is a fragile vessel on dangerous seas.

The chairman was a model of probity, a proud lion among lowly jackals.

In both cases, the comparison is purely imaginative. Metaphor, indeed, will help an author to impress an audience by projecting a creative and versatile authorial voice. Just as importantly, perhaps, metaphor can quickly distill strong emotional meanings that would be diluted through the use of other phrasings. The "nation" in the first example is clearly in the midst of a considerable and perilous conflict, while the "chairman" in the second is clearly superior to the people who surround him. Yet these meanings are made just as obvious—and are made MORE emotionally resonant—through the use of metaphor.

Open-Ended Question

An open-ended question is a question that is used to genuinely provoke a variety of answers or possibilities. (In contrast, a rhetorical question is a question designed to elicit a single answer that is difficult to challenge or refute.) Though potentially disorderly, open-ended questions can serve a variety of purposes for exceptionally skilled writers: these questions can engage a reader's imagination, help a reader to relate to subject matter through personal reflection, and show that the author is unafraid of different, complex possibilities.

> **Have you ever seen the look on the face of a child who has just undergone a life-altering surgery? In my work, I see looks of this sort every week, every day.**

Notice that the author does not provide a set answer to the question: the reader, instead, is left to ponder the importance of a "life-altering surgery" and the strong emotions that surround such a surgery. Open-ended questions can serve other purposes, too: in particular, they can urge the reader to ponder outcomes and repercussions.

> **We are a nation addicted to these devices; we walk with them before us, sleep with them beside us, talk to them more than we talk to other people. Is there any way out?**

Although the writer's tone is mostly negative, the question raises a positive possibility This combination of tones keeps the concluding question from being merely rhetorical and encourages the idea that genuinely different outcomes, positive and negative, ARE plausible.

Parallelism

The technique known as parallelism is, like alliteration and anaphora, a form of repetition that creates passion and emphasis. Yet parallelism involves the repetition of entire grammatical constructions, not simply the repetition of letters or words. Recurring grammatical units of this sort have the added virtue of creating strong and memorable driving rhythms within a work of prose, as in the example below.

> **I say this both because I cannot remain silent and because I cannot feign cowardice. I acknowledge the challenges before me: to build consensus within**

my party, to foster hope within my country, and to strengthen cooperation within the international community.

Parallelism can involve somewhat involved paired phrases (as in the "I cannot" constructions in the first sentence), or can involve lists of items or actions (as in the three infinitive constructions in the second sentence). Yet notice that the author does not always repeat word choice. In the second sentence, for example, the author uses three different verbs ("build . . . foster . . . strengthen") but uses the same STRUCTURE to give them emphasis and place them clearly in series.

RHETORICAL QUESTION

A rhetorical question is a question that involves a self-evident answer. Within an essay, such a question may function in a few different ways: changing an author's tone and creating a heightened moment of emotion are but two of the functions of a rhetorical question, such as the question below.

> **The research was backed by impeccable methodology, was impossible to refute on theoretical grounds, and was in line with thirty years of previous inquiry. What was Cullen thinking, in raising such small objections?**

The reader is led to dismiss Cullen's position, since the fairly obvious answer to the rhetorical question is that Cullen's approach was incorrect. In fact, another virtue of rhetorical questions is that they allow an author to quickly and subtly pinpoint specific perspectives as difficult to defend or maintain. It would be illogical, indeed, to answer the rhetorical question above with praise of Cullen.

SECOND-PERSON ADDRESS

The use of "you" to address a reader is known as second-person address. This device is especially useful in creating a sense of connection between an author and his or her audience; often, second-person address indicates a bond premised on empathy or on some other form of shared perspective, as in the example below.

> **You have probably seen flowers just like these, remarkable in their brilliant colors but even more remarkable in another way: they have medicinal properties that, if exploited properly, could save your life.**

Indeed, the reader may never have seen the "flowers" described, or any flowers like them. But the virtue of second-person address is that it encourages the reader to vividly imagine and relate to specific scenarios, emotions, and ideas. In other cases, a reader can be encouraged to take direct action, or to relate to the motives and beliefs (whether positive or negative) of the author.

> **So I appeal to you. You know what is right, you have seen years of work, years of heartbreak. You know that this is the time to take action.**

In this second excerpt, the author does not give commands (which might alienate a reader). The use of second-person address, rather, offers a more subtle way of encouraging the reader to be proactive and to relate to a specific set of emotions.

SENSORY DESCRIPTION (NON-VISUAL)

Although many of the most prominent descriptions in SAT Essays will rely on the sense of sight, other sensory powers will occasionally be brought into play. By describing sound, taste, touch, and smell, an author can insert a reader directly into an emotionally powerful scene. Consider, in light of these tactics, the following excerpt.

> **I sat there completely at peace. The caressing aromas of ginger and pumpkin wafted towards me, the leather of the chair was firm and supple beneath my fingers. What joy it would be to stay here, to sip that luxuriously crisp coffee forever, and never leave.**

Notice that the author does not actually provide visuals, and focuses instead on the scents of "ginger and pumpkin", the solidarity and texture of "leather", and the taste of "coffee". Yet these details perform valuable functions. Each one of these specific descriptions helps to create a scene that is vivid enough for the reader, imaginatively, to enter. And together, the details create a single strong impression of satisfaction and repose, allowing the reader to readily understand the author's exact emotional state.

SHIFTING TONES

At key points in an essay, an author may shift from one strong tone or attitude to another: from positive to negative, from subdued to impassioned, from speculative pragmatic. These are but a few of the examples that shifts in tone can take. Such a shift will create an element of surprise that will engage and intrigue the reader, as in the excerpt below.

> **I believed all this about humanity's place in the world, premised my life as a researcher on a belief that natural resources were ours to use, ours to benefit from—until all my premises were brought crashing down.**

Here, the author shifts away from confidence and indicates that an entire way of thinking has been abandoned. Changes in tone often grab the reader's attention with such rapid pivots; the use of a dash, indeed, is a popular tactic for registering such changes. Yet such changes can also be more subtle.

> **Quarterly revenues had decreased, same-store sales had stagnated, and nonetheless the directors of the board insisted that the entire business was on the right track. Yeah, sure. Who were they fooling?**

In this case, the strongest shift is from an formal to an informal writing style. This shift indeed makes the writing more striking and dramatic, but also has the advantage of introducing a conversational voice that makes a somewhat dry and technical issue easier to approach.

Short Sentences

A sophisticated writer will often use short sentences for strategic purposes. Somewhat like exclamations, short sentences can interrupt the flow of a formal essay with powerful effect: they can suggest an author's passion, lend emphasis to specific points, and (if used properly) leave an impression of variety and eloquence.

> **I was there. We were strong. We were unafraid. And by some strange premonition, we knew that all the hopes we had accumulated would reach their fruition as we gathered, in the twilight, on that rainy autumn day.**

The three short sentences that begin this excerpt serve a few different functions. The spell out a series of emotions with supreme clarity, and they quickly define the author as a member of a broader group. A longer description could, in fact, simply become a distraction. But notice also that the author follows these three sentences with a longer sentence that uses advanced vocabulary to create an elegant contrast.

Simile

A direct comparison that uses "like" or "as" to clearly pair off two items or ideas can be classified as a simile. (Keep in mind that a metaphor will often involve similar comparisons, but does NOT actually use "like" or "as" to establish a relationship.) Similes serve a few functions: they can, for instance, clarify a meaning or an emotion in a quick, immediately understandable manner.

> **The entire process was as much fun as being thrown out a window and landing on a pile of garbage.**

Here, the author uses "as" to create a comparison that spells out a strong negative tone. Yet a simile can also serve the purpose of offering a more neutral image, but in a manner that again is immediate and understandable.

> **Such a political party is like a great zeppelin, moving forward at a stately and leisurely pace.**

In this instance, the "political party" is not assigned a particularly strong positive or negative connotation. Yet the image of the "great zeppelin" indicates another important feature: how the political party acts and makes progress under normal circumstances.

Symbolism

The general strategy of creating a strong and somewhat detailed parallel between two items is known as symbolism. In some ways, symbolism is similar to other devices that rely on comparison: metaphors and similes are among the primary means of introducing symbolism. Yet symbolism can be placed in a category of its own because, typically, it is notably intricate and complex. A symbol may be open to a few different interpretations, may recur at meaningful points within an essay, and may be surrounded by considerable analysis on the author's part.

> **Indeed, a wind is blowing. It is sweeping through these tired streets, breathing life into even the tiniest trees and shrubs, rousing even the oldest and frailest from their tired beds. A wind is blowing from across the tumultuous mountains, calling us to both war and peace. That wind has a name: "revolution."**

Here, the wind symbolizes a broader social movement. However, the actions of the wind are too complicated and varied for the wind simply to be considered a metaphor. It is even debatable whether the wind's actions ("war and peace") are primarily negative or positive. What is not debatable is that the author uses this symbol to call attention to a major idea and to communicate both personal creativity (through command of language) and social consciousness (through the passion for a moment in history that the "wind" communicates).

VISUAL DESCRIPTION

By describing visual elements—size, shape, color, texture, movement—an author can accomplish a few different goals. Visual description is a powerful means of creating mental pictures that activate a reader's imagination. Such strong impressions can make readers feel as though they are witnessing events or episodes in a direct, visceral fashion. Moreover, visual description can help readers to latch onto problems by moving an essay away from explanation or analysis and into narrative and storytelling—which are the modes of expression that many readers find most accessible and memorable.

> **Her eyes—luminous indigo eyes such as I had never seen before—seemed to stare past everyone else. As she took out a chapped and faded red plastic bowl, in which was nestled a long wooden spoon as long as my forearm, I knew what I needed to do. I needed to offer San and the other children who thronged that mission more than a few smiles and games of soccer beneath the drooping palm trees. Those children would become my life.**

The visual descriptions above help the reader to readily connect to the scene and context that the author is describing. Notice, also, the precision of some of the colors and details that the narrator remembers. Specificity of the sort exhibited above allows the author to demonstrate a strong emotional investment in the topic of the essay; the details are recalled so firmly because the scene and the broader topic are loaded with emotional significance.

PATHOS: ESSAY GLOSSARY
PART II, EMOTION TERMS

ADMIRATION

Expressions of admiration can serve a few different purposes in SAT Essay passages. Some authors will pinpoint people, organizations, or initiatives that they admire in the hope that the reader will feel the same admiration for worthwhile ideas and accomplishments. Other authors will use expressions of admiration to profess and clarify their own loyalties—or to pinpoint, by way of contrast, ideas that do

NOT deserve admiration of any sort.

> **I frankly do not know which to praise more: his ability to take risks in a mood of supreme calm and confidence, or his intuitions concerning the future of commerce and technology. Wondrous though his successes may seem, for me there is little wonder that these qualities made Jeff Bezos the kind of once-in-a-generation businessman he is. Few others possess these talents: fewer still would have the nerve to make the best possible use of them.**

In this excerpt, the author voices clear admiration and approval for "Jeff Bezos". But this praise—rather than simply calling attention to the author's own loyalties—serves valuable strategic purposes as well. The admiring discussion of Bezos doubles as an opportunity for the author to define the qualities that are supremely useful in the world of modern business. Bezos's qualities are also exposed as relatively rare; the author, thus, also finds an opportunity to subtly criticize those who do NOT possess the qualities that are singled out for admiration.

DISDAIN AND DISAPPROVAL

To elucidate their own principles and to sway the reader AGAINST specific ideas, authors will often adopt tones of disdain and disapproval. Keep in mind that these emotions, though strong, are not as extreme as some of the other negative emotions that will be at an author's disposal (such as Fear and Panic, or Hatred and Revulsion). Ultimately, disdain and disapproval are designed to serve a carefully balanced group of objectives: to designate the author's position as superior to an opposite position, to inspire the reader to dislike that opposite position, and to project an authorial personality that is composed, controlled, and committed to a strong stance.

> **So it was that an entire approach to the study of literature was based on the worst of motives: self-promotion, empty rhetoric, the search for easy and unwarranted professional security. But worst served of all were the students. They suffered through seminars led by professors who embraced these dubious values, and emerged worse off than if they had never taken English courses at all.**

This excerpt involves strong vocabulary ("worst", "empty") that readily indicates how the reader is meant to react: with strong disapproval. Note, though, that the author's disdain is based on a reasonable set of values and criteria. Despite the sheer strength of these emotions, they are ultimately backed up by a logical argument about the clearly negative effects of the approach to literary study that the author despises.

EMPATHY

The quality of being able to directly understand another person's perspective or viewpoint—in considerable detail—is known as empathy. As used in SAT Essay passages, displays of empathy can take a few different forms: an author may record a long series of impressions that can be attributed to another person, or may write a few paragraphs entirely from the perspective of that other person. Empathy often demonstrates moral and intellectual engagement, but should not be confused with some of the other emotions (namely Sympathy) that appear in SAT Essay passages. An author typically "sympathizes" with the less fortunate, but can "empathize" with a larger variety of people—friends, enemies, subordinates, and superiors.

> **Think of what is must be like to inhabit Raymond's position. On the one hand, there are all the benefits that would come from selling the bistro to a larger services and management company—visibility, connections, opportunities for growth. On the other, there is the fact that he will be sacrificing the business he built from the ground up to a future that, though apparently promising, is ultimately uncertain.**

To get the reader to connect to "Raymond", the passage above begins with direct address. Yet most of the discussion is a third-person overview of the emotionally-intense possibilities (prosperity versus uncertainty) that Raymond himself is considering. The benefit of using empathy, in this instance and others, is that this emotional appeal encourages readers to think through the stakes and significance of particular problems. It thus becomes possible to directly access the strong emotions that are felt by an entirely different person.

FEAR AND PANIC

Among the most strikingly negative emotions that will appear within SAT Essays are fear and panic. Normally, these emotions would indicate a sense of horror or a loss of control, but SAT Essay authors can be adept at using fear and panic to complement points that are both positive and rational. Strategic uses of such strong negatives can inspire readers to feel strong, almost immediate aversion to specific possibilities, events, or ideas. But fear and panic can also be paired against uses of ethos and logos to show that an author, rather than being mastered by strong and potentially despairing emotion, can powerfully combine emotional engagement with good logical and moral sense.

> **Suddenly, the workers heard an ominous creaking sound. They looked up in horror as first one beam, then another swung loose, as the entire structure began to sway. They rushed for the ropes and elevators, but it was too late. Within fifteen minutes, shoddy materials spelled the doom of a thirty-story office building and took the lives of forty-seven workers. But surely this was an aberration, yes? Not at all: it is but one of many similar tragedies, each one a product of the same negligence.**

The author of the excerpt above has sounded a strong note of fear and panic by describing a scenario (the collapse of a building) that would naturally fill most readers with intense fear. Yet there is often more to the emotions of fear and panic than strong initial descriptions. Here, these negative emotions are meant to extend **beyond** the unsettling anecdote. The reader is meant, ultimately, to fear that "similar tragedies" could repeat themselves and continue to claim the lives of unsuspecting workers.

HATRED AND REVULSION

At times, it will be necessary for an author to offer a strong and unequivocal condemnation. The emotions of hatred and revulsion may seem extreme—too extreme, perhaps, for certain logical and rational arguments—but are nonetheless potent devices when used wisely. An author who expresses hatred can, simultaneously, express a moral courage that readers will admire. And a tone of hatred and revulsion is a way of showing that some ideas are so destructive or so absurd that they are in fact beyond the acceptable bounds of morality.

> **Such people are beyond rational negotiation, beyond moral reproach. They have dragged our national discourse on race relations into a gutter so foul that it defies any sort of description. These so-called "vigilantes" are the descendants not of a school of thought, but of the unthinking bigotry that has plagued us with its dishonesty, its violence, and its disregard for law and order since the end of the Civil War.**

In the statements above, the author does not in fact offer much in the way of balanced or evenhanded argument when considering the "people". To do so, in fact, would go AGAINST the author's purpose. The "people" are so clearly deserving of hatred and revulsion that "rational" measures are inappropriate. While such strength of emotion on the author's part would be difficult to justify in some cases, the completely negative nature of the "people"—promoters of bigotry, violence, and discord—makes such strength of emotion perfectly justifiable here.

IRONY AND DRY HUMOR

Although some forms of emotion used by SAT Essay authors will be striking and potentially divisive, other forms will be more subtle, but still effective in swaying readers' thoughts and opinions. One example of such emotional subtlety is the use of irony and dry humor. By exhibiting a sophisticated awareness of nuanced and lightly comical situations, a writer can give the impression that he or she is witty, clever, and perceptive. These strengths of personality can help win readers over to the larger argument (since it comes from a humorous and intelligent author), or can simply enliven writing that would otherwise be thoroughly analytical or intense (and perhaps somewhat more alienating).

> **And what, you may ask, did the members of the Marchant family intend to do after winning all that money? Build a private villa somewhere in the Maldives? Start a candy company? Buy a pony for everybody in town, and everybody in the next town, and everybody in the next one? They could do anything they wanted, certainly, except invest it in wisely-chosen stocks and bonds and continue to lead humble, productive lives.**

Here, the author maintains a mostly calm and meticulous tone when presenting details. However, the details of what the "Marchant family" intends are meant to strike the reader as ridiculous—and as sharply contrasting with the reasonable course of action that the author calls attention to towards the end of this excerpt. Taken together, the author's statements use a whimsical and humorous tone to call attention to an important inconsistency or irony within the family's behavior: although given the potential to live in a comfortable and reasonable manner, the members of the Marchant family may be inclined to make absurd choices instead.

OPTIMISM

A tone of optimism is naturally appealing in a few different ways. The positive character traits that accompany optimism—a proactive vision of the future, a belief that constructive steps can be taken— are designed to inspire readers in a clear, immediate fashion. Moreover, expressions of optimism can give an author's argument a sense of practicality and purpose. Many of the essays that you will encounter on the SAT involve substantial negative or critical portions; intelligent authors, however, know that such critiques must lead to meaningful solutions—especially if readers want to end with an emotion other than hopelessness or futility.

> **I believe that we can do better. Even the worst of the practices that we have seen— unaccountable price increases, searches for bizarre tax shelters—even these can be corrected, quickly and efficiently. Indeed, we will live to see a time when the entire medical and pharmaceutical industry re-connects with a truly humanitarian and philanthropic mission. That time will be here soon, much sooner than we think.**

Note that the author's tone is not purely positive. Rather, by complementing an analysis of the negatives within the "medical and pharmaceutical industry" with a vision of a positive future, the author projects a sense of optimism that is more thoughtful and meaningful than monotonous positivity possibly could be. After all, an author who is clearly aware of negatives but STILL envisions a positive future could not be easily accused of misplaced idealism—and is INSTEAD projecting thoughtful yet strong optimism.

PITY AND SADNESS

Some of the SAT Essay passages that you encounter will make stark, memorable uses of the emotions of pity and sadness. While few authors will be THOROUGHLY melancholy in terms of writing voice and writing style, INDIVIDUAL instances of these negative emotions can guide a reader to persons, groups, and events that deserve strongly negative responses. A reader may be encouraged to see a situation in all its bleakness so that the situation can be remedied; a reader may also be led to feel pity for a person who is neglected so that such a person becomes, for the first time, an object of contemplation.

> **Outside a Presbyterian church on 68th Street huddles an old woman. She has all the unmistakable signs of homelessness about her: a cardboard box with a few weathered changes of clothes, a cardboard sign broadcasting her plight, an old coffee cup for donations of loose dollars and change. She doesn't exist, for most of the bustling New Yorkers who stride past. But she once existed for rooms upon rooms of eager young college students. She was once Professor Starks, respected, loved, admired. Today, she has no name, except "that old homeless woman outside the church."**

The author's sense that "Professor Starks" is in a supremely pitiful situation is unmistakable here; beyond calling attention to the material deprivations that Professor Starks faces, the author points out occurrences (the loss of a respectable career) and tendencies (the neglect of the pedestrians) that are designed to stir up melancholy emotions. Yet the point of this discussion is, ultimately, to do more than to activate some of the reader's strongest emotions. Like other examples of pity and sadness, this instance alerts the reader to a problem and, perhaps, challenges the reader to take action against a saddening misfortune.

SENSE OF CONNECTION

While some writers establish strong connections to the people they are writing about (through

Empathy), other writers use pathos devices to connect directly with READERS. The intention, with sense of connection, is to make the reader feel that the writer is approachable, accessible, and straightforward; sometimes, the author's specific experiences will even align with the reader's. When engineered properly, this sense of connection between author and audience can be extremely powerful. Sense of connection can help readers to feel that a complex argument is well within their grasp or command, and can help an author to complement stronger emotions (such as Hatred and Revulsion) with a personable and appealing manner of writing.

> **I know what you are thinking: could such an experience really be so magical? Yet think back on your own childhood, to the places that mattered to you. It could have been a creek with a few ducks floating past, a soccer field in the open air, or a bustling square surrounded by skyscrapers—one of these places, or a place like it, was where you first felt your lifelong passion crystallize. That place, for me, was that planetarium on the outskirts of my hometown.**

In this excerpt, the author uses a few different devices that can establish a meaningful sense of connection between author and audience. First, direct second-person address and an easy colloquial style both enable the author to seem approachable. Second, the author discusses content ("childhood") that would be alien to few readers, and does so in a manner that allows the readers to reflect on their own thoughts. In this manner, the author promotes a specific position about the role of the "planetarium" by enabling readers to see—in a straightforward manner, and through reference to their own experience—why the "planetarium" is particularly significant.

Shock and Disbelief

The emotions of shock and disbelief can be deployed by SAT Essay authors in any one of a large number of fashions. These attitudes may (and often do) appear in discussions of results and occurrences that are so amazingly horrible that, at least temporarily, analysis becomes impossible. Yet shock and disbelief are among the few pathos emotions that take both negative AND positive slants. A moment of shock may indeed register an author's amazement at a resounding success, an unexpected change for the better, or a sight of stunning beauty.

> **The first time I saw the Great Barrier Reef, I had—for the first time in my life—no words at my disposal. I could float there in the azure water, watching as families of indigo fish skittered past, veering back and forth through an infinite world of red and orange and purple coral. The second time I saw the Great Barrier Reef, I was once again left without words. This time, there were no words for the heartbreak I felt, as I looked on at the ravages. The fish were gone. The coral had been bleached a skeletal white. The Reef was dying.**

Here, the author establishes two different types of shock and disbelief (first positive, then negative) by using vivid images to explain a reaction. These images are also meant to evoke strong, at times shocked reactions from the reader. Note also that shock and disbelief can be produced through strong shifts of tone, from negative to positive or positive to negative. In the excerpt above, for instance, the reader may be stunned by the dramatic change in the state of the reef: this shock and disbelief is registered by the abrupt change from a positive tone to a negative tone that occurs between the first and the second paragraph.

EXERCISES: PATHOS TERMS

DIRECTIONS: Briefly identify the **pathos style** employed in each excerpt, then identify the **pathos emotion** that the excerpt is meant to evoke.

ANSWER BANK, QUESTIONS 1-5

Direct Observation	Elevated Vocabulary	Collective Voice
Anaphora	Second Person	
Admiration	Sense of Connection	Shock and Disbelief
Empathy	Hatred and Revulsion	

1) Never in my life—I repeat, never in my life, never for a second—had I thought such a gross miscarriage of basic justice remotely possible.

STYLE: _____ EMOTION: _____

2) We've all been in situations of this sort, the kind of scenarios that make us wonder about everything our parents told us about the value of formal education.

STYLE: _____ EMOTION: _____

3) There he was, standing right on the podium: smug, pompous, pathetic, a man whose exalted position in no way corresponded to the base and despicable motives that brought him fame.

STYLE: _____ EMOTION: _____

4) You can imagine it, how it felt when Rita finally experienced the kind of small victory that you might witness every day.

STYLE: _____ EMOTION: _____

5) Irrefutable though some propositions may seem, the entire scenario is little more than a superficial simulacrum of a more intricate truth.

STYLE: _____ EMOTION: _____

ANSWER BANK, QUESTIONS 6-10

Alliteration	Simile	Metaphor
Symbolism	Sensory Description (Non-Visual)	
Irony and Dry Humor	Disdain and Disapproval	Optimism
Pity and Sadness	Fear and Panic	

6) With a plethora of pithy plosives, Professor Prune professed particularly profound pedantry.

STYLE: _____ EMOTION: _____

7) All they could detect was the scraping of knives, the rank smell of blood, the sounds of pain that spelled their doom.

STYLE: _____ EMOTION: _____

8) The whole project was like a circus without a ringmaster and with far too many clowns.

STYLE: _____ EMOTION: _____

9) It wasn't just a loss: the results of the campaign were a bloodbath, a massacre of the best intentions of some of the finest politicians this country had ever produced.

STYLE: _____ EMOTION: _____

10) I watched as the pigeons rose in flight over the park, less like pigeons than like so many weathered doves of peace, hearkening a better and brighter tomorrow.

STYLE: _____ EMOTION: _____

ANSWER BANK, QUESTIONS 11-15

Second Person	Exclamations	Dramatic Verbs
Italics for Emphasis	Parallelism	

Optimism	Disdain and Disapproval	Irony and Dry Humor
Fear and Panic	Sense of Connection	

11) You know what I have been through; you have been with me—sometimes in the flesh, sometimes in spirit—through all my failures and all my successes.

STYLE: _____ EMOTION: _____

12) They find themselves not only isolated from their fellow human beings, but also dogged by terror at every turn; not only menaced by silent enemies, but also threatened by their closest friends.

STYLE: _____ EMOTION: _____

13) And now they are trying to solve a new crisis with the same tired methods. Pathetic! Simply pathetic!

STYLE: _____ EMOTION: _____

14) These problems persist *for now*, but for the future, for posterity, for the struggle that *really* matters, it remains possible to keep faith in a common humanity alive.

STYLE: _____ EMOTION: _____

15) He roared, he raged, he cursed his adversaries to the highest heavens. In short, it was the strangest response to losing a game of Chinese checkers that I had ever seen.

STYLE: _____ EMOTION: _____

Answer Bank, Questions 16-20

Dramatic Adjectives	Rhetorical Question	Colloquial Expressions
Visual Description	Shifting Tones	
Hatred and Revulsion	Shock and Disbelief	Pity and Sadness
Empathy	Admiration	

16) Imagine what it was like to be Sister Eunice, to be alienated for so long from all that you had loved—and to suddenly see such beloved traditions resoundingly restored.

Style: _____ Emotion: _____

17) Yet little Marla sat there on the cruel steps of the building, deserted, helpless, and forgotten.

Style: _____ Emotion: _____

18) How he found a way to yet again "put the horse before the cart" is well beyond my comprehension.

Style: _____ Emotion: _____

19) His khaki uniform crisp, his medals shining, he stood tall and faced down his enemies.

Style: _____ Emotion: _____

20) Has there ever been, in the well-documented history of this once-revered Congress, such a gross insult to basic human decency?

Style: _____ Emotion: _____

Answers on the Next Page

ANSWERS: PATHOS TERMS

1) Style: Anaphora
Emotion: Shock and Disbelief

2) Style: Collective Voice
Emotion: Sense of Connection

3) Style: Direct Observation
Emotion: Hatred and Revulsion

4) Style: Second Person
Emotion: Empathy

5) Style: Elevated Vocabulary
Emotion: Admiration

6) Style: Alliteration
Emotion: Irony and Dry Humor

7) Style: Sensory Description (Non-Visual)
Emotion: Fear and Panic

8) Style: Simile
Emotion: Disdain and Disapproval

9) Style: Metaphor
Emotion: Pity and Sadness

10) Style: Symbolism
Emotion: Optimism

11) Style: Second Person
Emotion: Sense of Connection

12) Style: Parallelism
Emotion: Fear and Panic

13) Style: Exclamations

Emotion: Disdain and Disapproval

14) Style: Italics for Emphasis

Emotion: Optimism

15) Style: Dramatic Verbs

Emotion: Irony and Dry Humor

16) Style: Shifting Tones

Emotion: Empathy

17) Style: Dramatic Adjectives

Emotion: Pity and Sadness

18) Style: Colloquial Expressions

Emotion: Shock and Disbelief

19) Style: Visual Description

Emotion: Admiration

20) Style: Rhetorical Question

Emotion: Hatred and Revulsion

TURN TO NEXT PAGE FOR CHAPTER 8

CHAPTER EIGHT
ETHOS BODY PARAGRAPH

ETHOS BODY PARAGRAPH
TOPIC SENTENCE

The ethos body paragraph will be your shortest body paragraph, but that doesn't mean that you will skimp on anything. You must still have a strong topic sentence. Since ethos is about establishing that the author is a credible source, we are going to incorporate that concept in our topic sentence.

Example:

Lenhard's background further adds to how convincing her argument is.

ETHOS BODY PARAGRAPH
SUPPORT AND ANALYSIS

The purpose of the ethos body paragraph is to demonstrate the author's credibility. In order to do so, you must provide support, both with quotes and your own analysis. Often, it is difficult to find support for ethos, but one simple way to show credibility is to establish that the author has a wide breadth of knowledge concerning this topic, and is maybe even actively trying to do something about the issue he/she is discussing.

 Remember: Do not confuse ethos with logos. Citing a credible source (like *The New York Times*) bolsters the author's **argument**—NOT his or her personal credibility. Examples of personal credibility are outlined and discussed in this chapter.

> Example:
>
> *The reader learns early on in the essay that Lenhard is not simply a layperson when it comes to this issue. She tells us that she has first hand knowledge by way of working for a "consulting and research company, Mari Gallagher," that conquers this very problem. Lenhard writes in the second paragraph, "Community and health organizations, like mine, are searching for ways to improve the diets of America's food deserts." This shows that her company, herself included, is working "in an effort to eliminate the high levels of obesity and chronic diseases that [food deserts] foster." A reader is more likely to believe her because she knows more than the average person knows about this problem and is actually doing something to help mitigate it.*

ETHOS BODY PARAGRAPH
CLOSING SENTENCE

The ethos body paragraph closing sentence is as important as the topic sentence. By the time you have come to the end of your ethos body paragraph, you should have shown that the author is a credible source. Your closing sentence will reflect this sense of credibility.

Remember: You should not end with a quote.

Example:
The fact that she is knowledgeable and active in the food desert arena helps lend credibility to her argument.

Now, BRING IT ALL TOGETHER!

Lenhard's background further adds to how convincing her argument is. The reader learns early on in the essay that Lenhard is not simply a layperson when it comes to this issue. She tells us that she has firsthand knowledge by way of working for a "consulting and research company, Mari Gallagher," that conquers this very problem. Lenhard writes in the second paragraph, "Community and health organizations, like mine, are searching for ways to improve the diets of America's food deserts." This shows that her company, herself included, is working "in an effort to eliminate the high levels of obesity and chronic diseases that [food deserts] foster." A reader is more likely to believe her because she knows more than the average person knows about this problem and is actually doing something to help mitigate it. The fact that she is knowledgeable and active in the food desert arena helps lend credibility to her argument.

WRITING TIP:

Words and phrases that are often used in ethos body paragraphs:

◊ "the author displays confidence in his or her delivery"
◊ "the author utilizes personal knowledge when explaining…"
◊ "the author shows the reader that he or she has firsthand knowledge regarding…"
◊ "the author convinces/persuades the reader…"

ETHOS BODY PARAGRAPH TEMPLATE

If you are still uncertain about how to write an ethos body paragraph, we have included a simple template that you can follow. You just have to fill in the blanks. This template will work for MOST passages, but if you find that you need to modify it, do not change the overall structure and order of the sentences, as this is the most logical and effective organization for the ethos body paragraph.

ETHOS BODY PARAGRAPH

[AUTHOR]'s background further adds to how convincing her argument is. The reader learns early on in the essay that [AUTHOR] is not simply a layperson when it comes to this issue. [He or She] tells us that [he or she] has [CHOOSE: intensive/detailed/firsthand] knowledge by [WHAT DOES THE AUTHOR DO TO DEMONSTRATE KNOWLEDGE AND AUTHORITY?_____]. As [AUTHOR] writes, [QUOTE THAT DEMONSTRATES KNOWLEDGE AND AUTHORITY_____]. This shows that [he or she], as an engaged writer, is [QUOTE THAT DEMONSTRATES THE AUTHOR'S COMMITMENT TO THE ISSUE]. A reader is more likely to believe [him or her] because [he or she] knows more than the average person knows about this problem and is actually [OTHER STRENGTH OF THE AUTHOR'S POSITION]. The fact that [he or she] is knowledgeable and [OTHER WAY TO CHARACTERIZE THE AUTHOR] helps lend credibility to [his or her] argument.

ETHOS: ESSAY GLOSSARY

ANECDOTAL INVOLVEMENT

It is easy to see how and why some SAT Essay authors choose their topics: these authors have direct, meaningful experience of particular issues, and have personal stories and accounts to share. Anecdotal involvement of this sort is significant in a few different ways. An author who can provide an autobiographical narrative about an issue is, presumably, providing highly accurate firsthand facts. Such an author would also have a strong personal stake in a problem that, at some point, took form in a concrete event.

> **I remember it as though it had all happened yesterday: the seething crowd of curious onlookers in the back, the few true enthusiasts crowding towards the front. I stood in the wings, with my bandmates, while Springsteen wailed away on the mic and Clarence wailed away at the saxophone. That was what it was like at the Stone Pony, watching the glorious birth pains of one of our era's greatest musicians.**

In the excerpt above, the author provides a specific anecdote about a meaningful concert featuring Bruce Springsteen. It is clear that the author admires Springsteen as "one of our era's greatest musicians", but it is the author's presence at a clearly-remembered event that gives the author the credibility necessary to make such a strongly positive assessment.

APPROVAL OF OTHER AUTHORITIES

By showing that other authorities approve of his or her argument, an author can build credibility in a few different ways. A thesis that is supported by recognized experts must naturally fulfill high standards of rigor and erudition: after all, those other experts would be in the best possible position to DEFEAT an argument in their field. Calling upon other authorities also indicates that the author is speaking as an expert among experts, or is a high-achieving and thus credible individual.

> **Years of inquiry by the National Institute of Mental Health led up to the pioneering work (1989) by Charlew and Sen. These two were the first to fully articulate an idea that, today, is an indisputable truth: even administering sugar pills "disguised" as medicine can have some positive effect on a patient's health. For Charlew and Sen, there is nothing wrong, ethically or morally, with a strategic "placebo effect" as a psychiatric tool.**

Note that the author of the above passage does not use a first-person voice, but DOES stake out a strong stance in favor of "an indispensable truth". This "truth" is supported both by the author and by a body of research that culminated in the work of Charlew and Sen. On account of the body of expertise that backs the author's conclusions, few readers would be logically inclined to dismiss the author's claims as unsubstantiated—while MANY readers would find the author well-read and well-informed.

APPROVAL OF THE COMMUNITY

An author can naturally build credibility by demonstrating that his or her ideas are shared by a significant number of people. By invoking the approval of a community, an author can impart a sense of social acceptability and common sense to even a complex or unexpected argument. Note, of course, that a community will NOT normally be made up entirely of experts. Yet this reality can be played to an author's advantage: an argument that is endorsed by everyday people is, naturally, an argument that is broadly applicable and apparently sensible.

> **Together, my neighbors and I developed a commonsense approach to what, until then, had been an intractable problem. We realized that our local recycling center could only do so much; however, by *combining* their efforts with ours, we could keep hundreds of cubic feet of metal and plastic from finding their way into local landfills.**

Here, the author appeals to a highly discrete group (the "neighbors" who collaborated on a solution) but nonetheless evokes broad, important values, such as cooperation and pragmatism. Still, the communities invoked by SAT Essay authors can be much bigger. An entire ethnic, cultural, or socioeconomic group would, technically, be considered a single community.

CANDOR AND STRAIGHTFORWARDNESS

Some of the authors whose work is featured on the SAT Essay will profess strong, explicit standards of honesty. By adopting a position of candor and straightforwardness, an author gleans a few different advantages. Such an author will appear trustworthy, and may be able to persuade readers to accept even difficult, surprising, or controversial positions on faith. Such an author will also have an easier time characterizing his or her foes as unreliable or dishonest.

> **I am not going to lie to you; there is nothing easy about the path that we have chosen. But neither will I veil the true rewards of pursuing dignity and righteousness in the face of such adversity. Our trials will be severe, our way lonely, and our destination full of peace.**

In this excerpt, the author does not actually provide specifics regarding background and qualifications. Instead, we learn that this is an author who is determined not "to lie" to the audience, and who can explain both positives and negatives in stark terms. Because the author is willing to take a full, honest view of the situation—and is willing to acknowledge difficulties and drawbacks—the reader can feel confident that the testimony comes from someone who is reliable and morally righteous.

CREDENTIALS

Among the most obvious uses of ethos on SAT Essays is the tactic of providing clear credentials, qualifications, or other "resume-style" evidence of an author's strong background. Recognized positions, formal employment, degrees, and certificates are a few of the different types of credentials that an author may reveal. Information of this sort shows that an author's expertise is intensive enough to warrant the trust and recognition of other people who are, themselves, authorities within a specific discipline or pursuit.

> **I have worked as a Certified Financial Planner for the past thirty-seven years. I was employed Barton and Traintor, a firm with a veritable army of analysts and portfolio managers, before setting out on my own and creating the firm that now bears my name. And through all this, I have never once been tempted to buy bonds. Worst investment possible. Period.**

The author whose testimony appears in this excerpt is clearly a well-recognized finance and investment professional; both facts about specific qualifications and past employment are deployed in order to build the author's credibility. Thus, it is entirely reasonable to accept and trust this author's advice about what investments to make (and which ones to avoid). In fact, even if an author's ideas are somewhat surprising, those ideas become much easier to sell to a reader if they come from a source with highly specific and tangible credentials.

DIRECT OBSERVATION

Very often, authors build credibility regarding a particular topic or issue by listing phenomena, events, or trends that they have observed. These observations may not amount to actual narratives (or Anecdotes), but will certainly enhance an author's ability to win over members of his or her audience. Even small observations can demonstrate the author's precision and participation.

> **Over time, I watched as Jeremy turned from a spirited young man into a shell of his former self. His pattern was tragic, but it was no different from the pattern I had witnessed in my other patients. Deprived of mobility and independence, these young people first make valiant attempts to live with their spinal injuries, but begin to be afflicted by pangs of despair after a few months.**

In this excerpt, the author calls attention to a "pattern" that is exemplified by a single young man, "Jeremy", who has been placed under observation. Because the author has firsthand experience, AND can relate this experience to a thoughtful overall analysis, the author's credibility becomes almost impossible to challenge. Note, though, that direct observation can take other forms: for instance, records of highly precise physical details would prove that an author is conscientious, meticulous, and thus credible.

EDUCATION

References to an author's training, studies, and intellectual life generally can lend authority to an SAT Essay. Extensive education in an issue can demonstrate, with little trouble, that an author has established a firm body of knowledge and is drawing authoritative conclusions. But even an author who has studied an issue with passion and devotion (and perhaps WITHOUT really attaining recognition) can demonstrate a strong stake in that issue and, therefore, a strong sense of ethos.

I didn't realize it until I was pursuing my second master's degree, but there *was* something about Rothko's paintings that made them emotionally accessible. Before I knew it, I had the core of my master's thesis ready—and I came armed, equipped with years spent investigating the same literature, myth, and legend that Rothko himself loved.

The author featured in the excerpt above invokes a few different forms of education. Most obviously, the author calls attention to the "second master's degree" that led to the ideas about Rothko's paintings. While formal degrees are a potent way to demonstrate qualification and expertise, an author can also evoke education as an intensive, admirable process of learning and inquiry. This author indeed does so, calling attention to a background of rigorous scholarly knowledge in "literature, myth, and legend".

EXPLICIT EXPERTISE

On occasion, an author will define exactly what his or her field of expertise is. These fields can be as different as genetics, airplane design, and world cuisine, yet for an author to state EXACTLY what he or she can authoritatively discuss is a powerful tactic. After all, stating expertise shows a high level of confidence in one's identity and learning, AND efficiently leads to discussions of Credentials, Education, and Past Accomplishments.

Some of these problems, naturally, may seem obscure. But among Jane Austen aficionados such as myself—we who have read and religiously re-read all seven novels, consume Jane Austen biographies, doggedly dissect any Jane Austen-inspired movie, however obscure—such problems are the root of life itself.

It is clear from this testimony that the author is an expert in a well-defined topic, the life and work of novelist Jane Austen. This discussion of explicit expertise, moreover, is aided by the author's explicit definition of a "Jane Austen aficionado". We can see based on the author's testimony that a specialized body of knowledge is in play, and that the author can both sum up this body of knowledge and discuss it in a familiar and comfortable manner.

IMPLIED EXPERTISE

Some SAT Essay authors will refrain completely from discussing their own backgrounds. Instead, they will deploy statistics, quotations, technical terms, and analysis of research in a way that ONLY an expert logically could. The presence of these devices is a reliable signal of implied expertise, even when the facts of the author's career, accomplishments, and interests are not spelled out in any direct manner.

The practice known today as "Gerrymandering" derives its name from Elbridge Gerry (1744-1814), a governor of Massachusetts, and from the word "salamander." This tactic of dividing voting districts into unusual shapes to consolidate hostile voting blocs (and give one's own party a statewide advantage) only grows more infamous by the year. Democrats have Gerrymandered Maryland in a particularly shameless fashion, while Republicans have been equally shameless in their Gerrymandering of North Carolina.

In this excerpt, the author provides a detailed definition of a term ("Gerrymandering") that would be familiar to an expert in politics, along with an overview of both distant and recent history. Nowhere does the author explicitly state political or scholarly credentials (or even use the first person). Instead, the rigor of the author's information designates this author as a credible source and a figure whose expertise deserves respect.

MORAL COURAGE

An author who takes a counterintuitive, unpopular, or even dangerous stance can demonstrate a strong sense of ethos by doing so. The moral courage required to take accept such risks is a quality that many readers will admire, and that will cause the author to emerge as a moral authority in their eyes. Moreover, an author would only, logically, exhibit moral courage for the sake of a worthwhile argument. Such a stance is a sign that the author's position is valid, important, or pressing enough to merit somewhat extreme measures.

> **I was among the first to speak out against these threats to marine wildlife. Politically, it was not a wise move, and indeed it was one reason why my re-election effort resulted in a narrow but nonetheless devastating loss. But I am proud of the campaign I ran; I am convinced that setting the groundwork for a somewhat expensive but completely essential wildlife preservation effort was worth the political cost, any political cost.**

Here, the author pairs off two different alternatives to establish a position of moral superiority. Instead of being driven by personal gain, the author's actions were explained by a "somewhat expensive but completely essential" effort. The reader is thus led to respect the author's willingness to accept consequences and make sacrifices, and is encouraged to see the author as a person brave enough (and credible enough) to admit that easy choices are not always best in the long run.

MORAL VALUES SYSTEM

It is possible to strengthen an argument by relating it to an accepted set of ideals, principles, and values. The use of such a moral values system within an SAT Essay passage can show that a writer's arguments are valid and credible because they fit into traditions and ways of thinking that have ALREADY been shown to be righteous and meaningful. A writer can also indicate that he or she is a conscientious, disciplined individual (and thus win the reader's respect) by affiliating himself or herself with specific moral codes.

> **I could, indeed, have pursued more aggressive methods. Doing so, however, would have violated the first principle of my career: do not inflict any harm, not any whatsoever. What kind of a leader would I have been, setting such a precedent for double-dealing, going against the very code I had passed down?**

In this excerpt, the author discusses a specific moral principle ("do not inflict any harm") in a manner that is designed to enhance credibility. The author points out that the "first principle" of his moral code is related to his position as a leader; the author is both morally upright and ultimately responsible for others, and thus occupies a virtuous and authoritative position. Moreover, the idea of "double-dealing" is placed in complete contrast to the author's values. Indeed, some authors will establish strong and compelling ethical values by showing what kinds of values are wrongheaded or unacceptable.

PAST ACCOMPLISHMENTS

The authors whose essays appear on the SAT will often list the specific successes and victories that they have scored, from verifications of scientific theories to formal awards and honors. Mentioning past accomplishments of this sort can add potency to an argument in a few ways. Such accomplishments show that an author can work adeptly within established procedures and standards of behavior, and suggest that the author will be capable of future manifestations of aptitude and prowess.

> **Two years ago, I set the land speed record for a two-wheeled vehicle, breaking a record that had been on the books for over thirteen years. One year ago, I drove cross-country in a motorcycle in the shortest time it has ever taken an American to cross this great nation. Through all this dare-devilishness, I have always worn a helmet. *Not* wearing one would have been the single stupidest, the single most fatal, decision of my career.**

Note that the author of the above passage is not necessarily a leader or a scholar; instead, this author has set records that a reader is meant to regard as impressive. Such past renown puts the author in an excellent position to explain why people in similar pursuits—at virtually all skill levels, from amateurs to experts—should follow his good example. After all, the author's earlier accomplishments can in some respect be related to the fact that he has "always worn a helmet".

PERSONAL STAKE

The personal stake that motivates an author to address a specific topic or issue can take a variety of forms. An author may write about a subject that is of clear and present concern to his or her community, that involves great benefits or great disadvantages to society as a whole, or that speaks to his or her particular activities and passions. No matter what form this version of ethos takes, a personal stake demonstrates that an author has a strong emotional or ethical investment in the topic at hand—and wants to ensure the best conceivable outcome.

> **I say this not as a bystander, but as someone who would have garnered immeasurable advantages from school choice programs. My childhood would have been easier, happier, and academically better if I could have moved beyond the crime and discord of my home community to pursue my primary education elsewhere. My own children should have such mobility and such advantages, as should any children, all children in troubled hometowns such as mine.**

An author who exhibits a personal stake in an issue may, of course, show why he or she is personally affected and thus has every reason to follow the best possible course of action. However, the author of the excerpt above has children who are potentially affected by "school choice programs" and is linked to communities that themselves have a stake in the matter—thus demonstrating a much broader, much more urgent stake in the entire scenario. An author who is an upstanding representative of the well-being of others can establish an especially powerful sense of credibility and authority.

PRACTICALITY

It is possible to criticize some of the plans, proposals, and systems of values that arise in argumentative essays as impossible to fulfill, or as overly idealistic. Skilled authors, however, can both avoid these criticisms and tap into a powerful form of ethos by appealing to practicality. An author who makes it clear that his or her ideas are grounded in real-life experience and workable principles—sometimes by CRITICIZING impractical measures—is an author who deserves to be trusted on account of his or her sense of how the world really works.

> **We need to cut through empty theorizing of the sort that makes current wildlife conservation policy a laughingstock. We need to stop allowing emotion to skew science, and we need to stop disregarding proven empirical models and replacing them with outlandish, apocalyptic imaginings. Research institutes such as the Felton Foundation and the International Large Mammal Population Project have developed statistical models that can allow us, for instance, to monitor and protect caribou populations. That rigor is what separates them from the bodies of agitated non-specialists who too often pass as "researchers."**

In this excerpt, the author establishes credibility by endorsing "statistical models" that have clear practical applications and that are driven by results. Yet the author's condemnation of "empty theorizing" and of other measures that are NOT practical is equally persuasive. Thus, readers should be led to trust this pragmatic and discerning author, and should be led to distrust the individuals who (in stark contrast to the author herself) have made the unwise move of "disregarding proven empirical models".

PROACTIVE SOLUTIONS

By offering a specific solution to a problem or dilemma, an author can earn a reader's trust in any one of a few different ways. Authors who are capable of formulating proactive solutions exhibit analytical and decision-making skills that will only enhance credibility and indicate expertise. Moreover, if an author provides an intelligent solution to a strongly negative or seeming irresolvable situation, that author's ingenuity and clarity of thought can become a source of reverence.

> **The best way to improve financial literacy among the elderly is, quite simply, to weave financial literacy education into everyday life. Few American nursing homes make seminars on saving and budgeting late in life part of their activities programs; this deficiency should be remedied immediately, and can be, through networking with local businesspeople and volunteers.**

The author featured in this excerpt is supremely authoritative, since she is capable of identifying "the best way to improve financial literacy among the elderly". For an author, proposing a solution of ANY sort should be a means of proving trustworthiness and clarity of thought. However, providing the BEST solution is a means of indicating that an author had worked through other alternatives and, through intelligence and expertise, has arrived at an optimal approach.

EXERCISES: Ethos Terms

DIRECTIONS: Briefly identify the type of ethos employed in the excerpt.

ANSWER BANK, QUESTIONS 1-5

Education	Past Accomplishments	Implied Expertise
Approval of the Community	Candor and Straightforwardness	

1) Let me be completely honest: it was, quite simply, the worst period of my life.

TYPE: _____

2) Hitting that golf ball past the 300-yard sign for the first time is a feeling like no other.

TYPE: _____

3) My studies at the University of Toronto caused me to stumble upon the curious fact that octopuses have lifetimes of only one or two years.

TYPE: _____

4) Our entire county is up in arms over such restrictions.

TYPE: _____

5) This is the first time in twenty years that I have seen a company's stock price increase so dramatically despite five consecutive quarterly losses.

TYPE: _____

ANSWER BANK, QUESTIONS 6-10

Moral Courage	Explicit Expertise	Practicality
Proactive Solutions	Anecdotal Involvement	

6) It may be the unpopular thing for me to do, but it is undoubtedly the right thing for me to do.

TYPE: _____

7) I remember what it was like to be a part of those early Gates Foundation initiatives, to travel halfway across the world equipped with little more than one backpack and a new sense of purpose.

TYPE: _____

8) The only pragmatic method is to wait and see whether the two sides of this dispute have any interest in starting their own negotiations.

TYPE: _____

9) As the head of the Johns Hopkins Department of Biomedical Engineering, I routinely serve on faculty committees of just this sort.

TYPE: _____

10) I am writing not to suggest but to *demand* that we organize a boycott, and do so immediately, before these injustices spiral farther out of control.

TYPE: _____

ANSWER BANK, QUESTIONS 11-15

Credentials	Moral Courage	Moral Values System
Direct Observation	Personal Stake	

11) I am proud to say that I have, in record time, completed all the necessary steps to become an Emergency Medical Technician.

TYPE: _____

12) If such an expedition fails, my hopes of attaining true renown as a researcher (not to mention my investment of time, money, and patience) will be lost along with it.

TYPE: _____

13) However harsh the consequences of my actions, I am willing to accept my fate.

TYPE: _____

14) The idea that no woman, ever, should be paid less than a man to do the same job has been one of the central tenets of my career.

TYPE: _____

110

15) Every day I took careful measurements to see if even a minor tremor had shaken the area.

Type: _____

ANSWER BANK, QUESTIONS 16-20

Explicit Expertise	Past Accomplishments	Education
Anecdotal Involvement	Approval of Other Authorities	

16) My record has been well above average: in fact, where surgeries like this are concerned, I have the best success rate of any surgeon in the Tri-State Area.

Type: _____

17) I can tell you everything you would ever want to know about how evaluative methods such as this one came into being over the last thirty years.

Type: _____

18) I was there, right there just about two hundred feet away, when the zeppelin exploded into flames.

Type: _____

19) Although I studied medicine as an undergraduate, I was ultimately able to use the critical thinking skills I had attained to complete a PhD in philosophy.

Type: _____

20) I am but one of the thirty-seven musicians whose names you will find attached to this petition.

Type: _____

ANSWERS ON THE NEXT PAGE

ANSWERS: ETHOS TERMS

1) Type: Candor and Straightforwardness

2) Type: Past Accomplishments

3) Type: Education

4) Type: Approval of the Community

5) Type: Implied Expertise

6) Type: Moral Courage

7) Type: Anecdotal Involvement

8) Type: Practicality

9) Type: Explicit Expertise

10) Type: Proactive Solutions

11) Type: Credentials

12) Type: Personal Stake

13) Type: Moral Courage

14) Type: Moral Values System

15) Type: Direct Observation

16) Type: Past Accomplishments

17) Type: Explicit Expertise

18) Type: Anecdotal Involvement

19) Type: Education

20) Type: Approval of Other Authorities

CHAPTER NINE
CONCLUSION

WHAT TO WRITE TO AVOID REDUNDANCY

With this book, our job is to give you all the "bells and whistles" so that you can get the highest score possible. One such trick is to avoid a redundant conclusion. This may make you wonder: what could I possibly put in the conclusion? The answer is simple: in YOUR CONCLUSION you should address the AUTHOR'S CONCLUSION.

Think of it this way: if the author were running a mile instead of forming an argument, he or she would sprint the last 100 meters. This sprint would constitute his or her last push to win. Similarly, the way an author concludes the passage is his or her last push to get you to agree with his or her argument, and in that way to win.

In your conclusion, you are going to write about what the author's last push is and, ultimately, about why it's effective.

This last push may take different forms. It may be a SOLUTION TO THE PROBLEM, a CALL TO ARMS, an APPEAL TO NATIONALISM, etc.

 Remember: Pay attention to how the author concludes his/her argument while annotating so that you do not waste time rereading the end of the passage.

Example:

*In the **SAMPLE** Passage, Lenhard utilizes the **SOLUTION TO THE PROBLEM** type of ending.*

CONCLUSION SUPPORT AND ANALYSIS

Although this is a conclusion and therefore is meant to be fairly concise, you must still provide some support and analysis.

> **Example:**
>
> *Ultimately, Lenhard concludes that because "people have heavily ingrained eating and food shopping habits…more than one measure will be needed to initiate change." But she doesn't leave the reader hanging at this point; she provides an answer to the problem, writing, "With hope, homegrown initiatives can supplement government programs." And the reason we, as readers, buy her solution is that by the time she gives it, she's already persuaded us of her argument; we are already convinced that there is a food desert problem and her solution comes at a time when the reader is receptive to, and even "hankering for" it.*

9 CONCLUSION CLOSING SENTENCE

You must end the conclusion paragraph with a closing sentence. If you do not, your conclusion will read almost like another body paragraph. The format for this sentence is simple and can be easily mimicked.

 Remember: In your closing sentence, you must incorporate what all three body paragraphs are about, as well how the author ends the passage.

Example:

If her logic, language, and credibility don't win over the reader, certainly, her last attempt at cleverly maneuvering a solution to the problem does the trick.

Now, BRING IT ALL TOGETHER!

Ultimately, Lenhard concludes that because "people have heavily ingrained eating and food shopping habits…more than one measure will be needed to initiate change." But she doesn't leave the reader hanging at this point; she provides an answer to the problem, writing, "With hope, homegrown initiatives can supplement government programs." And the reason we, as readers, buy her solution is that by the time she gives it, she's already persuaded us of her argument; we are already convinced that there is a food desert problem and her solution comes at a time when the reader is receptive to, and even "hankering for" it. If her logic, language, and credibility don't win over the reader, certainly, her last attempt at cleverly maneuvering a solution to the problem does the trick.

CONCLUSION TEMPLATE

If you are still uncertain about how to write a concluding paragraph, we have included a simple template that you can follow. You just have to fill in the blanks. This template will work for MOST passages, but if you that find you need to modify it, do not change the overall structure and order of the sentences, as this is the most logical and effective organization for the conclusion.

CONCLUSION

Ultimately, [AUTHOR] concludes that [QUOTE THAT SUMS UP THE MAIN ARGUMENT (OR HOOK)_____]. But [he or she] doesn't leave the reader hanging at this point; [he or she] provides an answer to the problem, writing, [QUOTE THAT ADDRESSES THE PROBLEM (OR HOOK)_____]. And the reason we, as readers, accept the author's closing statements is that by the time [he or she] gives them, [he's or she's] already persuaded us of [his or her] argument; we are already convinced that [AUTHOR'S THESIS_____] and [his or her] solution comes at a time when the reader is receptive to it. If [his or her] logic, language, and credibility don't win over the reader, certainly, [his or her] final maneuver of [WHAT IS THE TACTIC IN THE ESSAY'S CONCLUSION?] does the trick.

SAT Essay Vocabulary

Diversifying and Enhancing
SAT Essay Vocabulary

Word Choice Essentials

Before you immerse yourself in SAT Essay practice, you should be aware of the standards of vocabulary dictated by the College Board rubric—and should work with a few main concepts that we at IES will guide you through. For a top Writing score, your vocabulary MUST be diverse and impressive. You do not need to use an overwhelming number of sophisticated words, but you DO need to establish variety in the words you choose.

Unfortunately, many students become over-reliant on a few words that are repeated much too often. Perhaps the greatest offenders are "persuade" and "argument," and with good reason: these are words that occur prominently in the Main Idea box that follows each essay.

To avoid such repetition, simply follow a two-step process:

1) Determine whether you are over-using specific essay-related words

2) Switch them out for other, more impressive words that are synonymous

Here is how you might do something of this sort for "persuade":

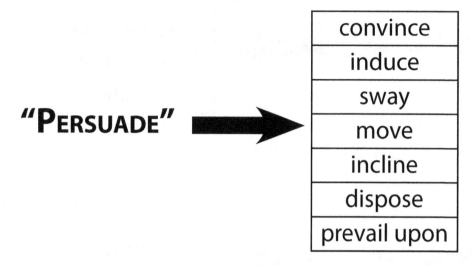

The word "argument can be handled similarly:

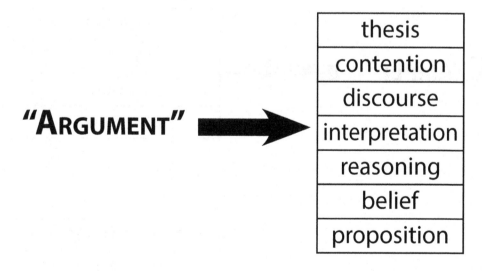

DIVERSIFYING AND ENHANCING
LOGOS VOCABULARY

"GOOD LOGIC"

rationale	conception
discernment	perceptiveness
cogitation	deliberation
scrutiny	acumen

"STATES"

claims	posits
attests	alleges
affirms	indicates
declares	professes

"EXAMPLE"

specimen	archetype
case study	illustration
paragon	instance
occurrence	justification

"PROVES"

demonstrates	corroborates
substantiates	ascertains
evinces	verifies
confirms	authenticates

DIVERSIFYING AND ENHANCING
PATHOS VOCABULARY

**"TO CAUSE"
(AN EMOTION)**

engender	trigger
incite	evoke
spark	generate
stimulate	give rise to

**"STRONG"
(EMOTION)**

vivid	compelling
visceral	stark
pronounced	unalloyed
poignant	overpowering

"FEELING"

sensation	sentiment
consciousness	impression
awareness	perception
mood	intimation

"DICTION"

word choice	vocabulary
language	phraseology
inflection	delivery
eloquence	elocution

DIVERSIFYING AND ENHANCING

ETHOS VOCABULARY

"CREDIBILITY" →

authenticity	plausibility
tenability	exactitude
rectitude	fidelity
dependability	legitimacy

"EXPERIENCE" →

exposure	pragmatism
cognizance	apprehension
refinement	participation
personal stake	involvement

"EXPERT" →

adept	erudite
proficient	masterful
deft	qualified
virtuosic	cultivated

"ANECDOTE" →

firsthand account	testimony
incident	narrative
reminiscence	episode
confession	retrospection

GRAMMAR AND STYLE MASTERY

GRAMMAR AND STYLE MASTERY: REFINING THE SAT ESSAY

According to the official College Board Essay grading rubric, you will need to create an essay that is "free or virtually free of errors" in order to obtain a top Writing Component score. Outstanding grammar, punctuation, sentence structure, and word choice will help you to achieve this goal. Moreover, these writing strengths will add clarity and precision to your argument, potentially strengthening your Reading and Analysis scores as well.

This chapter is designed to introduce you to some of the most common grammar and style pitfalls that we at IES have seen on the SAT Essay. Correct them, and control the test!

SPELLING AND WORD CHOICE ERRORS

Among the most common and potentially most damaging errors on the SAT Essay are misspellings of common English words. For example:

... arguement ✗   ... argument ✓

... peice ✗   ... piece ✓

Watch out for similar errors that involve extra and unnecessary vowels, flipped "ie" or "ei" combinations, or only a single letter when two letters are needed ("excelent" instead of "excellent," "pasage" instead of "passage"). Even if you know the correct spelling, you may commit these errors if you are writing hastily and inattentively.

Other spelling errors will cause the reader to question if you know the right word for what you are trying to communicate. These "diction" errors include common mix-ups involving ideas; here are a few of the most frequent.

effect ("result")	vs.	affect ("to influence")
precede ("to go before")	vs.	proceed ("continue")
complement ("go together")	vs.	compliment ("praise")

> **✔ Quick Tips**
>
> Sometimes students will distort a single word in different ways. For instance, it is fairly common to see the word "definitely" mis-written as "definitely" (wrong vowel) or "defiantly" (diction error). Know which words are your weaknesses, and know precisely *why*.

To avoid errors such as these, proceed carefully and make sure that you are using the correct word for the given situation or context. You can consult the IES SAT Grammar Workbook for a more complete list.

Make sure also not to commit the common writing error of mistaking a possessive for a contraction, or the other way around: mixing up "its" (possessive) for "it's" (contraction of "it is") for example. Train yourself to apply such distinctions quickly and with flawless accuracy, in this case and in those listed below.

your (possessive)	you're (contraction, "you are")	
their (possessive)	they're (contraction, "they are")	there (place or situation)
to (direction)	too (addition)	two (number)

Agreement Errors: Subject-Verb and Subject-Pronoun

Subject-verb agreement is one of the major topics tested on the SAT Writing and Language multiple-choice test. Nonetheless, SAT Essay students may have difficulty applying subject-verb rules while coordinating the rest of the essay for maximum clarity. Consider the following examples.

> **There is many reasons behind the author's argument that "pop music is by no means detrimental to today's youth."** ✗

> **These anecdotes, which the author presents by using a clear and decisive voice, persuades the readers that the argument is morally sound.** ✗

Read the sentences slowly. The subject of the first is "reasons"; the subject of the second is "anecdotes". The verbs clearly do not agree, but can quickly be fixed.

> **There _are_ many reasons behind the author's argument that "pop music is by no means detrimental to today's youth."** ✓

> **These anecdotes, which the author presents by using a clear and decisive voice, _persuade_ the readers that the argument is morally sound.** ✓

Subject-pronoun errors occur in a few major forms that you must train yourself to avoid. First, never refer to a group or collective that takes a grammatically SINGULAR noun—"committee," "country," "family," "army," and indeed "group" —using "they." ALWAYS use "it." Second, never refer to a single person as "they." This usage may be common in everyday speech, but on the SAT it is completely incorrect grammar.

✔ Quick Tips

Make sure, in terms of subject-pronoun, that you NEVER refer to the author as "they" unless an article has two authors. Always use "he" or "she" for correct grammar. If for any reason you are unsure of the author's gender, check the reference box that contains the Main Idea.

Sentence Structure Errors: References

Writing errors may also arise when you are referring back to the passage itself, or to the author of the passage. Consider the following two sentences.

> **In Susan Galbraith's "Closing Sesame Street," it is about how pre-school education has improved considerably in the recent past.** ✗

> **In "Closing Sesame Street" by Susan Galbraith, she says that pre-school education has improved considerably in the recent past.** ✗

Both sentences express ideas awkwardly by introducing NEEDLESS backwards references ("it is about" in the first, "she says" in the second). Instead of attempting to write a sophisticated sentence and ending up with a mis-coordinated one, ELIMINATE redundant references and make sure that the ideas flow smoothly.

> **In "Closing Sesame Street," _Susan Galbraith explains that_ pre-school education has improved considerably in the recent past.** ✓

STYLE ERRORS: IRRITATING TRANSITIONS

There are two types of paragraph-to-paragraph transitions that SAT readers find particularly objectionable. The first type involves "numbering" transitions that introduce the three body paragraphs:

> **"First, . . . Second, . . . Third,"** ✕

> **"Firstly, . . . Secondly, . . . Thirdly,"** ✕

Essay readers find these redundant and annoying: it will be clear to any reader what paragraph goes in what order. Try, instead, for sophisticated transitions that capture the FUNCTIONS of the paragraphs. If two paragraphs are somewhat similar in topic, link them with a transition:

> **"Moreover" or "Furthermore" or "Building on this technique,"** ✓

If you are shifting topic considerably, try a transition that calls attention to the departure or contrast:

> **"However, the author also . . . " or "Shifting tactics, the author then . . . "** ✓

Beyond avoiding these pitfalls, NEVER begin your conclusion paragraph with "In conclusion," or any variation on this phrase ("In summation," "To conclude," etc.). This is the second error type that readers find especially objectionable. It will be obvious to any remotely intelligent reader that the conclusion has been reached, making such phrases awkward and pointless. Instead, simply begin the conclusion assertively by using a strong declarative sentence. You can also use a more elegant transition such as "Ultimately," though make sure that it flows well with the previous paragraph.

STYLE ERRORS: SENTENCE LENGTH

See if you can figure out the stylistic problem with the following sentences.

> **The author states that driverless cars will never be viable. Current driverless and semi-autonomous cars are unsafe. Furthermore, drivers are often "unwilling to learn new tricks." Yet this is only the beginning of Shelstein's larger argument.** ✕

The sentences use perfect grammar, spelling, and punctuation; they are also logically connected. However, they are all ALMOST EXACTLY the same length. A choppy effect is the result—a result that may cause an SAT reader to question your attention to detail.

> ### ✔ Quick Tips
>
> Some students run an unusual risk: they write fairly long sentences, but the sentences are STILL all roughly the same length. To avoid this danger, re-read your work. If you find that your sentences are consistently too long, use shorter sentences for points of emphasis.

To combat this effect, re-visit your essays, see if you have patches of similar-length sentences, and split or combine as needed to create variety. Consider the following quick yet considerable improvements.

For the author, driverless cars will never be viable. Current driverless and semi-autonomous cars are _unsafe, and drivers themselves_ are often "unwilling to learn new tricks." Yet this is only the beginning of Shelstein's larger argument. ✓

STYLE ERRORS: SENTENCE PATTERNS

In addition to establishing variety by writing sentences of different lengths, you should be able to create sentences that follow significantly different structures. Doing so is a valuable step towards an outstanding Writing score. To see how varying sentence patterns can be accomplished, consider the following excerpt.

> **The author states that forest fires can, in fact, cause forests to regenerate. New nutrients can enter the soil. Trees that have been destroyed can be replaced by younger, fresher trees after the fire has run its course.** ✕

This excerpt demonstrates good grammar and good variety in sentence length. However, because every sentence begins using exactly the same structure (simple subject-verb), the effect is still one of unpleasant repetition.

Consider, now, the following revision of the excerpt above.

✔ Quick Tips

A good rule of thumb is to write one sentence that begins with a transition, descriptive phrase, or subordinate clause for every sentence that begins with a simple subject-verb combination (see above). If you find this difficult, try changing the ratio in a manner that favors simple-subject verb sentences but still incorporates a fair number of sentences that use other openings.

> **In fact, the author states that forest fires can cause forests to regenerate. New nutrients can enter the soil. After the fire has run its course, trees that have been destroyed can be replaced by younger, fresher trees.** ✓

The author has done little more than change the position of transitional and descriptive phrases. However, the new version demonstrates greater attention to detail and will more likely impress the reader: after all, it indicates comfort with different and somewhat varied sentence structures.

Making sure that you use varied sentence structures will also help you to avoid another danger: over-use of the same vocabulary, INCLUDING vocabulary from the essay prompt. Consider the following excerpt.

> **The author states that little can be done to reverse the harmful effects of social media. Technology is growing at a fast pace and the author states that technology "harms our basic ability to communicate." The author persuades the audience of this idea using a bizarre anecdote.** ✕

Phrases such as "The author states" and "The author persuades" can be badly over-used. While checking for variety in sentence structure, make sure that you ALSO vary your vocabulary sufficiently. (Also, do not unvaryingly refer to the author as "the author"; re-naming the author periodically can also help your style.) The following example returns to the quotation above and corrects all of these deficiencies.

> **The author asserts that little can be done to reverse the harmful effects of social media. Technology, which is growing at a fast pace, indeed "harms our basic ability to communicate." Using a bizarre anecdote, Sheryl Summers sways her audience to accept exactly this viewpoint.** ✓

Style Errors: Vocabulary Level

Vocabulary errors on the SAT Essay take two forms: 1) needlessly advanced vocabulary and 2) overly colloquial vocabulary. In an attempt to impress readers, students often write sentences such as the following:

> **To compellingly progress her argument, the author uses a plethora of strategies involving examplification.** ✗

This sentence contains an awkward and faulty usage ("progress the argument"), a needlessly advanced and showy word ("plethora"), and an advanced-sounding but actually nonexistent word ("examplification"). There is nothing, except perhaps its structure, that is impressive about the sentence above.

The lesson here is that direct and lucid wording is your best resort. Consider the improvement below:

> **To compellingly make her argument, the author uses multiple strategies involving specific examples.** ✓

This sentence is clear and sensible. ONLY use advanced vocabulary when you are comfortable with the words and are certain that they will enhance your meaning.

The other problem that students run into, needlessly conversational vocabulary, can be broken with effective self-discipline. Phrases such as "a big deal" and "last but not least," and over-uses of empty words such as "very," "really," and "thing" or "something," will undermine your argument and alienate readers who are looking for you to demonstrate sophisticated word choice.

> ✔ **Quick Tips**
>
> For needlessly advanced vocabulary, two of the worst offenders are "plethora" and "myriad." Both of these words are over-used as stand-ins for the word "many." Readers are NOT impressed by this usage; simply use "many" and allow your ideas to speak for themselves.

TIME FOR REVIEW: Now that you know which grammar and style errors will be especially high-priority on the SAT Essay, test your skills with the error-identification exercises on the pages that follow.

GRAMMAR AND STYLE: EXERCISE 1

DIRECTIONS: Circle the error in the sentence, and write the error type and the correct phrasing on the lines below.

Example

> This essay prominently uses the rhetorical technique of ~~examplification.~~ ✗
>
> VOCABULARY ERROR: CHANGE TO *exemplification* ✓

1) After considering a series of faulty proposed solutions, the author presents their anecdote to the problem.

ERROR TYPES: _____ CORRECT PHRASING: _____

2) In Bill Cheswick's "One, Two, Tree," it is the author saying that children can learn basic number and logic skills from playing outdoors.

ERROR TYPES: _____ CORRECT PHRASING: _____

3) It can be concluded from the author's arguement that, ultimately, its impossible to reform the contemporary journalism industry.

ERROR TYPES: _____ CORRECT PHRASING: _____

4) After complementing recognized experts, the author goes on to explain how there outstanding ideas are nonetheless open to modification.

ERROR TYPES: _____ CORRECT PHRASING: _____

5) The comprehensive list of possible FDA reforms convince the reader that the author is a recognized dairy industry expert.

ERROR TYPES: _____ CORRECT PHRASING: _____

6) Operating under the assumption that a pieceful solution must be pursued, Martin Luther King encourages his plethora supporters to stage a protest.

ERROR TYPES: _____ CORRECT PHRASING: _____

7) The author profusely motivates ethos by speaking definately: "I reject" and "I protest" are two phrases that occur frequently in the essay.

ERROR TYPES: _____ CORRECT PHRASING: _____

8) Some of the reasons that Sam Polk believes that money is a corrupting influence is based on events from Polk's own troubled life on Wall Street.

ERROR TYPES: _____ CORRECT PHRASING: _____

9) There is little that the reader can do too make such policies not such a huge thing, at least in the view of Dwight D. Eisenhower.

ERROR TYPES: _____ CORRECT PHRASING: _____

10) Honeywell's ideas about film viewership is based on his assumption that "you can easily access films online, even if your in you're own home."

ERROR TYPES: _____ CORRECT PHRASING: _____

11) Referring to the period when Pol Pot dictatored Cambodia, the author explains that the atrocities in the country had few real procedents.

ERROR TYPES: _____ CORRECT PHRASING: _____

12) In "Mother Tongue," it is Amy Tan arguing that the phrase "broken English" is deeply problematic.

ERROR TYPES: _____ CORRECT PHRASING: _____

13) The main idea of Beha's passage, in summation, is that "immersion in the New York literary scene is an excelent preperation for entering other careers," including law and marketing.

ERROR TYPES: _____ CORRECT PHRASING: _____

14) The author, indeed, is convinced that the committee must reform their practices or "such wanton pollution will only continue to be ignored."

ERROR TYPES: _____ CORRECT PHRASING: _____

15) In conclusion, Radziwell's argument culminates with a final synopsis of the affects of college-level creative writing programs.

ERROR TYPES: _____ CORRECT PHRASING: _____

GRAMMAR AND STYLE, EXERCISE 2

DIRECTIONS: Briefly note what major stylistic flaws are present in each excerpt, and write an improved version in the space provided.

Example

This essay states "nobody is perfect." The author wants us to embrace our flaws. Also, the author believes that acknowledging imperfection is a sign of strength. ✗

ERROR TYPE: Repetitive sentence openings, too many short sentences

REVISION: "Nobody is perfect," claims the author, who wants us to embrace our flaws. Acknowledging imperfection, according to this essay, is in fact a sign of strength. ✓

1) The author states that programs such as Microsoft Word should be free to all users. This software helps both businesses and consumers to perform essential tasks. The author argues that free programs will eventually make Microsoft Word irrelevant.

ERROR TYPES: _____

REVISED PHRASING: _____

_____

_____

_____

2) Nobody are willing to take responsibility for cleaning up urban trash, according to Susan Cary. To call attention to this hard truth, the author builds their case by citing statistics from their own research and by citing the research of two other experts who is widely respected.

ERROR TYPES: _____

REVISED PHRASING: _____

_____

_____

_____

3) Acording to Thomas T. Earnwright, "their's no reason we can't focuss on the real problems in contemporary healthcare." Throughout his essay, Earnwright shows the unfortinate consaquences of devoting to little attention to the most substantial healthcare issues.

ERROR TYPES: _____

REVISED PHRASING: _____

_____

_____

_____

4) Patel's criticisms of Apple are harsh: unless the company changes their methods, they will lose their position as a leader within the electronic devices market. In fact, without a new course, their will be a fair chance that "Apple's market share will only erode over the next two decades."

ERROR TYPES: _____

REVISED PHRASING: _____

_____

_____

_____

5) Brunetti is a good believer in the idea that office spaces can be efficiently rented out after-hours. She persuades her audience using personal examples from her own life as "an experienced supply-chain consultant." She also persuades her audience by using a humorous tone throughout her essay.

ERROR TYPES: _____

REVISED PHRASING: _____

_____

_____

_____

6) In the first paragraph, the author says that global warming must be addressed. However, the author says that contemporary politicians have also "exaggerated global warming problems. The author of "Too Much Climate Certitude" by Rory Hollistein argues that we must take a more cautious and "refreshingly skeptical" approach.

ERROR TYPES: _____

REVISED PHRASING: _____

_____

_____

_____

7) Henrietta So takes her position for myriad reasons. First, she believes that adult schools can lift up underprivileged communities. Second, she believes that adult schools are more cost-efficient than YMCA programs. Third, she believes that colleges too often neglect the practical skills that are taught in adult schools.

ERROR TYPES: _____

REVISED PHRASING: _____

_____

_____

_____

8) According to the author, meaningful reform is unlikely. Excessive bureaucracy "hampers any sort of innovation." If this bureaucracy can be phased out, reform is possible.

ERROR TYPES: _____

REVISED PHRASING: _____

_____

_____

_____

9) It is in "Hollowing Out Coal Country" where the author Burt Elon Lee shows how enviornmental reform impacts small communities in destructive ways. Lee's arguement is based on a profuse amount of rhetorical strategies involving interviews with Coal Country residents.

ERROR TYPES: _____

REVISED PHRASING: _____

_____

_____

_____

10) In conclusion, Victoria Roy persuades her audience to accept her opinion that "elected politicians should serve shorter terms as a matter of principal." To this end, she purposes shorter term limits for federal legislators.

ERROR TYPES: _____

REVISED PHRASING: _____

_____

_____

_____

ANSWERS ON THE NEXT PAGE

ANSWERS: GRAMMAR AND STYLE

EXERCISE 1:

1) After considering a series of faulty proposed solutions, the author presents **his antidote** to the problem. (Subject-Pronoun, Word Choice)

2) In "One, Two, Tree," **author Bill Cheswick demonstrates** that children can learn basic number and logic skills from playing outdoors. (Reference Error)

3) It can be concluded from the author's **argument** that, ultimately, **it's** impossible to reform the contemporary journalism industry. (Spelling, Word Choice)

4) After **complimenting** recognized experts, the author goes on to explain how **their** outstanding ideas are nonetheless open to modification. (Diction, Word Choice)

5) The comprehensive list of possible FDA reforms **convinces** the reader that the author is a recognized dairy industry expert. (Subject-Verb)

6) Operating under the assumption that a **peaceful** solution must be pursued, Martin Luther King encourages his **many** supporters to stage a protest. (Spelling, Needlessly Advanced Vocabulary)

7) The author **repeatedly appeals to** ethos by speaking **defiantly**: "I reject" and "I protest" are two phrases that occur frequently in the essay. (Needlessly Advanced Vocabulary, Diction and Spelling)

8) Some of the reasons that Sam Polk believes that money is a corrupting influence **are** based on events from Polk's own troubled life on Wall Street. (Subject-Verb)

9) There is little that the reader can do **to** make such policies **insignificant**, at least in the view of Dwight D. Eisenhower. (Word Choice, Overly Colloquial Vocabulary)

10) Honeywell's ideas about film viewership **are** based on his assumption that "you can easily access films online, even if **you're** in **your** own home." (Subject-Verb, Word Choice)

11) Referring to the period when Pol Pot **was dictator of** Cambodia, the author explains that the atrocities in the country had few real **precedents**. (Nonexistent and Supposedly Advanced Vocabulary, Word Choice)

12) In "Mother Tongue," **Amy Tan argues** that the phrase "broken English" is deeply problematic. (Reference Error)

13) The main idea of Beha's **passage is** that "immersion in the New York literary scene is an **excellent preparation** for entering other careers," including law and marketing. (Irritating Transition, Spelling)

14) The author, indeed, is convinced that the committee must reform **its** practices or "such wanton pollution will only continue to be ignored." (Subject-Pronoun)

15) **Thus,** Radziwell's argument culminates with a final synopsis of the **effects** of college-level creative writing programs. (Irritating Transition, Diction)

EXERCISE 2:

1) REVISION: **According to the author,** programs such as Microsoft Word should be free to all **users, since such** software helps both businesses and consumers to perform essential tasks. The author **conjectures** that free programs will eventually make Microsoft Word irrelevant.

ERROR TYPES: Sentence Length, Sentence Structure, Repeated Vocabulary

2) REVISION: Nobody **is** willing to take responsibility for cleaning up urban trash, according to Susan Cary. To call attention to this hard truth, the author builds **her** case by citing statistics from **her** own research and by citing the research of two other experts who **are** widely respected.

ERROR TYPES: Subject-Verb, Subject-Pronoun

3) REVISION: **According** to Thomas T. Earnwright, "**there's** no reason we can't **focus** on the real problems in contemporary healthcare." Throughout his essay, Earnwright shows the **unfortunate consequences** of devoting **too** little attention to the most substantial healthcare issues.

ERROR TYPES: Spelling, Word Choice

4) REVISION: Patel's criticisms of Apple are harsh: unless the company changes **its** methods, **it** will lose **its** position as a leader within the electronic devices market. In fact, without a new course, **there** will be a fair chance that "Apple's market share will only erode over the next two decades."

ERROR TYPES: Word Choice, Subject-Pronoun

5) Brunetti is **an advocate of** the idea that office spaces can be efficiently rented out after-hours. **To demonstrate her direct knowledge, she employs** personal examples from her own life as "an experienced supply-chain consultant." She also **wins over her readers** by using a humorous tone throughout her essay.

ERROR TYPES: Overly Colloquial Vocabulary, Over-Use of Phrases from the Prompts

6) In the first paragraph, **Rory Holstein emphasizes** that global warming must be addressed. However, **he then explains** that contemporary politicians have also "exaggerated global warming problems. **Indeed, throughout "Too Much Climate Certitude," Holstein** argues that we must take a more cautious and "refreshingly skeptical" approach.

ERROR TYPES: Repeated Vocabulary, Reference Error

7) Henrietta So takes her position for **a variety of** reasons: she believes that adult schools can lift up underprivileged **communities and that** adult schools are more cost-efficient than YMCA programs. **Moreover,** colleges too often neglect the practical skills that are taught in adult **schools, according to So**.

ERROR TYPES: Needlessly Advanced Vocabulary, Irritating Transitions, Sentence Structure.

8) According to the author, meaningful reform is **unlikely because** bureaucracy "hampers any sort of innovation." If this bureaucracy can be phased out, reform is possible.

ERROR TYPES: Unvarying Sentence Length

9) **In "Hollowing Out Coal Country," Burt Elon Lee** shows how **environmental** reform impacts small communities in destructive ways. Lee's **argument** is based on **a number** of rhetorical strategies involving interviews with Coal Country residents.

ERROR TYPES: Reference Error, Spelling, Needlessly Advanced Vocabulary

10) **Ultimately,** Victoria Roy sways her audience to accept her opinion that "elected politicians should serve shorter terms as a matter of **principle**." To this end, she **proposes** shorter term limits for federal legislators.

ERROR TYPES: Irritating Transition, Word Choice

SAT® Practice Essay #01

ESSAY BOOK

DIRECTIONS

The essay gives you an opportunity to show how effectively you can read and comprehend a passage and write an essay analyzing the passage. In your essay, you should demonstrate that you have read the passage carefully, present a clear and logical analysis, and use language precisely

Your essay must be written on the lines provided in your answer booklet; except for the Planning Page of your answer booklet, you will receive no other paper on which to write. You will have enough space if you write on every line, avoid wide margins, and keep your handwriting to a reasonable size. Remember that people who are not familiar with your handwriting will read what you write. Try to write or print so that what you are writing is legible to those readers.

You have 50 minutes to read the passage and write an essay in response to the prompt provided in this booklet.

REMINDERS

— Do not write your essay in this booklet. Only what you write on the lined pages of your answer booklet will be evaluated.

— An off-topic essay will not be evaluated.

Learn more about IES Test Prep's Essay offerings at **iestestprep.com**

This cover is representative of what you'll see on test day.

Adapted from Gabrielle Lenhard's, "Stepping Towards a Better Balance." © 2015 by IES Publications.

1 From *homo sapien* harpoons to the Samsung Galaxy, mankind has created tools to help itself complete tasks more efficiently. As the "tool" is perfected, it takes on more basic responsibility of physical action or computation. While this frees the operator to think on a higher level, and quickens production, it also creates a primarily sedentary worker. In combination with the millions of American manufacturing jobs being steadily outsourced, the evolution of technology has resulted in an economy dominated by desk jobs. To combat this, American companies must develop more balanced work environments for their employees, as they recognize the major health risks posed by deskbound positions.

2 As the head of a human resources department, I have received many complaints from employees about their backs aching after sitting in a, rather uncomfortable, standard office chair at their desks for over 8 hours a day. Part of me wants to rally for more ergonomic seating for the whole company, but that would be simply putting a Band-Aid on a bullet wound; the problem isn't the chair, it's sitting in it.

3 The average American spends 13 hours a day in his chair, with only a remaining few spent actually moving or standing. Dr. James Levine, an endocrinologist and Co-Director of the Mayo Clinic program Obesity Solutions, has discovered through years of studying the sedentary lifestyle that sitting most directly slows down the metabolism. This causes weight gain and the myriad of associated cardiovascular problems, diabetes, cancers, and arthritis. Individuals who exercise rigorously, for an hour or so a day, can be afflicted by the same repercussions on a lesser scale, if their other waking hours remain largely inactive. Thus, small changes in habit may have the most success in battling the health risks of desk jobs.

4 To test this theory, James Levine and his associates developed what they call "Magic Underwear," fundamentally a pair of spandex with motion sensors. They then analyzed groups of individuals wearing the device in agricultural settings compared to urban ones, and people in analogous American environments with a monitored calorie intake. Conclusively, those who used a greater amount of energy going about their everyday lives remained leaner.

5 Among the simplest measures that American companies can take to activate the everyday routines of office workers is the standing desk or walking meetings. Online blogger Gina

Trapani works from home, and made a New Year's resolution to switch to a standing desk in 2011. A full year later, she had no plans to switch back. Gina stands for the majority of the day, reporting that she has also increased her motion from pacing and fidgeting. In her first few weeks of using the standing desk, she lost 3 to 5 pounds.

6 However, Gina admits that she would be less inclined to use a standing desk in a corporate office, surrounded by a "sea of sitters." She adeptly recognizes the impact of odd man out syndrome on office health. Certain companies have found that onsite wellness centers can incentivize by providing a communal environment. The proximity alone can be enough motivation to exercise, but many programs also offer reductions in health premiums for those dedicated to pumping the iron. Company gyms, like those at Verizon, Discovery, and Cisco, can serve as meeting places that invigorate the daily routine and as more relaxed settings that build co-worker relationships.

7 For certain individuals, this onsite option is unattractive. They favor gym time as an escape from the workplace, and others may be too embarrassed by their physiques to utilize the privilege. More creative workplace health initiatives can foster the right kind of friendly competition. FitBit, for example, is a wrist device that keeps track of daily calories burned, steps taken, and overall time spent active. The Fitbit Wellness Division partners with corporations to create programs that focus on rewarding participation. Since Texas medical center Houston Methodist partnered with Fitbit Wellness in 2014, it has distributed over 11,000 trackers among 4,000 employees. One of the first step challenges organized by Houston Methodist tasked workers with "over-stepping their superiors," initiating engagement and socialization between the CEO's and staff.

8 Over time, a healthy work environment benefits the employer and the individual equally. Overweight men and women miss a greater number of work days per year due to illness or injury on average, and healthy employees have higher productivity than those who continue to work while sick. American employers are beginning to recognize the relationship between wellness and performance. About 79% of companies offer health improvement plans, and 54% of those are incentive-driven exercise programs. Dr. Ron Goetzel, a Senior Scientist at the Institute for Health and Productivity Studies, stresses that "companies are a microcosm of society." Using this logic, the same components that make up a balanced community must be present in a workplace to sustain successful employees. A healthy employee can be the hallmark of both success and happiness.

Write an essay in which you explain how Gabrielle Lenhard builds an argument to persuade the audience that more balanced work environments are helpful to both the employee and the employer. In your essay, analyze how the author uses one or more of the features listed in the box above (or features of your own choice) to strengthen the logic and persuasiveness of her argument. Be sure that your essay focuses on the most relevant features of the passage.

Your essay should not explain whether you agree with the author's claims, but rather explain how the author builds an argument to persuade the audience.

ESSAY 1

IMPORTANT: **USE A NO. 2 PENCIL. DO NOT WRITE OUTSIDE THE BORDER!**
Words written outside the essay book or written in ink **WILL NOT APPEAR** in the copy
sent to be scored, and your score will be affected.

PLANNING PAGE   You may plan your essay in the unlined planning space below, but only use the lined pages following this one to write your essay. Any work on the planning page will not be scored.

Use pages 5 through 8 for your ESSAY ———————▶

FOR PLANNING ONLY

Use pages 5 through 8 for your ESSAY ———————▶

You may continue on the next page.

You may continue on the next page.

You may continue on the next page.

You may continue on the next page.

You may continue on the next page.

STOP.

SAT® Practice Essay #02

ESSAY BOOK

DIRECTIONS

The essay gives you an opportunity to show how effectively you can read and comprehend a passage and write an essay analyzing the passage. In your essay, you should demonstrate that you have read the passage carefully, present a clear and logical analysis, and use language precisely

Your essay must be written on the lines provided in your answer booklet; except for the Planning Page of your answer booklet, you will receive no other paper on which to write. You will have enough space if you write on every line, avoid wide margins, and keep your handwriting to a reasonable size. Remember that people who are not familiar with your handwriting will read what you write. Try to write or print so that what you are writing is legible to those readers.

You have 50 minutes to read the passage and write an essay in response to the prompt provided in this booklet.

As you read the passage below, consider how the author uses

◇ evidence, such as facts or examples, to support claims.

◇ reasoning to develop ideas and connect claims and evidence.

◇ stylistic or persuasive elements, such as word choice or appeals to emotion, to add power to the ideas expressed.

Adapted from Nelson Randall, "How to Make Money and Not Do Anything Stupid."

1 Investing in the stock market can be described as the art of making money by doing nothing—and the less you do, the more money you make. I'm not joking about this (entirely). Nor am I trying to depict investors, investment bankers, and financial managers as unfairly-rewarded do-nothings; movies such as *The Wolf of Wall Street* and blogs such as Goldman Sachs Elevator have been doing that for years (and still haven't ruined the romance of big-time investing). I'm actually giving you a sound piece of advice, whether you're an activist investor with hundreds of millions at your disposal or a college student with a couple thousand dollars in an E-Trade account. Buy stocks and sit on them. Forever.

2 The principle of approaching investments as an exclusively long-term game is nothing new. Warren Buffett, who is widely regarded as the most successful investment businessman of the twentieth century, famously noted that "the stock market is designed to transfer money from the active to the patient." For much of his career, Buffet's investment approach was to pour money into noted brands and well-structured companies and watch them gain strength over time. The idea is to find sound investments that may not do much day to day, but that will excel decade to decade. As Buffet noted elsewhere, "it's far better to buy a wonderful company at a fair price than a fair company at a wonderful price."

3 I know that this doesn't sound like an exciting way to play the stock market. But the alternative requires nerves of steel and will probably lose you money anyway.

4 All investors (myself included) dream of putting money on a stock and watching it double, triple, or skyrocket in a few days. The truth is that this seldom happens; in forty years of investing it never once happened to me. (Late in 2014 I bought shares of the biomedical company Incyte, which doubled in value roughly five months after I made my purchase. That was the closest I ever came.) But the belief that it could happen is what propels many non-specialists into the activity known as "day trading"—investing based not on long-term investment quality but on making daily buys and sells in the hopes of accumulating a profit.

5 Day traders make investments based not on company fundamentals, but on market volatility. If a good company is poised to lose value, day traders will sell; if a terrible company is poised to gain value, day traders will buy. In fact, some day traders focus exclusively on relatively terrible companies and have had enormous luck doing so.

6   Consider the story of Tim Grittani, who began trading a few thousand dollars worth of penny stocks in 2011 and had amassed $1 million by 2014. Grittani learned how to rapidly leverage the fortunes of small, volatile companies from Tim Sykes, who, according to a CNN story about Sykes and Grittani, "is famous for turning his Bar Mitzvah gift money of about $12,000 into millions by day-trading penny stocks while in college." CNN doesn't cover the droves of people who lose money on penny stocks and day trading, though the Securities and Exchange Commission does caution investors that "investors in penny stocks should be prepared for the possibility that they may lose their whole investment."

7   The pitfalls of day trading, penny stocks, and excessive day-to-day financial posturing are evident to many. Perhaps these realities are not evident enough, though, in a world transformed by the Internet and increasingly prone to media-driven fantasies. Accessible investment platforms such as E-Trade do not really make investment expertise more accessible, and such expertise may not even be the point. Since 2008, hedge funds, which rely on professional day trading as a fundamental business strategy, have underperformed the stock market at large; late in 2011, over 80% of hedge funds were operating at a loss. You would do better to pick household name companies you like and trust, put some money on them, and stick around—which is what I have done, buying stock in telecommunications companies, chemical companies, companies that provide auto parts, companies that manufacture toilet paper. Exciting? No. But seeing firsthand how the stock market transfers money "from the active to the patient" has its own quiet thrill.

Write an essay in which you explain how Nelson Randall builds an argument to persuade his audience that long-term stock investments are worthwhile. In your essay, analyze how the author uses one or more of the features listed in the box above (or features of your own choice) to strengthen the logic and persuasiveness of his argument. Be sure that your essay focuses on the most relevant features of the passage.

Your essay should not explain whether you agree with the author's claims, but rather explain how the author builds an argument to persuade the audience.

ESSAY 1

IMPORTANT: **USE A NO. 2 PENCIL. DO NOT WRITE OUTSIDE THE BORDER!**
Words written outside the essay book or written in ink **WILL NOT APPEAR** in the copy sent to be scored, and your score will be affected.

PLANNING PAGE You may plan your essay in the unlined planning space below, but only use the lined pages following this one to write your essay. Any work on the planning page will not be scored.

Use pages 5 through 8 for your ESSAY ⟶

FOR PLANNING ONLY

Use pages 5 through 8 for your ESSAY ⟶

BEGIN YOUR ESSAY HERE.

You may continue on the next page.

You may continue on the next page.

STOP.

ies
TEST
PREP

SAT® Practice Essay #03

ESSAY BOOK

DIRECTIONS

The essay gives you an opportunity to show how effectively you can read and comprehend a passage and write an essay analyzing the passage. In your essay, you should demonstrate that you have read the passage carefully, present a clear and logical analysis, and use language precisely

Your essay must be written on the lines provided in your answer booklet; except for the Planning Page of your answer booklet, you will receive no other paper on which to write. You will have enough space if you write on every line, avoid wide margins, and keep your handwriting to a reasonable size. Remember that people who are not familiar with your handwriting will read what you write. Try to write or print so that what you are writing is legible to those readers.

You have 50 minutes to read the passage and write an essay in response to the prompt provided in this booklet.

REMINDERS

— Do not write your essay in this booklet. Only what you write on the lined pages of your answer booklet will be evaluated.

— An off-topic essay will not be evaluated.

Learn more about IES Test Prep's Essay offerings at **iestestprep.com**

This cover is representative of what you'll see on test day.

THIS TEST BOOKLET MUST NOT BE TAKEN FROM THE ROOM. UNAUTHORIZED REPRODUCTION OR USE OF ANY PART OF THIS BOOKLET IS PROHIBITED.

As you read the passage below, consider how the author uses

◇ evidence, such as facts or examples, to support claims.

◇ reasoning to develop ideas and connect claims and evidence.

◇ stylistic or persuasive elements, such as word choice or appeals to emotion, to add power to the ideas expressed.

Adapted from Tallis Moore's "Brain Drain: The Dangers of Pop-Psych." © 2015 by IES Publications.

1   Are you right-brained or left-brained? Both Internet and print media have long been smitten with the notion that there are two types of people in the world: the right-brained, who are more creative, empathetic, and spatially-minded, and the left-brained, who are more rational, analytic, and linguistically gifted. It's certainly an appealing idea. If it were true, a simple quiz could tell us our strengths and weaknesses—a valuable personal insight in just five minutes! But the brain is the most mysterious and intricate machine that science has yet encountered. Could such a simple, sweeping claim be true?

2   As a professor of psychology, I begin every first day of class by asking my students who is right-brained and who is left-brained. Inevitably, students raise their hands for one or the other. I have yet to meet that precocious student that raises his or her hand for both or, at the very least, challenges this question. I still hope for the day I meet the student who asks me, "who says I can't be a compassionate, trilingual CPA who paints watercolor landscapes on the weekend?" Indeed, "who says?"

3   For the answer, we must travel back to the 1960s, when a team of researchers under Roger Sperry conducted a series of studies on epilepsy patients, who had been treated with a surgical procedure that severed the left and right hemispheres of the brain from each other by cutting the corpus callosum. Their clever tests found that, in isolation, the two hemispheres had different levels of involvement in a variety of tasks, such as math, language, and drawing. Without a doubt, the studies showed that there are notable differences between the hemispheres, at least when they're unable to communicate with each other.

4   Popular psychology took the idea and ran with it. Before long, the complex differences that Sperry and his team had enumerated were distilled into a more easily digestible concept, the left/right dichotomy we're familiar with today. Artists are right-brained, and economists are left-brained. It caught on like wildfire.

5   However, since the 1960s, the vast majority of relevant research has either undermined or directly contradicted this notion. A recent study at the University of Utah, analyzing over 1,000 brains, found no evidence that the subjects were more attuned to their right or left hemispheres. "It is not the case that the left hemisphere is associated with logic or reasoning

SAT® Practice Essay #03

ESSAY BOOK

DIRECTIONS

The essay gives you an opportunity to show how effectively you can read and comprehend a passage and write an essay analyzing the passage. In your essay, you should demonstrate that you have read the passage carefully, present a clear and logical analysis, and use language precisely

Your essay must be written on the lines provided in your answer booklet; except for the Planning Page of your answer booklet, you will receive no other paper on which to write. You will have enough space if you write on every line, avoid wide margins, and keep your handwriting to a reasonable size. Remember that people who are not familiar with your handwriting will read what you write. Try to write or print so that what you are writing is legible to those readers.

You have 50 minutes to read the passage and write an essay in response to the prompt provided in this booklet.

As you read the passage below, consider how the author uses

◇ evidence, such as facts or examples, to support claims.
◇ reasoning to develop ideas and connect claims and evidence.
◇ stylistic or persuasive elements, such as word choice or appeals to emotion, to add power to the ideas expressed.

Adapted from Tallis Moore's "Brain Drain: The Dangers of Pop-Psych." © 2015 by IES Publications.

1 Are you right-brained or left-brained? Both Internet and print media have long been smitten with the notion that there are two types of people in the world: the right-brained, who are more creative, empathetic, and spatially-minded, and the left-brained, who are more rational, analytic, and linguistically gifted. It's certainly an appealing idea. If it were true, a simple quiz could tell us our strengths and weaknesses—a valuable personal insight in just five minutes! But the brain is the most mysterious and intricate machine that science has yet encountered. Could such a simple, sweeping claim be true?

2 As a professor of psychology, I begin every first day of class by asking my students who is right-brained and who is left-brained. Inevitably, students raise their hands for one or the other. I have yet to meet that precocious student that raises his or her hand for both or, at the very least, challenges this question. I still hope for the day I meet the student who asks me, "who says I can't be a compassionate, trilingual CPA who paints watercolor landscapes on the weekend?" Indeed, "who says?"

3 For the answer, we must travel back to the 1960s, when a team of researchers under Roger Sperry conducted a series of studies on epilepsy patients, who had been treated with a surgical procedure that severed the left and right hemispheres of the brain from each other by cutting the corpus callosum. Their clever tests found that, in isolation, the two hemispheres had different levels of involvement in a variety of tasks, such as math, language, and drawing. Without a doubt, the studies showed that there are notable differences between the hemispheres, at least when they're unable to communicate with each other.

4 Popular psychology took the idea and ran with it. Before long, the complex differences that Sperry and his team had enumerated were distilled into a more easily digestible concept, the left/right dichotomy we're familiar with today. Artists are right-brained, and economists are left-brained. It caught on like wildfire.

5 However, since the 1960s, the vast majority of relevant research has either undermined or directly contradicted this notion. A recent study at the University of Utah, analyzing over 1,000 brains, found no evidence that the subjects were more attuned to their right or left hemispheres. "It is not the case that the left hemisphere is associated with logic or reasoning

more than the right," said Dr. Jeff Anderson, lead author of the study. "Also, creativity is no more processed in the right hemisphere than the left."

6 How would one even define the amorphous terms used by the myth's proponents, such as "creative" and "rational?" Creativity is particularly hard to measure in a laboratory setting. You can't just give your subjects a paintbrush, and have the researchers judge the paintings on a scale from one to ten; art is, by definition, subjective.

7 Even math, something that most people would firmly place under the "rational" column, is quite the mixed bag. It includes a number of discrete skills, such as counting, calculating, estimating, and memory, each arising from processes that take place in both hemispheres. "Damage to either hemisphere can cause difficulties with math," according to Dr. Kara Federmeier, a professor at the University of Illinois. "This kind of pattern, in which both hemispheres of the brain make critical contributions, holds for most types of cognitive skills. It takes two hemispheres to be logical—or to be creative."

8 There is some solid research that outlines striking differences between the hemispheres. But such differences are rarely straightforward enough for popular science, and often vary wildly from person to person. For example, Broca's area, a structure that controls much of our ability to speak, exists only on the left hemisphere. Unless, of course, you're left handed, in which case it's just as likely to show up on your right side. And before you conclude that the left hemisphere has more aptitude for language, keep in mind that other activities, such as reading and comprehending speech, are much more widely distributed between the two halves.

9 Given the wealth of data opposing the myth of the left/right brain dichotomy, why does it enjoy such vigorous persistence, showing up everywhere from Oprah's "O" Magazine to CNN headlines? Part of it may be that, even if it's not good science, it's an excellent metaphor. Surely you know people who fit cleanly into the left-brain or right-brain personality types, and perhaps it's easier and more practical to think of them in this way. But by putting people in boxes, we risk ignoring the human being underneath the type. No personality test, whether it's a Buzzfeed quiz or a Myers-Briggs assessment, can truly capture the fascinating complexity of the mind. As Neil deGrasse Tyson said, "Don't call me left brained, right brained. Call me human."

Write an essay in which you explain how Tallis Moore builds an argument to persuade the audience that the pop-psych theory about the "left brain and right brain" is ultimately inaccurate. In your essay, analyze how the author uses one or more of the features listed in the box above (or features of your own choice) to strengthen the logic and persuasiveness of his argument. Be sure that your essay focuses on the most relevant features of the passage.

Your essay should not explain whether you agree with the author's claims, but rather explain how the author builds an argument to persuade the audience.

ESSAY 1

☐ I understand that my essay (without my name) may be reproduced in other IES Test Prep and IES Publications materials. If I mark this box, I grant permission to produce my essay for purposes beyond score reporting and assessment of my writing skills, including (but not limited to) publication without payment or royalties in an IES Publications book. Marking this box will have no effect on my score, nor will it prevent my essay from being made available for viewing at an IES campus.

IMPORTANT: **USE A NO. 2 PENCIL. DO NOT WRITE OUTSIDE THE BORDER!**
Words written outside the essay book or written in ink **WILL NOT APPEAR** in the copy sent to be scored, and your score will be affected.

PLANNING PAGE You may plan your essay in the unlined planning space below, but only use the lined pages following this one to write your essay. Any work on the planning page will not be scored.

Use pages 5 through 8 for your ESSAY ⟶

FOR PLANNING ONLY

Use pages 5 through 8 for your ESSAY ⟶

BEGIN YOUR ESSAY HERE.

You may continue on the next page.

You may continue on the next page.

You may continue on the next page.

ies
TEST
PREP

SAT® Practice Essay #04

ESSAY BOOK

DIRECTIONS

The essay gives you an opportunity to show how effectively you can read and comprehend a passage and write an essay analyzing the passage. In your essay, you should demonstrate that you have read the passage carefully, present a clear and logical analysis, and use language precisely

Your essay must be written on the lines provided in your answer booklet; except for the Planning Page of your answer booklet, you will receive no other paper on which to write. You will have enough space if you write on every line, avoid wide margins, and keep your handwriting to a reasonable size. Remember that people who are not familiar with your handwriting will read what you write. Try to write or print so that what you are writing is legible to those readers.

You have 50 minutes to read the passage and write an essay in response to the prompt provided in this booklet.

As you read the passage below, consider how the author uses

◇ evidence, such as facts or examples, to support claims.

◇ reasoning to develop ideas and connect claims and evidence.

◇ stylistic or persuasive elements, such as word choice or appeals to emotion, to add power to the ideas expressed.

Adapted from Patrick Kennedy, "The Adjunct Future." © 2015 IES Publications, Inc. Originally published December 1, 2014. Patrick Kennedy is a professor and editor.

1 Academics and journalists alike were thrown into an uproar early in the autumn of 2013. The cause: a story in the *Pittsburgh Post-Gazette* titled "The Death of an Adjunct" and accompanied by the subtitle "Margaret Mary Vojtko, an adjunct professor of French for 25 years, died underpaid and underappreciated at age 83." Written by an attorney named Daniel Kovalik, the article described Vojtko's struggles to afford cancer treatment and basic upkeep on her home. In the "best of times" (Kovalik's scathingly, aptly ironic judgment), she was "not even clearing $25,000 per year." In the worst of times, her salary placed her well below the U.S. poverty line (just over $11,000 in the year of Vojtko's death). The media was stunned to learn that Vojtko was a scholar and a teacher, and further reports of the saddening living conditions faced by American professors have proliferated in the years since her story was brought to public attention. Today, a basic Google search of "adjunct professors on food stamps" can yield hours worth of reading material.

2 Where did the education industry go so horribly wrong?

3 Start with the statistics. In 2013, the *New York Times* published the finding that 76% of all college professors in the United States are "adjuncts"—instructors who receive no tenure and no health benefits and who are paid primarily on a course-by-course basis. A January 2014 study by the House of Representatives adds to this the troubling fact that most adjuncts, in the mold of Margaret Mary Vojtko, earn below the U. S. poverty line. To make ends meet, adjuncts frequently travel from one campus to another, distant campus. Such time-consuming travel dilutes adjunct salaries, and fast: an adjunct can earn $2500 for a course that meets for fifteen weeks, 3.5 hours per week. That comes out to roughly $48 per hour, but only without factoring in travel, grading, lesson planning, conferences with other faculty, and office hours with students. These many unpaid activities can turn what looks like a $48 per hour salary on paper to a barely-minimum-wage salary in reality.

4 In fact, the entire adjunct situation is a strange study of how poorly theory and practice can line up. Using adjuncts, in theory, is a brilliant idea. Universities have often been criticized for shelling out six-figure salaries to "superstar" professors who publish primarily in obscure academic journals and have no real commitment to actually teaching students. An adjunct

needs to teach well in order to thrive and, again in theory, will usually bring to the table some meaningful real-world experience and a firm spirit of resourcefulness and pragmatism. And this is just where the theory fails, on multiple levels.

5 Anyone who enters adjunct teaching should be aware of the basic economics of the profession; if you haven't crunched the salary numbers I provided a few paragraphs up, don't even think about being an adjunct professor. Don't think about it if you don't have good time management skills. And don't think about it if you expect adjuncting to be anything more than an accompaniment to your primary employment; adjuncting isn't and probably won't ever be structured that way.

6 For many years, my father was a part-time professor at a law school a few towns over; at present, I am an adjunct professor in an English, writing, and career development program. But my father was a full-time patent lawyer and I am a full-time editor and journalist. College teaching was never a career consideration for me because I learned, early enough in my own college education and mostly through my own research, that the economics of college and university teaching are mostly awful on the teacher's end. From a financial standpoint, such teaching pays off only if you can lecture largely from memory and streamline your grading and administrative work to a few hours a week—aptitudes that I developed in graduate school and have put to use ever since. Most adjuncts are never instructed in these realities. That needs to change: there needs to be better mentoring of college students who are interested in teaching careers, and greater honesty from department heads and human resources departments about the challenges incoming adjuncts face. It is too late to save Margaret Mary Vojtko, but not too late to help younger adjuncts who face the same perils.

Write an essay in which you explain how Patrick Kennedy builds an argument to persuade his audience that college students considering educational careers should be better informed to the realities of that career choice. In your essay, analyze how the author uses one or more of the features listed in the box above (or features of your own choice) to strengthen the logic and persuasiveness of his argument. Be sure that your essay focuses on the most relevant features of the passage.

Your essay should not explain whether you agree with the author's claims, but rather explain how the author builds an argument to persuade the audience.

ESSAY 1

☐ I understand that my essay (without my name) may be reproduced in other IES Test Prep and IES Publications materials. If I mark this box, I grant permission to produce my essay for purposes beyond score reporting and assessment of my writing skills, including (but not limited to) publication without payment or royalties in an IES Publications book. Marking this box will have no effect on my score, nor will it prevent my essay from being made available for viewing at an IES campus.

IMPORTANT: **USE A NO. 2 PENCIL. DO NOT WRITE OUTSIDE THE BORDER!**
Words written outside the essay book or written in ink **WILL NOT APPEAR** in the copy sent to be scored, and your score will be affected.

PLANNING PAGE   You may plan your essay in the unlined planning space below, but only use the lined pages following this one to write your essay. Any work on the planning page will not be scored.

Use pages 5 through 8 for your ESSAY ➯

FOR PLANNING ONLY

Use pages 5 through 8 for your ESSAY ➯

BEGIN YOUR ESSAY HERE.

You may continue on the next page.

You may continue on the next page.

BEGIN YOUR ESSAY HERE.

You may continue on the next page.

You may continue on the next page.

You may continue on the next page.

STOP.

SAT® Practice Essay #05

ESSAY BOOK

DIRECTIONS

The essay gives you an opportunity to show how effectively you can read and comprehend a passage and write an essay analyzing the passage. In your essay, you should demonstrate that you have read the passage carefully, present a clear and logical analysis, and use language precisely

Your essay must be written on the lines provided in your answer booklet; except for the Planning Page of your answer booklet, you will receive no other paper on which to write. You will have enough space if you write on every line, avoid wide margins, and keep your handwriting to a reasonable size. Remember that people who are not familiar with your handwriting will read what you write. Try to write or print so that what you are writing is legible to those readers.

You have 50 minutes to read the passage and write an essay in response to the prompt provided in this booklet.

As you read the passage below, consider how the author uses

◇ evidence, such as facts or examples, to support claims.

◇ reasoning to develop ideas and connect claims and evidence.

◇ stylistic or persuasive elements, such as word choice or appeals to emotion, to add power to the ideas expressed.

Adapted from Danielle Barkley, "The Sharing Economy Myth" © 2015 by IES Publications.

1 Of the directions I was given at an early age, the injunction to "share!" remains one of the most vivid. Whether it was the purple crayon or the most sought after piece of the train set, objects to which access was desirable were used to implement a lesson in one variety of economic organization. Oddly, the values that this lesson reinforced often seem to have little cultural traction outside of the world of childhood. While sharing as an abstract principle is emphasized as important for social harmony, private ownership is more often the expected practice, and the one to which significant cultural weight is attached. The same child who is urged to let her friend play with her plush animal is also reminded through myriad and subtle messages that, someday, owning her own car will connote freedom and owning her own home will advertise her success and stability.

2 Because of the cultural and psychological complexity of attitudes surrounding sharing, ownership, and professionalism, the contemporary phenomenon known as the sharing economy has been hotly debated. Most often, "sharing economy" is used to refer to a framework in which an individual allows strangers to access something he or she owns, but on a temporary basis and for a fee. These exchanges can occur on a direct level, particularly with the help of the Internet, yet the most widely publicized elements of the sharing economy are organizations that act as intermediaries for peer-to-peer transactions. Air Bnb and Uber, which allow individuals to share access to accommodations and vehicles (respectively), represent two of the best-known success stories from the rise of the sharing economy. According to the research firm PwC, in 2015 five major sharing economy segments (finance, online staffing, accommodation, car sharing, and music or video streaming) boasted a combined global worth of approximately $15 billion dollars, with a projected increase in worth of up to $335 billion by 2025.

3 In principle, these innovative practices—facilitated by a digital communication platforms, by ratings and reviews that create the impression that the individuals accessing shared services can be assured of reasonable quality—seem quite promising. However, while the sharing economy may initially allow individuals to access services at competitive rates, its costs are actually considerable—and risk eroding our existing understanding of what sharing means and why it matters. "Sharing economy" itself is a misnomer. Sharing tends to imply either voluntarily granting access without remuneration, or operating on a barter system.

4   The sharing economy, which some have suggested re-naming "collaborative consumption," relies on profit as the primary motivation. Especially in cases in which exchanges are facilitated through a corporate structure, there is little evidence to suggest that the profit generated is distributed any more equitably than has historically been the case.

5   That individuals are motivated to rent out spare rooms or to use their vehicles to transport others also speaks less to a desire to share resources than to the urge to survive in a struggling economy. In 2014, 3.7 million Americans had been unemployed for six months or longer. Even for those with some employment, the gap between full-time and part-time employment has widened since 2010, and hourly wages (adjusted for inflation) have declined. As Kevin Roose writes, "A huge precondition for the sharing economy has been a depressed labor market, in which lots of people are trying to fill holes in their income by monetizing their stuff and their labor in creative ways." At the same time, the sharing economy is quickly becoming notorious for low standards of safety and consumer protection. The peer-to-peer aspect of the sharing economy means that, under this model, risk can be shifted entirely onto the consumer, with little to no effort made to monitor the individuals providing services. Though relatively rare, cases in which individuals have been assaulted by drivers or accommodation hosts point to an extreme version of the negative potential of unregulated exchanges.

6   The notion of sharing has historically hinged on the principle of voluntarily granting access based on personal connection or social contract. Associating "sharing" with profit-driven exchange dilutes these values, especially since the sharing economy provides little stability to either workers or consumers. Peer-to-peer economic exchanges may well have a place in the future growth of certain industries, but conflating these practices with the practices we learn in order to be empathetic members of productive communities makes the already-mixed messages about the value of sharing even more muddled.

Write an essay in which you explain how Danielle Barkley builds an argument to persuade the audience that the concept of the sharing economy is actually misleading. In your essay, analyze how the author uses one or more of the features listed in the box above (or features of your own choice) to strengthen the logic and persuasiveness of her argument. Be sure that your essay focuses on the most relevant features of the passage.

Your essay should not explain whether you agree with the author's claims, but rather explain how the author builds an argument to persuade the audience.

ESSAY 1

IMPORTANT: **USE A NO. 2 PENCIL. DO NOT WRITE OUTSIDE THE BORDER!**
Words written outside the essay book or written in ink **WILL NOT APPEAR** in the copy sent to be scored, and your score will be affected.

PLANNING PAGE You may plan your essay in the unlined planning space below, but only use the lined pages following this one to write your essay. Any work on the planning page will not be scored.

Use pages 5 through 8 for your ESSAY ⟶

FOR PLANNING ONLY

Use pages 5 through 8 for your ESSAY ⟶

BEGIN YOUR ESSAY HERE.

You may continue on the next page.

You may continue on the next page.

STOP.

SAT® Practice Essay #06

ESSAY BOOK

DIRECTIONS

The essay gives you an opportunity to show how effectively you can read and comprehend a passage and write an essay analyzing the passage. In your essay, you should demonstrate that you have read the passage carefully, present a clear and logical analysis, and use language precisely

Your essay must be written on the lines provided in your answer booklet; except for the Planning Page of your answer booklet, you will receive no other paper on which to write. You will have enough space if you write on every line, avoid wide margins, and keep your handwriting to a reasonable size. Remember that people who are not familiar with your handwriting will read what you write. Try to write or print so that what you are writing is legible to those readers.

You have 50 minutes to read the passage and write an essay in response to the prompt provided in this booklet.

REMINDERS

— Do not write your essay in this booklet. Only what you write on the lined pages of your answer booklet will be evaluated.

— An off-topic essay will not be evaluated.

Learn more about IES Test Prep's Essay offerings at **iestestprep.com**

This cover is representative of what you'll see on test day.

THIS TEST BOOKLET MUST NOT BE TAKEN FROM THE ROOM. UNAUTHORIZED REPRODUCTION OR USE OF ANY PART OF THIS BOOKLET IS PROHIBITED.

As you read the passage below, consider how the author uses

◇ evidence, such as facts or examples, to support claims.

◇ reasoning to develop ideas and connect claims and evidence.

◇ stylistic or persuasive elements, such as word choice or appeals to emotion, to add power to the ideas expressed.

Adapted from Larry Bernstein, "Sleep No More: Unrested and Restless in the American Economy." © 2015 by IES Publications.

1 Are you tired? It's not surprising if you are. According to a Gallup poll, the average American adult gets just 6.8 hours of sleep a night, while doctors recommend 7-9 hours per night for people aged 21-65.

2 However, don't take these findings as proof that all Americans are turning into sleep-deprived zombies. (The average American, after all, is on the tail end of that 7-9 hours range.) Take it from Dr. Sudhansu Chokroverty, the co-chair of neurology and program director for clinical neurophysiology and sleep medicine at the New Jersey Neuroscience Institute. Dr. Chokroverty says that many people can function with 6 hours of sleep, while some need 9 hours or more: "The amount of sleep needed to function the next day varies from individual to individual, and is determined genetically and hereditarily."

3 Another reason for some people needing less sleep than others is the quality of sleep one is getting. That's right, not all sleep is created equal. There are three stages of sleep, with stage III, slow-wave deep sleep, being the most restorative of all. As people age, they tend to get less stage III sleep. Yet Dr. Robert Simpson, an assistant professor in the University of Utah's division of pulmonary medicine and a sleep medicine specialist, has determined that health plays a greater role in quality of sleep than age. "If we track people over time and ask them, 'How's your sleep?' the degree to which it deteriorates or improves over time tends to mirror their overall health," says Dr. Simpson.

4 Enough Americans, though, seem to be getting little enough sleep for serious long-term consequences to start arising. Simpson is right: health and sleep cannot be separated. The situation throughout America isn't exactly a sleeplessness apocalypse, but it can't be brushed off. Lifestyle risks are involved. "Sleeping too little and too much are both associated with increased risk of mortality and a range of other adverse health issues: cardiovascular disease, possibly cancer, and also impaired psychological well-being," says Lauren Hale, editor of the journal *Sleep Health* and associate professor of preventative medicine at Stony Brook University. Day-to-day sleep loss can build up to these repercussions, and others.

5 Now, everyone has suffered through a bad night of sleep, or simply had a night of less-than-usual sleep: if you're in high school or college, you've probably had many such nights.

SAT® Practice Essay #06

ESSAY BOOK

DIRECTIONS

The essay gives you an opportunity to show how effectively you can read and comprehend a passage and write an essay analyzing the passage. In your essay, you should demonstrate that you have read the passage carefully, present a clear and logical analysis, and use language precisely

Your essay must be written on the lines provided in your answer booklet; except for the Planning Page of your answer booklet, you will receive no other paper on which to write. You will have enough space if you write on every line, avoid wide margins, and keep your handwriting to a reasonable size. Remember that people who are not familiar with your handwriting will read what you write. Try to write or print so that what you are writing is legible to those readers.

You have 50 minutes to read the passage and write an essay in response to the prompt provided in this booklet.

REMINDERS

— Do not write your essay in this booklet. Only what you write on the lined pages of your answer booklet will be evaluated.

— An off-topic essay will not be evaluated.

Learn more about IES Test Prep's Essay offerings at **iestestprep.com**

This cover is representative of what you'll see on test day.

THIS TEST BOOKLET MUST NOT BE TAKEN FROM THE ROOM. UNAUTHORIZED REPRODUCTION OR USE OF ANY PART OF THIS BOOKLET IS PROHIBITED.

As you read the passage below, consider how the author uses

◇ evidence, such as facts or examples, to support claims.

◇ reasoning to develop ideas and connect claims and evidence.

◇ stylistic or persuasive elements, such as word choice or appeals to emotion, to add power to the ideas expressed.

Adapted from Larry Bernstein, "Sleep No More: Unrested and Restless in the American Economy." © 2015 by IES Publications.

1   Are you tired? It's not surprising if you are. According to a Gallup poll, the average American adult gets just 6.8 hours of sleep a night, while doctors recommend 7-9 hours per night for people aged 21-65.

2   However, don't take these findings as proof that all Americans are turning into sleep-deprived zombies. (The average American, after all, is on the tail end of that 7-9 hours range.) Take it from Dr. Sudhansu Chokroverty, the co-chair of neurology and program director for clinical neurophysiology and sleep medicine at the New Jersey Neuroscience Institute. Dr. Chokroverty says that many people can function with 6 hours of sleep, while some need 9 hours or more: "The amount of sleep needed to function the next day varies from individual to individual, and is determined genetically and hereditarily."

3   Another reason for some people needing less sleep than others is the quality of sleep one is getting. That's right, not all sleep is created equal. There are three stages of sleep, with stage III, slow-wave deep sleep, being the most restorative of all. As people age, they tend to get less stage III sleep. Yet Dr. Robert Simpson, an assistant professor in the University of Utah's division of pulmonary medicine and a sleep medicine specialist, has determined that health plays a greater role in quality of sleep than age. "If we track people over time and ask them, 'How's your sleep?' the degree to which it deteriorates or improves over time tends to mirror their overall health," says Dr. Simpson.

4   Enough Americans, though, seem to be getting little enough sleep for serious long-term consequences to start arising. Simpson is right: health and sleep cannot be separated. The situation throughout America isn't exactly a sleeplessness apocalypse, but it can't be brushed off. Lifestyle risks are involved. "Sleeping too little and too much are both associated with increased risk of mortality and a range of other adverse health issues: cardiovascular disease, possibly cancer, and also impaired psychological well-being," says Lauren Hale, editor of the journal *Sleep Health* and associate professor of preventative medicine at Stony Brook University. Day-to-day sleep loss can build up to these repercussions, and others.

5   Now, everyone has suffered through a bad night of sleep, or simply had a night of less-than-usual sleep: if you're in high school or college, you've probably had many such nights.

However, if humans regularly get inadequate sleep, they do not function well and their most basic everyday activities are impacted. People become accident prone, less productive, fatigued, less perceptive, and susceptible to poor judgement. These seemingly minor effects can have dramatic impacts. Drowsy driving causes 20 percent (some put the number as high as 33 percent) of all motor vehicle crashes. In the United States, such drowsy driving leads to approximately one million damaged cars, 500,000 injuries, and 8,000 deaths each year. Sleep deprivation has also caused massive catastrophes. It has been pointed to as a significant factor in the 1979 nuclear accident at Three Mile Island, the 1986 nuclear meltdown at Chernobyl, the grounding of the Exxon Valdez oil tanker, and the explosion of the space shuttle Challenger.

6   The destructive impact of sleeplessness is also evident in the business world. Approximately one third of American workers show up to their places of employment without having had enough sleep. In today's economy, many of those workers are in jobs that require them to rely on their mental and social skills—the very skills that are most impacted by their inadequate sleep. Tired workers, naturally, are less productive workers. To quantify all this, a Singapore Management University research team found that, on any given day, workers waste an extra 8.4 minutes online for every hour of interrupted sleep the previous night.

7   Such sleep-related problems with productivity have a significant economic impact. One study in Australia calculated the cost of sleeplessness at 0.8 percent of the country's gross domestic product. Closer to home, Harvard University scientists estimated that sleep deprivation costs U.S. companies $63.2 billion in lost productivity per year. Employees who suffer from insomnia (a sleep disorder characterized by difficulty falling asleep, staying asleep, or both) lose an average of 11.3 days of productive time per year; this loss costs employers an average of $2,280 per employee. The value of a good night's sleep is clear, whether we put a number on it or not.

Write an essay in which you explain how Larry Bernstein builds an argument to persuade the audience that lack of sleep affects the economy. In your essay, analyze how the author uses one or more of the features listed in the box above (or features of your own choice) to strengthen the logic and persuasiveness of his argument. Be sure that your essay focuses on the most relevant features of the passage.

Your essay should not explain whether you agree with the author's claims, but rather explain how the author builds an argument to persuade the audience.

ESSAY 1

IMPORTANT: **USE A NO. 2 PENCIL. DO NOT WRITE OUTSIDE THE BORDER!**
Words written outside the essay book or written in ink **WILL NOT APPEAR** in the copy sent to be scored, and your score will be affected.

PLANNING PAGE You may plan your essay in the unlined planning space below, but only use the lined pages following this one to write your essay. Any work on the planning page will not be scored.

Use pages 5 through 8 for your ESSAY ⟶

FOR PLANNING ONLY

Use pages 5 through 8 for your ESSAY ⟶

BEGIN YOUR ESSAY HERE.

You may continue on the next page.

You may continue on the next page.

You may continue on the next page.

STOP.

SAT ®Practice Essay #07

ESSAY BOOK

DIRECTIONS

The essay gives you an opportunity to show how effectively you can read and comprehend a passage and write an essay analyzing the passage. In your essay, you should demonstrate that you have read the passage carefully, present a clear and logical analysis, and use language precisely

Your essay must be written on the lines provided in your answer booklet; except for the Planning Page of your answer booklet, you will receive no other paper on which to write. You will have enough space if you write on every line, avoid wide margins, and keep your handwriting to a reasonable size. Remember that people who are not familiar with your handwriting will read what you write. Try to write or print so that what you are writing is legible to those readers.

You have 50 minutes to read the passage and write an essay in response to the prompt provided in this booklet.

REMINDERS

— Do not write your essay in this booklet. Only what you write on the lined pages of your answer booklet will be evaluated.

— An off-topic essay will not be evaluated.

Learn more about IES Test Prep's Essay offerings at **iestestprep.com**

This cover is representative of what you'll see on test day.

THIS TEST BOOKLET MUST NOT BE TAKEN FROM THE ROOM. UNAUTHORIZED REPRODUCTION OR USE OF ANY PART OF THIS BOOKLET IS PROHIBITED.

As you read the passage below, consider how Chris Holliday uses

◇ evidence, such as facts or examples, to support claims.

◇ reasoning to develop ideas and connect claims and evidence.

◇ stylistic or persuasive elements, such as word choice or appeals to emotion, to add power to the ideas expressed.

Adapted from Chris Holliday, "Everything Goes: How the 1960s Made the World Modern." © 2015 IES Publications. Originally published April 10, 2014. Chris Holliday is an expert in Shakespearean drama who has written extensively on the role of the arts in politics and society.

1 In the summer of 1956, I went camping with the Boy Scouts. I had never done so before. We went to the South of England and set up our tents about three miles from a town, in a big field with woods and a stream nearby. During the day, we went hiking and fishing. At night, we settled into our sleeping bags under canvas tents and fell asleep to the music floating in from a nearby traveling fair. Most of the songs were pretty familiar until, one night, I found myself the only one in my tent still awake and heard a new sound that animated me. It was raw, edgy, and rebellious. It was Elvis Presley.

2 Musically, of course, this was really where the sixties started. The sounds of Elvis, Jerry Lee Lewis, Buddy Holly, and, above all, the Gibson Les Paul electric guitar carried music from early Rock 'n' Roll to the development of Hard Rock, by way of Motown and the Blues. In England, where I grew up, the kids were ready: no young teenager could afford to miss a chord. After Elvis, the Beatles and the Rolling Stones stole the scene for everyone: they inflamed the young and infuriated the old with their attitudes so free, daring, and demanding—on and offstage. You could neither ignore them nor dismiss them. The same can be said of much of the sixties: despite the trivia, the celebrities, the fashion, and other seeming flippancies, this was the decade that molded the modern world. Anyone who lived through it all became more self-aware, more perceptive—even if all we see, in hindsight, is a psychedelic good time.

3 Ah, the fashions. Most men noticed that women's skirts became shorter and tops skimpier as the decade developed, but men themselves were also becoming more adventurous in dress. I distinctly remember wearing Cuban heeled boots and long, limp-collared and full-sleeved shirts in paisley, not to mention bell-bottom trousers. I let my hair grow, though not quite to my shoulders, for I was always a conservative at heart. Still, I thought I looked "groovy" as I tottered down the street, an overweight bear, sweating at every pore. But who cared? The energy of that decade's celebrities was infectious. Everybody wanted to follow (or, in my case, lumber after) the trends.

4 It was all a bit of fun really, and there really had not been much of that since World War II ended in 1945. Perhaps it is difficult to realize this now, but in the sixties, there were still cities in the UK where the evidence of the bombings conducted by German planes was still evident. It was only in the sixties that the streets of England began to take on a Technicolor aspect, abandoning the drab dullness and feeble, failed cheer they had exhibited until then. Even British films were improving: the first James Bond movie came out in 1962, starring Sean Connery—seedy, flippant, and absolutely mesmerizing. That was a break from the monotone, repressed, repetitive movies of the time, most of them depictions of how British do-gooders had won the war. Cautious attitudes were replaced by optimism, by confidence. People began to say what they thought. Satire was popular, as television shows began to mock the pomposity of politicians—along with almost everything else. Things were going to be different from then on.

5 I celebrated my twenty-first birthday in 1963 by going to the theatre to see a revue that had been written by a friend of mine. Lots of silly sketches, some satirical acts, some old jokes revisited, a couple of funny songs, and cleverly worked dance routines. Great fun. There was one sketch I shall never forget. The curtain rose to reveal a typical middle-class kitchen where a man was preparing his meal. There was a radio on the table, playing the music from an actual broadcast. As the man sat down to eat his breakfast, the music on the radio faded and an announcer began to speak: "We interrupt this program to take you to the news studio for a breaking announcement." The actor reached over and switched off the radio. We chuckled: that was the usual reaction to such interruptions. After the show ended to tumultuous applause and I left the theatre, the streets outside were crowded with vendors selling special editions of a local newspaper.

6 "American President Kennedy Assassinated" was the headline.

> Write an essay in which you explain how Chris Holliday builds an argument to persuade his audience that the sixties were an enjoyable yet historically important period of history. In your essay, analyze how Holliday uses one or more of the features listed in the box above (or features of your own choice) to strengthen the logic and persuasiveness of his argument. Be sure that your essay focuses on the most relevant features of the passage.
>
> Your essay should not explain whether you agree with Holliday's claims, but rather explain how Holliday builds an argument to persuade his audience.

ESSAY 1

☐ I understand that my essay (without my name) may be reproduced in other IES Test Prep and IES Publications materials. If I mark this box, I grant permission to produce my essay for purposes beyond score reporting and assessment of my writing skills, including (but not limited to) publication without payment or royalties in an IES Publications book. Marking this box will have no effect on my score, nor will it prevent my essay from being made available for viewing at an IES campus.

IMPORTANT: **USE A NO. 2 PENCIL. DO NOT WRITE OUTSIDE THE BORDER!**
Words written outside the essay book or written in ink **WILL NOT APPEAR** in the copy sent to be scored, and your score will be affected.

PLANNING PAGE You may plan your essay in the unlined planning space below, but only use the lined pages following this one to write your essay. Any work on the planning page will not be scored.

Use pages 5 through 8 for your ESSAY ⟶

FOR PLANNING ONLY

Use pages 5 through 8 for your ESSAY ⟶

BEGIN YOUR ESSAY HERE.

You may continue on the next page.

You may continue on the next page.

BEGIN YOUR ESSAY HERE.

You may continue on the next page.

You may continue on the next page.

You may continue on the next page.

STOP.

SAT® Practice Essay #08

ESSAY BOOK

DIRECTIONS

The essay gives you an opportunity to show how effectively you can read and comprehend a passage and write an essay analyzing the passage. In your essay, you should demonstrate that you have read the passage carefully, present a clear and logical analysis, and use language precisely

Your essay must be written on the lines provided in your answer booklet; except for the Planning Page of your answer booklet, you will receive no other paper on which to write. You will have enough space if you write on every line, avoid wide margins, and keep your handwriting to a reasonable size. Remember that people who are not familiar with your handwriting will read what you write. Try to write or print so that what you are writing is legible to those readers.

You have 50 minutes to read the passage and write an essay in response to the prompt provided in this booklet.

REMINDERS

— Do not write your essay in this booklet. Only what you write on the lined pages of your answer booklet will be evaluated.

— An off-topic essay will not be evaluated.

Learn more about IES Test Prep's Essay offerings at **iestestprep.com**

This cover is representative of what you'll see on test day.

THIS TEST BOOKLET MUST NOT BE TAKEN FROM THE ROOM. UNAUTHORIZED REPRODUCTION OR USE OF ANY PART OF THIS BOOKLET IS PROHIBITED.

As you read the passage below, consider how the author uses

◇ evidence, such as facts or examples, to support claims.

◇ reasoning to develop ideas and connect claims and evidence.

◇ stylistic or persuasive elements, such as word choice or appeals to emotion, to add power to the ideas expressed.

Adapted from Ralphael Cael's "The Founding Fathers v. The Climate Change Skeptics." A Postdoctoral Fellow at UC Berkeley, Cael focuses his research on climate change politics throughout history.

1   The United States has in recent years become a stronghold for climate change skepticism, especially since the U.S. government's declaration in 2001 that it would not participate in the Kyoto Protocol. Thus, it might surprise you to learn that our country's founders were keen observers of climatic trends and might even be counted among the first climate change activists.

2   From the start, the project to colonize North America had proceeded on the understanding that climate followed latitude; so dependent was climate on the angle of the sun to the Earth's surface, it was believed, that the word "climate" was defined in terms of parallels of latitude. New England was expected to be as mild as England, and Virginia as hot as Italy and Spain. Surprised by harsh conditions in the New World, however, a great number of the early settlers did not outlast their first winter in the colonies. Many of the survivors returned to Europe, and in fact, the majority of the seventeenth-century colonies in North America were abandoned.

3   A view formed in Europe that the New World was inferior to the Old. In particular, it was believed that the climate of the colonies caused physical and mental degeneration. The respected French naturalist Georges-Louis Leclerc explained in his encyclopedia of natural history that "all animals of the New World were much smaller than those of the Old. This great diminution in size, whatever maybe the cause, is a primary kind of degeneration." He speculated that the difference in climate might be the cause.

4   In the New World, refuting such theories became a matter of patriotism. Building on the ideas of John Evelyn, John Woodward, Jean-Baptiste Dubos, and David Hume—who all believed that the clearing and cultivation of land in Europe accounted for the temperate climate that had enabled the Enlightenment—the colonists set about arguing that their settlement was causing a gradual increase in temperatures and improvement of the flora and fauna of North America.

5 One need hardly belabor the point that these early climate change advocates were wrong. Modern climate reconstructions show that there was a brief warming period in New England during the late 1700s, but the actual theories of the time were pre-scientific in the sense that they predate a scientific understanding of the greenhouse effect. It is true that the French scientist Edme Mariotte had, as early as 1681, noticed the greenhouse effect, but it was not until the 1760s and 1770s that the first systematic measurements were made, and it would still be another century before anyone imagined that human activities might influence atmospheric composition to such an extent that the climate might be modified.

6 Yet one should not belittle the efforts of these early climate change advocates. Fighting back against the European "degeneracy theory" was necessitated by pride as much as by a concern that this theory might negatively affect immigration and trade from Europe. The search for anti-degeneracy evidence, moreover, resulted in substantial contributions to zoology, and was instrumental to the foundation of modern meteorology and climatology. One might speculate, even, that the degeneracy controversy contributed to England's refusal to afford its North American colonial subjects representation in Parliament, and so helped spark the American Revolution. In this case, one might construe the Founders' climate change advocacy partly as an attempt to facilitate a peaceful resolution of their grievances.

7 Then as now, climate change had political implications; then as now, too, the proofs used by climate change skeptics can appear problematic. Much of the climate change skepticism of the seventeenth century was based on second- and third-hand accounts by travelers, and the skeptics rarely made efforts to justify their ideas experimentally.

8 The parallels between the past and present are quite obvious, and are of considerable use to us today. While modern climate change advocates and skeptics have become experts at pointing to each other's errors, each side is blind to its own faults. An episode in our history that bears such strong resemblance to our present encourages a rare opportunity to examine ourselves as though through the eyes of others. Today's anti-climate change activists may recognize in themselves some of the overzealousness of the Founding Fathers and therefore better guard against potential fallacies. Skeptics may recognize in themselves the often anti-scientific spirit of the degeneracy theorists, and consequently make greater efforts to engage constructively in the scientific enterprise. One can hope, at least.

Write an essay in which you explain how the author builds an argument to persuade the audience that historical climate change politics is pertinent today. In your essay, analyze how the author uses one or more of the features listed in the box above (or features of your own choice) to strengthen the logic and persuasiveness of his argument. Be sure that your essay focuses on the most relevant features of the passage.

Your essay should not explain whether you agree with the author's claims, but rather explain how the author builds an argument to persuade the audience.

ESSAY 1

IMPORTANT: **USE A NO. 2 PENCIL. DO NOT WRITE OUTSIDE THE BORDER!**
Words written outside the essay book or written in ink **WILL NOT APPEAR** in the copy sent to be scored, and your score will be affected.

PLANNING PAGE   You may plan your essay in the unlined planning space below, but only use the lined pages following this one to write your essay. Any work on the planning page will not be scored.

Use pages 5 through 8 for your ESSAY ⟶

FOR PLANNING ONLY

Use pages 5 through 8 for your ESSAY ⟶

BEGIN YOUR ESSAY HERE.

You may continue on the next page.

You may continue on the next page.

You may continue on the next page.

SAT® Practice Essay #09

ESSAY BOOK

DIRECTIONS

The essay gives you an opportunity to show how effectively you can read and comprehend a passage and write an essay analyzing the passage. In your essay, you should demonstrate that you have read the passage carefully, present a clear and logical analysis, and use language precisely

Your essay must be written on the lines provided in your answer booklet; except for the Planning Page of your answer booklet, you will receive no other paper on which to write. You will have enough space if you write on every line, avoid wide margins, and keep your handwriting to a reasonable size. Remember that people who are not familiar with your handwriting will read what you write. Try to write or print so that what you are writing is legible to those readers.

You have 50 minutes to read the passage and write an essay in response to the prompt provided in this booklet.

As you read the passage below, consider how the author uses

◇ evidence, such as facts or examples, to support claims.

◇ reasoning to develop ideas and connect claims and evidence.

◇ stylistic or persuasive elements, such as word choice or appeals to emotion, to add power to the ideas expressed.

Adapted from Sheila Chode's "Water, Water, Everywhere" © 2015 by IES Publications.

1 I have been privileged to witness my niece grow from a captivating infant into a charming young woman. From birth, her parents showered her with affection. They delighted in her achievements and bragged unashamedly when her grades put her at the top of her classes, which they often did. Full of pride, her parents encouraged her scholarly habits; her dietary choices, however, were left up to her. Her choices of beverages ranged from fruit juice to Gatorade to soda; I don't know that I ever saw her choose water. She grew from a chubby baby to an overweight child. Sometime during those formative years she entered the obese category. At twenty years old, she had not quite reached five feet tall, but she weighed more than 150 pounds.

2 This result would not have surprised many in the nutritional field. Over the last decade the mantra "make sure your child has plenty of fluids" has changed to "make sure your child drinks water." The benefits of staying hydrated are well known and wide ranging. A person's body is 75 percent water; the brain is 90 percent water. When a person becomes dehydrated, many of the body's vital functions are compromised. Severe dehydration can cause muscle cramps and lethargy and lead to heat stroke. Without enough water, the kidneys cannot function properly; a buildup of toxins in the body results and leads to general malaise.

3 It has become obvious in recent years that not all fluids are created equal. A study published in 2008 linked fruit juice consumption to increased risk of developing type 2 diabetes. The study found that women who drank a glass of fruit juice a day increased their risk of developing type 2 diabetes by 18 percent. (Interestingly, women who ate three pieces of fruit a day instead reduced their risk by the same percentage.) By replacing water with juice, a person consumes a considerable portion of calories, but very few vitamins or nutrients. Juices concentrate a fruit's sugars by removing the fiber that occurs naturally in a fruit. When the fiber is present, the body absorbs the sugar much more slowly, relieving the strain on the body's organs.

4 Unfortunately, many of the fluids consumed by children are even more harmful than natural juices, which are, at least, caffeine-free. A study in the Journal of Pediatrics found that five year-olds who regularly drank sugary soda showed more frequent signs of aggression and had more difficulty paying attention than those children who drank little or none. This paralleled the discoveries of an earlier study, which located signs of aggression in teens

SAT® Practice Essay #09

ESSAY BOOK

DIRECTIONS

The essay gives you an opportunity to show how effectively you can read and comprehend a passage and write an essay analyzing the passage. In your essay, you should demonstrate that you have read the passage carefully, present a clear and logical analysis, and use language precisely

Your essay must be written on the lines provided in your answer booklet; except for the Planning Page of your answer booklet, you will receive no other paper on which to write. You will have enough space if you write on every line, avoid wide margins, and keep your handwriting to a reasonable size. Remember that people who are not familiar with your handwriting will read what you write. Try to write or print so that what you are writing is legible to those readers.

You have 50 minutes to read the passage and write an essay in response to the prompt provided in this booklet.

REMINDERS

— Do not write your essay in this booklet. Only what you write on the lined pages of your answer booklet will be evaluated.

— An off-topic essay will not be evaluated.

Learn more about IES Test Prep's Essay offerings at **iestestprep.com**

This cover is representative of what you'll see on test day.

THIS TEST BOOKLET MUST NOT BE TAKEN FROM THE ROOM. UNAUTHORIZED REPRODUCTION OR USE OF ANY PART OF THIS BOOKLET IS PROHIBITED.

As you read the passage below, consider how the author uses

◇ evidence, such as facts or examples, to support claims.

◇ reasoning to develop ideas and connect claims and evidence.

◇ stylistic or persuasive elements, such as word choice or appeals to emotion, to add power to the ideas expressed.

Adapted from Sheila Chode's "Water, Water, Everywhere" © 2015 by IES Publications.

1 I have been privileged to witness my niece grow from a captivating infant into a charming young woman. From birth, her parents showered her with affection. They delighted in her achievements and bragged unashamedly when her grades put her at the top of her classes, which they often did. Full of pride, her parents encouraged her scholarly habits; her dietary choices, however, were left up to her. Her choices of beverages ranged from fruit juice to Gatorade to soda; I don't know that I ever saw her choose water. She grew from a chubby baby to an overweight child. Sometime during those formative years she entered the obese category. At twenty years old, she had not quite reached five feet tall, but she weighed more than 150 pounds.

2 This result would not have surprised many in the nutritional field. Over the last decade the mantra "make sure your child has plenty of fluids" has changed to "make sure your child drinks water." The benefits of staying hydrated are well known and wide ranging. A person's body is 75 percent water; the brain is 90 percent water. When a person becomes dehydrated, many of the body's vital functions are compromised. Severe dehydration can cause muscle cramps and lethargy and lead to heat stroke. Without enough water, the kidneys cannot function properly; a buildup of toxins in the body results and leads to general malaise.

3 It has become obvious in recent years that not all fluids are created equal. A study published in 2008 linked fruit juice consumption to increased risk of developing type 2 diabetes. The study found that women who drank a glass of fruit juice a day increased their risk of developing type 2 diabetes by 18 percent. (Interestingly, women who ate three pieces of fruit a day instead reduced their risk by the same percentage.) By replacing water with juice, a person consumes a considerable portion of calories, but very few vitamins or nutrients. Juices concentrate a fruit's sugars by removing the fiber that occurs naturally in a fruit. When the fiber is present, the body absorbs the sugar much more slowly, relieving the strain on the body's organs.

4 Unfortunately, many of the fluids consumed by children are even more harmful than natural juices, which are, at least, caffeine-free. A study in the Journal of Pediatrics found that five year-olds who regularly drank sugary soda showed more frequent signs of aggression and had more difficulty paying attention than those children who drank little or none. This paralleled the discoveries of an earlier study, which located signs of aggression in teens

who consumed sugary sodas in greater volume. That study linked sugary soda consumption with many mood-related issues, from fighting to feelings of sadness and hopelessness. The caffeine in these drinks is, most likely, one of the culprits, as it is known to affect the body's hormonal levels and is considered unsafe for children. Other substances sodas contain that could influence a child's mood include carbonated water, high-fructose corn syrup, aspartame, sodium benzoate, phosphoric acid, and citric acid.

5   The public health implications are troubling. According to the Harvard School of Public Health, two out of three adults and one out of three children in the United States are overweight or obese. This health crisis has resulted in our nation spending more than $190 billion annually on obesity-related health conditions. The rising consumption of sugary drinks has been directly linked to increased chances of obesity, type 2 diabetes, gout, and heart disease. In one study, the chances of becoming obese increased 60 percent for each additional 12-ounce soda that a child consumed.

6   For her part, my niece has excelled in many ways. She is attending college and continues to create a stellar academic record, thanks, in part, to habits established when she was young. Her other early habits, though, continue to haunt her. She suffers from joint pain, fatigue, diabetes, and various other medical complaints. How different would her life be today, if she had been taught early on to make healthful choices?

7   Many parents struggle to provide nice homes for their children. They seek out the best schools and embrace sacrifice so that their children don't have to do without. Those choices are admirable, but I wonder if one of the most important parenting decisions we can make is as simple as teaching our children to drink water.

Write an essay in which you explain how the author builds an argument to persuade the audience that parents should teach their children to consume more water compared to other fluids. In your essay, analyze how the author uses one or more of the features listed in the box above (or features of your own choice) to strengthen the logic and persuasiveness of her argument. Be sure that your essay focuses on the most relevant features of the passage.

Your essay should not explain whether you agree with the author's claims, but rather explain how the author builds an argument to persuade the audience.

ESSAY 1

☐ I understand that my essay (without my name) may be reproduced in other IES Test Prep and IES Publications materials. If I mark this box, I grant permission to produce my essay for purposes beyond score reporting and assessment of my writing skills, including (but not limited to) publication without payment or royalties in an IES Publications book. Marking this box will have no effect on my score, nor will it prevent my essay from being made available for viewing at an IES campus.

IMPORTANT: **USE A NO. 2 PENCIL. DO NOT WRITE OUTSIDE THE BORDER!**
Words written outside the essay book or written in ink **WILL NOT APPEAR** in the copy sent to be scored, and your score will be affected.

PLANNING PAGE   You may plan your essay in the unlined planning space below, but only use the lined pages following this one to write your essay. Any work on the planning page will not be scored.

Use pages 5 through 8 for your ESSAY ──────────➤

FOR PLANNING ONLY

Use pages 5 through 8 for your ESSAY ──────────➤

BEGIN YOUR ESSAY HERE.

You may continue on the next page.

You may continue on the next page.

STOP.

SAT® Practice Essay #10

ESSAY BOOK

DIRECTIONS

The essay gives you an opportunity to show how effectively you can read and comprehend a passage and write an essay analyzing the passage. In your essay, you should demonstrate that you have read the passage carefully, present a clear and logical analysis, and use language precisely

Your essay must be written on the lines provided in your answer booklet; except for the Planning Page of your answer booklet, you will receive no other paper on which to write. You will have enough space if you write on every line, avoid wide margins, and keep your handwriting to a reasonable size. Remember that people who are not familiar with your handwriting will read what you write. Try to write or print so that what you are writing is legible to those readers.

You have 50 minutes to read the passage and write an essay in response to the prompt provided in this booklet.

Adapted from Gabrielle Lenhard's "An America Hungry for Change." Lenhard is an urban sociologist.

1 Imagine a child arriving home for dinner to find a tub of Kentucky Fried Chicken on the table, rather than a home cooked meal with plenty of fruits and vegetables. And this occurs three times a week on average. Imagine living in a community where a raw cantaloupe could be considered exotic for its scarcity. For many geographic areas in the United States with limited access to fresh and nutritious food, the fried chicken phenomenon is a reality. Yet even the biggest fans of KFC need a balanced diet.

2 The U.S. Department of Agriculture has termed areas such as these "food deserts." More than 29.7 million Americans currently live in neighborhoods that qualify as food deserts, where fast food restaurants and convenience stores are the nearest, and primary, options for nourishment. My consulting and research company, Mari Gallagher, labels these as "fringe retailers." Resulting diets are high in sugar, fat, and salt—the calling card of processed comestibles. Community and health organizations, like mine, are searching for ways to improve the diets of America's food deserts in an effort to eliminate the high levels of obesity and chronic diseases that they foster.

3 The circumstances hindering the residents of food deserts are unique in each community. The distance of a mile or two in an urban area that relies heavily upon public transportation is more comparable to the distance of 10 miles in a rural community. While an overwhelming number of qualifying sites are low income, factors such as education, ethnicity, and dietary restrictions must also be taken into account. Thus, proposing broad solutions to the problem of inadequate nutrition is quite complex and challenging.

4 The 2011 presidential budget requested over 400 million dollars for a Healthy Food Financing Initiative (HFFI) to be launched. This program aims to open supermarkets and wholesome food retailers in food deserts across the nation. In addition to providing fresh food to nutritionally starved areas, the program purports that supermarkets can stimulate the economy of a disadvantaged area by creating jobs, fostering surrounding retail, and making the area more attractive to investors. In 2010, the neighborhood supermarket shut its doors in Highland Falls, New York. The town supported a weekly bus service to the nearest equivalent merchant 11 miles away as an alternative to the discontinued resource and fringe retailers. With financing from HFFI, a local couple was able to re-open the abandoned store, with

16,000 square feet of new or improved produce vending space—creating 27 jobs. Highland Falls is just one example of the many success stories that this government initiative boasts since its inception.

5   Yet, research does not firmly suggest that establishing a new grocery store in a food desert will change the diets of those people living in it. A study conducted by population health professor Steven Cummins observed the population of a food desert in Philadelphia after a new supermarket was opened. The study showed no changes in BMIs (body mass index) or the consumption levels of produce, and participants did not switch to better provisions. Rather, the community perception of access to food was changed; inhabitants had the sense that their area had improved.

6   There is limited data analyzing the effectiveness of implementing new retailers in food deserts, and Professor Cummins' study only examined one Philadelphia location for a period of 6 months. Meanwhile, an abundance of information links chronic conditions and a nutritionally challenged diet to those living in food deserts. It's possible that policy makers jumped to address a very real problem with a solution ill-tested for success. But one thing is clear. People have heavily ingrained eating and food shopping habits, and more than one measure will be needed to initiate change.

7   Citizens seeking to initiate their own change may help to fill the gaps between fresh food availability and affordability. Community farms and gardens provide one method of augmenting diets in disadvantaged, urban areas with the nutrients that fringe retailers do not offer. The Shawnee area of Louisville, Kentucky has hosted The People's Garden since 2011, an outpost of the local non-profit Louisville Grows. The organization has produced more than 3,000 pounds of produce to be circulated among local markets since 2012. Farms like these viscerally connect individuals to the foods that they are eating, inviting them to be active, educated participants in the process of food arriving on the dinner table.

8   With hope, homegrown initiatives can supplement government programs, satisfying a need for community specific solutions and helping to alleviate America's hankering for healthy options.

Write an essay in which you explain how the author builds an argument to persuade the audience that government health assisted programs are insufficient in providing quality nutrition. In your essay, analyze how the author uses one or more of the features listed in the box above (or features of your own choice) to strengthen the logic and persuasiveness of her argument. Be sure that your essay focuses on the most relevant features of the passage.

Your essay should not explain whether you agree with the author's claims, but rather explain how the author builds an argument to persuade the audience.

ESSAY 1

☐ I understand that my essay (without my name) may be reproduced in other IES Test Prep and IES Publications materials. If I mark this box, I grant permission to produce my essay for purposes beyond score reporting and assessment of my writing skills, including (but not limited to) publication without payment or royalties in an IES Publications book. Marking this box will have no effect on my score, nor will it prevent my essay from being made available for viewing at an IES campus.

IMPORTANT: **USE A NO. 2 PENCIL. DO NOT WRITE OUTSIDE THE BORDER!**
Words written outside the essay book or written in ink **WILL NOT APPEAR** in the copy sent to be scored, and your score will be affected.

PLANNING PAGE You may plan your essay in the unlined planning space below, but only use the lined pages following this one to write your essay. Any work on the planning page will not be scored.

Use pages 5 through 8 for your ESSAY ——————▶

FOR PLANNING ONLY

Use pages 5 through 8 for your ESSAY ——————▶

You may continue on the next page.

You may continue on the next page.

BEGIN YOUR ESSAY HERE.

You may continue on the next page.

You may continue on the next page.

You may continue on the next page.

STOP.

SAT® Practice Essay #11

ESSAY BOOK

DIRECTIONS

The essay gives you an opportunity to show how effectively you can read and comprehend a passage and write an essay analyzing the passage. In your essay, you should demonstrate that you have read the passage carefully, present a clear and logical analysis, and use language precisely

Your essay must be written on the lines provided in your answer booklet; except for the Planning Page of your answer booklet, you will receive no other paper on which to write. You will have enough space if you write on every line, avoid wide margins, and keep your handwriting to a reasonable size. Remember that people who are not familiar with your handwriting will read what you write. Try to write or print so that what you are writing is legible to those readers.

You have 50 minutes to read the passage and write an essay in response to the prompt provided in this booklet.

REMINDERS

— Do not write your essay in this booklet. Only what you write on the lined pages of your answer booklet will be evaluated.

— An off-topic essay will not be evaluated.

Learn more about IES Test Prep's Essay offerings at **iestestprep.com**

This cover is representative of what you'll see on test day.

THIS TEST BOOKLET MUST NOT BE TAKEN FROM THE ROOM. UNAUTHORIZED REPRODUCTION OR USE OF ANY PART OF THIS BOOKLET IS PROHIBITED.

As you read the passage below, consider how the author uses

◇ evidence, such as facts or examples, to support claims.

◇ reasoning to develop ideas and connect claims and evidence.

◇ stylistic or persuasive elements, such as word choice or appeals to emotion, to add power to the ideas expressed.

Adapted from Jonathan Holt's "Morbid Hybrid: Interbreeding as a Means of Species Depletion." Jonathan Holt is a biologist whose work has been central to species categorization practices within the scientific community.

1 Biodiversity, a measurement of the number of distinct species in an area, is the gold standard among ecologists and conservationists. According to the common wisdom, the more variety in an area, the better, and anything that reduces this variety is disastrous. Extinction is the best studied form of species depletion, but hybridization—the interbreeding and merging of two species—is just as loathed in our field. Recently, however, researchers have witnessed hybrid populations surviving, and even thriving, forcing us the re-examine the most fundamental tenets of biology.

2 In the past hundred years, a new creature has appeared on the American landscape: the coywolf. Roughly two-thirds coyote, one quarter wolf, and the rest dog, they've swept out from the Great Lakes region and colonized many of the eastern United States' recovering forests. From my various field studies, I have concluded that this animal's wolf genes provide both physical prowess and instinctive social coordination to hunt deer in packs, while the coyote and dog DNA instills scrappy survival skills necessary to live alongside human civilization. Just in the last hundred years, nature has cobbled together the perfect creature for the U.S.'s strange mix of wilderness, highway, and city. This is evolution in hyper-drive.

3 Previously, hybridization has been seen as useless at best, the "grossest blunder in sexual preference which we can conceive of," according to one of my colleagues. Many mixes, such as the mule, end up sterile—an evolutionary dead end. Others are horribly maladapted; one parent is specialized for one way of surviving, the other for an entirely different strategy, and the child ends up being sub-par at both tasks. Nature itself seems to do everything in its power to prevent interbreeding: similar species in the same area often develop markings, dances, or songs that separate one species from another during the breeding season. But creatures such as the coywolf show that hybridization can't be dismissed out of hand.

4 The central issue is that the idea of "species," the fundamental unit of both biology and biodiversity, is more fluid than we would like it to be. Species is typically defined as a group of organisms that can exchange genes, or breed, and produce fertile offspring—so does that mean that wolves, dogs, and coyotes must now be considered one species? On the other hand, chihuahuas and mastiffs certainly can't breed with each other, so should they be

considered separate? Darwin himself expressed skepticism about our reliance on "species," referring to "The vain search for the undiscovered and undiscoverable essence of the term."

5   Botanists could never ignore the utility of hybridization. With the way pollen spreads, crossbred plants are a mundane occurrence, both in agriculture and in the wild. But the closer we look, the more we realize that hybridization is central to animal evolution as well. As the ice caps melt, many "grolar" or "pizzly" bears have been sighted, mixes between polar bears and their more temperate cousins. A few have even proven to be second-generation, showing that sterility is not an issue with this new form. Such a creature could be uniquely suited to the forested tundra of places like Alaska, where the cold may dissuade grizzlies, but an omnivorous diet may be more efficient than the polar's reliance on seal blubber.

6   Close species, such as Galapagos finches, may even rely on hybridization to endure rapid changes in their environment. During the catastrophic storms of El Niño, one species was almost entirely wiped from the islands, unable to survive in the harsh new climate. However, their beaks were the only ones adapted to eating a certain type of seed; a niche was left empty. A hybrid developed between the dwindling species and a more hardy cousin, and now it thrives, effortlessly replacing its more pure ancestors.

7   Studies of the genomes of more stable species show signs of hybridization in the past. Clymene dolphins seem to have descended from two other Atlantic species. Minke whales, spadefoot toads, Antillean bats—the list goes on. The vast majority of humans even have sections of Neaderthal DNA. Perhaps, borrowing beneficial genes from neighboring species is simply another tool in evolution's box.

8   As is often the case, nature proves to be squirrelly, refusing to fit into our sterile rules and rigid boxes. Terms like 'species' are still necessary; without them, biologists would find it quite difficult to communicate. Sometimes, however, it's important to remember that biodiversity is just a number.

Write an essay in which you explain how the author builds an argument to persuade the audience that hybridization is not a threat to biodiversity. In your essay, analyze how the author uses one or more of the features listed in the box above (or features of your own choice) to strengthen the logic and persuasiveness of his argument. Be sure that your essay focuses on the most relevant features of the passage.

Your essay should not explain whether you agree with the author's claims, but rather explain how the author builds an argument to persuade the audience.

ESSAY 1

☐ I understand that my essay (without my name) may be reproduced in other IES Test Prep and IES Publications materials. If I mark this box, I grant permission to produce my essay for purposes beyond score reporting and assessment of my writing skills, including (but not limited to) publication without payment or royalties in an IES Publications book. Marking this box will have no effect on my score, nor will it prevent my essay from being made available for viewing at an IES campus.

IMPORTANT: **USE A NO. 2 PENCIL. DO NOT WRITE OUTSIDE THE BORDER!**
Words written outside the essay book or written in ink **WILL NOT APPEAR** in the copy sent to be scored, and your score will be affected.

PLANNING PAGE You may plan your essay in the unlined planning space below, but only use the lined pages following this one to write your essay. Any work on the planning page will not be scored.

Use pages 5 through 8 for your ESSAY ⟶

FOR PLANNING ONLY

Use pages 5 through 8 for your ESSAY ⟶

BEGIN YOUR ESSAY HERE.

You may continue on the next page.

SAT® Practice Essay #12

ESSAY BOOK

DIRECTIONS

The essay gives you an opportunity to show how effectively you can read and comprehend a passage and write an essay analyzing the passage. In your essay, you should demonstrate that you have read the passage carefully, present a clear and logical analysis, and use language precisely

Your essay must be written on the lines provided in your answer booklet; except for the Planning Page of your answer booklet, you will receive no other paper on which to write. You will have enough space if you write on every line, avoid wide margins, and keep your handwriting to a reasonable size. Remember that people who are not familiar with your handwriting will read what you write. Try to write or print so that what you are writing is legible to those readers.

You have 50 minutes to read the passage and write an essay in response to the prompt provided in this booklet.

As you read the passage below, consider how the author uses

◇ evidence, such as facts or examples, to support claims.

◇ reasoning to develop ideas and connect claims and evidence.

◇ stylistic or persuasive elements, such as word choice or appeals to emotion, to add power to the ideas expressed.

Adapted from Cynthia Helzner, "Nepotism Now?" © 2015 by IES Publications.

1   While applying for jobs, many of us have heard the old adage, "It's not what you know, it's whom you know." The commonness of this saying makes it all too clear that someone who has put in years of effort in education and employment may lose out on a position simply because he or she doesn't know "people in high places." For example, Dr. Gillian Evans of Manchester University opined that privileged children who have failed their exams or worked in unimpressive jobs may be hired above more qualified candidates. If we want our society to be one in which people can "work their way up" with hard work and education, do we really want to hire based on whom you know rather than what you know?

2   Nepotism is favoritism based on kinship (usually familial kinship, though the term can also include favoritism shown to friends and significant others). The archetypal form of nepotism is business nepotism, in which current or past employees' family members receive preference in the hiring process. Although nepotism is often seen as a fact of life rather than a form of job discrimination, in reality, considering any factors other than an applicant's qualifications (education, prior job experience, displays of aptitude during interviews and company tests, etc.) constitutes employment discrimination.

3   Why is nepotism so often accepted while other forms of job discrimination are not? Perhaps nepotism is given a free pass because we acknowledge that it is natural to want to help one's family members, and one's own children in particular. In fact, many parents say that they "would do anything" to help their kids. Surely, putting in a good word with the hiring committee, or perhaps even being on the hiring committee, would fall within the purview of what a parent might do to help his or her child get a job.

4   In some cases, namely small family businesses (restaurants, flower shops, barbershops, etc.), business nepotism may make sense. Family business owners often hire their children because those children are going to inherit the business anyway, and so they need to be taught first-hand how to run the business. Moreover, small companies often benefit from consistency of business practices. Hiring one's children can certainly help in that regard.

5   While business nepotism (or, put more politely, "helping your kids") may not have a discriminatory intent, it certainly has a discriminatory effect and should therefore be banned in government hiring processes, if not large company hiring as well. In contrast to a small family business, the government has a duty to treat all of its citizens equally and fairly. To not do so undermines public trust, diminishes the overall quality of the employment force, and replaces meritocracy (selection and promotion of the most qualified candidates) with oligarchy (selection and promotion of the candidates who have connections to those in power). Likewise, large companies have an interest in choosing high-quality workforces and maintaining public trust.

6   Imagine if you were to walk into a government agency or corporate headquarters and see that many of its summer interns were children of the employees. Would you trust that agency to administer its services fairly and impartially? Would you trust that corporation to behave in ethical ways?

7   According to a 2013 study of seventeen Connecticut government agencies, 108 of the 1,128 summer interns hired—almost one tenth of the total—were immediate family members (children, spouses, siblings, parents, or children's spouses) of full-time agency employees. In some of the agencies studied, the majority of the summer interns were immediate family members of agency employees.

8   Connecticut is not unique; nepotism in hiring is widespread. Clearly, we need a solution. New York City utilizes a lottery system for its Summer Youth Employment Program. This program is the largest in the U.S. to use the lottery system, but other municipalities (such as Medford, Massachusetts) use the lottery system as well.

9   While the lottery system prevents nepotism, it also prevents meritocracy. That may not be of grave significance for summer internships, but surely we would not want full-time employees to be chosen randomly. In short, the lottery system is not the widely applicable solution that we need. A better solution is that applicants' names should be redacted from their application materials (resumes, cover letters, transcripts, etc.). Moreover, no family members of applicants should be allowed to review applications or interview candidates. This solution would preserve meritocracy while hindering nepotism, resulting in a fairer hiring process.

Write an essay in which you explain how the author builds an argument to persuade the audience that employment should be based on meritocracy rather than nepotism. In your essay, analyze how the author uses one or more of the features listed in the box above (or features of your own choice) to strengthen the logic and persuasiveness of her argument. Be sure that your essay focuses on the most relevant features of the passage.

Your essay should not explain whether you agree with the author's claims, but rather explain how the author builds an argument to persuade the audience.

ESSAY 1

I understand that my essay (without my name) may be reproduced in other IES Test Prep and IES Publications materials. If I mark this box, I grant permission to produce my essay for purposes beyond score reporting and assessment of my writing skills, including (but not limited to) publication without payment or royalties in an IES Publications book. Marking this box will have no effect on my score, nor will it prevent my essay from being made available for viewing at an IES campus.

IMPORTANT: **USE A NO. 2 PENCIL. DO NOT WRITE OUTSIDE THE BORDER!**
Words written outside the essay book or written in ink **WILL NOT APPEAR** in the copy sent to be scored, and your score will be affected.

PLANNING PAGE   You may plan your essay in the unlined planning space below, but only use the lined pages following this one to write your essay. Any work on the planning page will not be scored.

Use pages 5 through 8 for your ESSAY ⟶

FOR PLANNING ONLY

Use pages 5 through 8 for your ESSAY ⟶

BEGIN YOUR ESSAY HERE.

You may continue on the next page.

You may continue on the next page.

You may continue on the next page.

STOP.

SAT® Practice Essay #13

ESSAY BOOK

DIRECTIONS

The essay gives you an opportunity to show how effectively you can read and comprehend a passage and write an essay analyzing the passage. In your essay, you should demonstrate that you have read the passage carefully, present a clear and logical analysis, and use language precisely

Your essay must be written on the lines provided in your answer booklet; except for the Planning Page of your answer booklet, you will receive no other paper on which to write. You will have enough space if you write on every line, avoid wide margins, and keep your handwriting to a reasonable size. Remember that people who are not familiar with your handwriting will read what you write. Try to write or print so that what you are writing is legible to those readers.

You have 50 minutes to read the passage and write an essay in response to the prompt provided in this booklet.

THIS TEST BOOKLET MUST NOT BE TAKEN FROM THE ROOM. UNAUTHORIZED REPRODUCTION OR USE OF ANY PART OF THIS BOOKLET IS PROHIBITED.

As you read the passage below, consider how the author uses

◇ evidence, such as facts or examples, to support claims.
◇ reasoning to develop ideas and connect claims and evidence.
◇ stylistic or persuasive elements, such as word choice or appeals to emotion, to add power to the ideas expressed.

Adapted from Derrick McQueen's "Polluter Pays" © 2015 by IES Publications.

1 Industrial waste comes in many forms: radioactive substances that decay and release carcinogens, greenhouse gases that contribute to global warming, toxic chemicals that leak into our groundwater and river systems, killing aquatic life and making our drinking water unsafe for consumption. Clearly, industrial waste is an enormously important problem, as its spread affects human health, environmental stability, and climate.

2 Unfortunately, environmental clean-up is very costly, often so costly that it is deemed "not worth it" by the owners of polluted property. Once land or water is polluted to a hazardous degree, it is too unsafe to use for almost any purpose. The value of the land thus plummets, often well into the negative if ownership expenses, such as property taxes, exceed the use value of the land. This can lead to abandonment of the land.

3 Abandonment is harmful not only to the owner who loses the land but also to the public at large. Unlike abandoned personal property, abandoned real estate cannot be taken over until many (often 20) years have passed. Unused property indeed reduces our collective productivity, and has the side effect of making usable land more expensive by reducing the number of competing parcels available.

4 One answer to the problem of polluted land is the "polluter pays principle," in which the polluter is held legally responsible for paying to clean up hazardous waste. This principle is equitable because it places the financial burden of clean-up on the party responsible for the mess rather than the party who happens to own the property. In some cases (for example, if a factory's liquid waste leaks into its own backyard), the polluter may be the landowner. In other cases, the landowner is an innocent bystander. For example, a factory may dump its toxic waste into a river, which then flows downstream to unrelated properties.

5 The benefits of cleaning up brownfields (areas of land which are so badly polluted by industrial waste that they became too toxic to use) go beyond the removal of toxic waste—a goal that, in and of itself, would justify the effort and cost. Additional benefits of land rehabilitation include job creation and increases in residential property values near brownfield sites. (Wouldn't you pay more to live in a house that was as far as possible from an ecosystem teeming with industrial waste?)

6 Rehabilitation of brownfields also reduces vehicle usage, which in turn reduces the amount of greenhouse gases emitted by automobiles. This reduction occurs because brownfields (often former industrial sites) are strategically located areas for industry. For example, a factory may have been built at a certain location because that location is relatively close to both the company's suppliers and a large population center from which company employees commute to the factory. By rehabilitating the property rather than relocating to a more distant site, such a company could maintain the short drive to suppliers and the short commute for company employees.

7 Perhaps the most widely known example of a polluter pays law is CERCLA, which created the Superfund program to clean up brownfields. Superfund has been very successful thus far, and with the number of brownfields still in need of rehabilitation, the Superfund program will continue to improve the safety and productivity of the American landscape. Superfund's brownfields program alone has assessed approximately 25,000 properties and has rehabilitated over 50,000 acres of land. Since 2006, programs operating under CERCLA have collectively assessed approximately 40,000 properties annually, and have completed almost 100,000 clean-ups, rehabilitating more than 900,000 acres of land.

8 This work is both priceless and pricey. Since the introduction of Superfund, billions of dollars directed towards cleanup efforts have been spent by companies that polluted the environment. For example, a recent settlement by the Kerr-McGee Corporation and its affiliates resulted in a $5.15 billion payment, of which approximately $4.4 billion will go toward environmental rehabilitation. Sadly, there are almost a half million brownfields in the United States, with an estimated total clean-up cost of up to one trillion dollars.

9 Without Superfund and similar programs, where would all of the money come from? The most likely answer is: nowhere. Few taxpayers and lawmakers would be willing to foot such an enormous bill to clean up land that does not directly impact them, and few companies would voluntarily pay to clean up their pollution. As the only real way to ensure action, "polluter pays" should be a reality, not simply a principle.

Write an essay in which you explain how the author builds an argument to persuade the audience that the "polluter pays principle" is the most viable solution to environmental preservation and cleanup. In your essay, analyze how the author uses one or more of the features listed in the box above (or features of your own choice) to strengthen the logic and persuasiveness of his argument. Be sure that your essay focuses on the most relevant features of the passage.

Your essay should not explain whether you agree with the author's claims, but rather explain how the author builds an argument to persuade the audience.

ESSAY 1

IMPORTANT: **USE A NO. 2 PENCIL. DO NOT WRITE OUTSIDE THE BORDER!**
Words written outside the essay book or written in ink **WILL NOT APPEAR** in the copy sent to be scored, and your score will be affected.

PLANNING PAGE You may plan your essay in the unlined planning space below, but only use the lined pages following this one to write your essay. Any work on the planning page will not be scored.

Use pages 5 through 8 for your ESSAY ⟶

FOR PLANNING ONLY

Use pages 5 through 8 for your ESSAY ⟶

BEGIN YOUR ESSAY HERE.

You may continue on the next page.

You may continue on the next page.

You may continue on the next page.

You may continue on the next page.

You may continue on the next page.

STOP.

SAT® Practice Essay #14

ESSAY BOOK

DIRECTIONS

The essay gives you an opportunity to show how effectively you can read and comprehend a passage and write an essay analyzing the passage. In your essay, you should demonstrate that you have read the passage carefully, present a clear and logical analysis, and use language precisely

Your essay must be written on the lines provided in your answer booklet; except for the Planning Page of your answer booklet, you will receive no other paper on which to write. You will have enough space if you write on every line, avoid wide margins, and keep your handwriting to a reasonable size. Remember that people who are not familiar with your handwriting will read what you write. Try to write or print so that what you are writing is legible to those readers.

You have 50 minutes to read the passage and write an essay in response to the prompt provided in this booklet.

REMINDERS

— Do not write your essay in this booklet. Only what you write on the lined pages of your answer booklet will be evaluated.

— An off-topic essay will not be evaluated.

Learn more about IES Test Prep's Essay offerings at **iestestprep.com**

This cover is representative of what you'll see on test day.

THIS TEST BOOKLET MUST NOT BE TAKEN FROM THE ROOM. UNAUTHORIZED REPRODUCTION OR USE OF ANY PART OF THIS BOOKLET IS PROHIBITED.

As you read the passage below, consider how the author uses

◇ evidence, such as facts or examples, to support claims.

◇ reasoning to develop ideas and connect claims and evidence.

◇ stylistic or persuasive elements, such as word choice or appeals to emotion, to add power to the ideas expressed.

Adapted from Matthew Gaertner's "The Leaning Tower of PISA" © 2015 by IES Publications.

1   In 2012, the media coverage that followed the results of tests administered by the Program for International Student Assessment (PISA) alarmed many Americans. The U.S. ranked 35th in mathematics, and 27th in science. Politicians, educators, parents, and students voiced a growing fear that American students are rapidly falling behind in STEM subjects (science, technology, engineering, and mathematics), and that this widening gap will lead to an economically crippling shortage of sufficiently educated applicants for jobs in STEM-related fields. It would seem logical then that to fill this growing demand for STEM workers, schools and educators in the US should devote more of their limited time and resources to STEM subjects.

2   However, the idea that American STEM educators suddenly cannot produce competent employees to fill jobs in STEM-related fields depends on assumptions worth interrogating. In fact, the results of the PISA tests are not shockingly low, and when considering the current job market for American STEM workers, the educational system in the U.S. is actually providing an ample number of graduates with STEM degrees each year.

3   Every three years the Program for International Student Assessment tests 15-year-old students from a growing number of educational systems around the world in various subjects, including reading, math, and science. In 2012, out of 65 educational systems, the U.S. ranked 35th in math, and 27th in science. If this number sounds low, consider that many of the educational systems at the top of the list represent much smaller and wealthier populations. There are a number of reasons we can expect more affluent populations to perform better in schools; factors such as greater school funding, additional resources such as tutors, and a higher likelihood of having a parent or guardian who went to college place students in affluent populations at an advantage. Educational systems like Hong Kong's can reasonably be expected to outperform the U.S. system, and many have for decades.

4   Since the PISA tests were initiated in 2000, the U.S. has never outranked Hong Kong, Belgium, or tens of other smaller educational systems. American PISA scores in STEM subjects are not the best in the world, but they are not decreasing rapidly, nor are they shockingly low considering that the U.S. provides education to a large and economically diverse population.

5   The Department of Commerce reported in 2010 that 7.6 million people were working in jobs related to STEM, which represents roughly 1 out of every 18 workers. 4.7 million of those workers had college degrees, and only 3.3 million of those graduates majored in STEM. This means that 1.4 million STEM workers went to college but majored in something else. In 2014 the Census Bureau reported that only 26% of those with bachelor's degrees in STEM related fields actually work in those fields now. Majoring in a STEM subject in college does not guarantee that students can or will find jobs in STEM, and not all STEM workers with college degrees majored in a STEM-related subject. The economic principle of supply and demand tells us that if there is a shortage of STEM workers, their services would be in high demand and their wages would rise.

6   But largely stagnant wages in many sectors of the STEM workforce suggest otherwise.

7   Many of the most specialized and educated STEM workers, such as engineers, have experienced relatively stagnant wages in recent decades compared to non-STEM workers, and also in comparison to STEM workers as a whole. This means that many of the STEM workers with degrees in non-STEM subjects have salaries that are growing more quickly than those of engineers who possess advanced educations in STEM subjects.

8   There is room for improvement in the American educational system, STEM subjects included. Certainly, American students could achieve higher-ranking PISA scores if the appropriate resources were devoted to that end. However, there is not a sudden shortage of highly-educated applicants for jobs in STEM fields, nor does our educational system struggle to produce an adequate number of graduates with advanced degrees in STEM fields. There is arguably a case to be made, rather, that salaries for many of the most desirable STEM jobs in the U.S. are lower than they might be if the market were less saturated than it is now.

9   Many American students should study and even pursue degrees in STEM subjects, but not at the expense of a well-rounded education, and certainly not based on the assumption that American employers are all in desperate need of more graduates with STEM degrees.

Write an essay in which you explain how the author builds an argument to persuade the audience that an increasing focus on STEM education is unnecessary. In your essay, analyze how the author uses one or more of the features listed in the box above (or features of your own choice) to strengthen the logic and persuasiveness of his argument. Be sure that your essay focuses on the most relevant features of the passage.

Your essay should not explain whether you agree with the author's claims, but rather explain how the author builds an argument to persuade the audience.

ESSAY 1

IMPORTANT: **USE A NO. 2 PENCIL. DO NOT WRITE OUTSIDE THE BORDER!**
Words written outside the essay book or written in ink **WILL NOT APPEAR** in the copy sent to be scored, and your score will be affected.

PLANNING PAGE You may plan your essay in the unlined planning space below, but only use the lined pages following this one to write your essay. Any work on the planning page will not be scored.

Use pages 5 through 8 for your ESSAY ⟶

FOR PLANNING ONLY

Use pages 5 through 8 for your ESSAY ⟶

BEGIN YOUR ESSAY HERE.

You may continue on the next page.

You may continue on the next page.

STOP.

SAT® Practice Essay #15

ESSAY BOOK

DIRECTIONS

The essay gives you an opportunity to show how effectively you can read and comprehend a passage and write an essay analyzing the passage. In your essay, you should demonstrate that you have read the passage carefully, present a clear and logical analysis, and use language precisely

Your essay must be written on the lines provided in your answer booklet; except for the Planning Page of your answer booklet, you will receive no other paper on which to write. You will have enough space if you write on every line, avoid wide margins, and keep your handwriting to a reasonable size. Remember that people who are not familiar with your handwriting will read what you write. Try to write or print so that what you are writing is legible to those readers.

You have 50 minutes to read the passage and write an essay in response to the prompt provided in this booklet.

REMINDERS

— Do not write your essay in this booklet. Only what you write on the lined pages of your answer booklet will be evaluated.

— An off-topic essay will not be evaluated.

Learn more about IES Test Prep's Essay offerings at **iestestprep.com**

This cover is representative of what you'll see on test day.

THIS TEST BOOKLET MUST NOT BE TAKEN FROM THE ROOM. UNAUTHORIZED REPRODUCTION OR USE OF ANY PART OF THIS BOOKLET IS PROHIBITED.

As you read the passage below, consider how the author uses

◇ evidence, such as facts or examples, to support claims.

◇ reasoning to develop ideas and connect claims and evidence.

◇ stylistic or persuasive elements, such as word choice or appeals to emotion, to add power to the ideas expressed.

Adapted from Gabrielle Lenhard's "Trash Talk" © 2015 by IES Publications.

1 When customers purchase items at a drug store in Los Angeles County, they are asked if they have brought their own bags or would like to purchase a paper bag for 10 cents. This practice results from the Single-Use Plastic Carryout Bag Ordinance and affects retailers selling perishable and other goods bagged in billions of plastic bags annually. Those bags use valuable resources to manufacture, have only a 5.2% rate of recycling, and cost the city millions of dollars to clean up when later littered upon the streets and waterways of L.A. After a year or so, the ordinance had about a 90% success rate, and cities around the country have since implemented similar programs.

2 The triumph of the L.A. Bag Ordinance, as well as its subsequent popularity, demonstrates a desire and willingness among the American people to instigate change. The country is moving towards reducing its waste footprint because companies and citizens alike recognize the environmental impact of their consumption. As a Senior Environmental Planner with consulting firm IFC International, preparing California Environmental Quality Act documents is frequently my line of work. I am proud to see officials taking into consideration the ecological and community impact of the projects they propose, but a great deal of room for improvement remains.

3 *Biocycle Magazine*, in conjunction with the Earth Engineering Center of Columbia University, publishes the most accurate survey of municipal solid waste (MSW) in the United States. According to recent data, "On average, 1.28 tons of MSW were generated per capita in 2008." This works out to about 7.01 pounds of trash daily, staggeringly higher than the Japanese national average of 2.5 pounds per day. In fact, our daily national average is higher than that of almost every other country on the planet and has nearly doubled since 1960.

4 America is a vast place, you might say. It has plenty of real estate in which dig another landfill, and existing landfills can last from decades to thousands of years more. However, this does not make landfills the most sustainable solution to an indefinite problem. Toxic substances are released as materials break down and leach into the soil and groundwater. And as organic substances decompose in confined spaces, they produce methane, a potent greenhouse gas.

SAT® Practice Essay #15

ESSAY BOOK

DIRECTIONS

The essay gives you an opportunity to show how effectively you can read and comprehend a passage and write an essay analyzing the passage. In your essay, you should demonstrate that you have read the passage carefully, present a clear and logical analysis, and use language precisely

Your essay must be written on the lines provided in your answer booklet; except for the Planning Page of your answer booklet, you will receive no other paper on which to write. You will have enough space if you write on every line, avoid wide margins, and keep your handwriting to a reasonable size. Remember that people who are not familiar with your handwriting will read what you write. Try to write or print so that what you are writing is legible to those readers.

You have 50 minutes to read the passage and write an essay in response to the prompt provided in this booklet.

As you read the passage below, consider how the author uses

◇ evidence, such as facts or examples, to support claims.

◇ reasoning to develop ideas and connect claims and evidence.

◇ stylistic or persuasive elements, such as word choice or appeals to emotion, to add power to the ideas expressed.

Adapted from Gabrielle Lenhard's "Trash Talk" © 2015 by IES Publications.

1 When customers purchase items at a drug store in Los Angeles County, they are asked if they have brought their own bags or would like to purchase a paper bag for 10 cents. This practice results from the Single-Use Plastic Carryout Bag Ordinance and affects retailers selling perishable and other goods bagged in billions of plastic bags annually. Those bags use valuable resources to manufacture, have only a 5.2% rate of recycling, and cost the city millions of dollars to clean up when later littered upon the streets and waterways of L.A. After a year or so, the ordinance had about a 90% success rate, and cities around the country have since implemented similar programs.

2 The triumph of the L.A. Bag Ordinance, as well as its subsequent popularity, demonstrates a desire and willingness among the American people to instigate change. The country is moving towards reducing its waste footprint because companies and citizens alike recognize the environmental impact of their consumption. As a Senior Environmental Planner with consulting firm IFC International, preparing California Environmental Quality Act documents is frequently my line of work. I am proud to see officials taking into consideration the ecological and community impact of the projects they propose, but a great deal of room for improvement remains.

3 *Biocycle Magazine*, in conjunction with the Earth Engineering Center of Columbia University, publishes the most accurate survey of municipal solid waste (MSW) in the United States. According to recent data, "On average, 1.28 tons of MSW were generated per capita in 2008." This works out to about 7.01 pounds of trash daily, staggeringly higher than the Japanese national average of 2.5 pounds per day. In fact, our daily national average is higher than that of almost every other country on the planet and has nearly doubled since 1960.

4 America is a vast place, you might say. It has plenty of real estate in which dig another landfill, and existing landfills can last from decades to thousands of years more. However, this does not make landfills the most sustainable solution to an indefinite problem. Toxic substances are released as materials break down and leach into the soil and groundwater. And as organic substances decompose in confined spaces, they produce methane, a potent greenhouse gas.

5   Electronic waste is particularly rich in noxious substances, and Dell is an excellent example of a company choosing to engage the environmental consequences of its products and manufacturing. Dell accepts any brand of used electronics at more than 2,000 Goodwill locations, as well as offering prepaid, return shipping labels for most of its own merchandise and printer supplies. Dell resells or recycles the collected materials responsibly, in opposition to the growing amount of e-waste illegally shipped to developing countries. To top this effort off, Dell has reduced its packaging by 12%, with continuing efforts involving redesign.

6   In addition to directly promoting environmental and civilian health, these measures yield greater company profits. Waste reduction is a business opportunity. Retail giant Walmart, for instance, shrank the packaging of one toy truck. A year later, the company had conserved 4,000 trees, 497 shipping loads, and one million gallons of oil transporting the toys from China to points of sale, a total 2.4 million dollars in savings. The incentive to reduce waste is clear for corporations and municipalities alike, but how are civilians spurred towards sustainability? Their trash is taken and transported out of sight and out of mind.

7   The idea of zero waste has been tackled by several major American cities, including Seattle, San Francisco, and Austin. In one possible method of achieving this goal, Seattle imposed a fine for depositing food scraps in trash receptacles. Noncompliance with this organics initiative would result in a $1 fine for residential homes and $50 for apartment buildings and businesses, a punishment for refusal to go green. Denizens recently sued the city over collectors going through garbage without warrants, and Seattle had to suspend the proposed fees until at least January 2016.

8   Austin, alternatively, has commercial recycling and residential composting rebate programs, and provides community classes to qualify for them. The city began the move towards zero waste in 2008 and hopes to achieve a 50% rate of diversion this year. This plan's success provides evidence that a focus on positive outcomes and education is key, as our nation develops new reduction, recycling, and decomposition practices. Indeed, the organizations and communities leading waste reduction in America are setting an example for every generation to come. I implore you too to join the nationwide trash talk.

Write an essay in which you explain how the author builds an argument to persuade the audience that engaging in collective initiatives for waste reduction will reduce the nation's garbage production. In your essay, analyze how the author uses one or more of the features listed in the box above (or features of your own choice) to strengthen the logic and persuasiveness of her argument. Be sure that your essay focuses on the most relevant features of the passage.

Your essay should not explain whether you agree with the author's claims, but rather explain how the author builds an argument to persuade the audience.

ESSAY 1

IMPORTANT: **USE A NO. 2 PENCIL. DO NOT WRITE OUTSIDE THE BORDER!**
Words written outside the essay book or written in ink **WILL NOT APPEAR** in the copy sent to be scored, and your score will be affected.

PLANNING PAGE   You may plan your essay in the unlined planning space below, but only use the lined pages following this one to write your essay. Any work on the planning page will not be scored.

Use pages 5 through 8 for your ESSAY ⟶

FOR PLANNING ONLY

Use pages 5 through 8 for your ESSAY ⟶

BEGIN YOUR ESSAY HERE.

You may continue on the next page.

You may continue on the next page.

You may continue on the next page.

SAT® Practice Essay #16

ESSAY BOOK

DIRECTIONS

The essay gives you an opportunity to show how effectively you can read and comprehend a passage and write an essay analyzing the passage. In your essay, you should demonstrate that you have read the passage carefully, present a clear and logical analysis, and use language precisely

Your essay must be written on the lines provided in your answer booklet; except for the Planning Page of your answer booklet, you will receive no other paper on which to write. You will have enough space if you write on every line, avoid wide margins, and keep your handwriting to a reasonable size. Remember that people who are not familiar with your handwriting will read what you write. Try to write or print so that what you are writing is legible to those readers.

You have 50 minutes to read the passage and write an essay in response to the prompt provided in this booklet.

As you read the passage below, consider how Robert F. Kennedy uses

◇ evidence, such as facts or examples, to support claims.

◇ reasoning to develop ideas and connect claims and evidence.

◇ stylistic or persuasive elements, such as word choice or appeals to emotion, to add power to the ideas expressed.

Adapted from Senator Robert F. Kennedy, Day of Affirmation Address. Delivered at Capetown University in South Africa, June 6, 1966.

1   The first element of this individual liberty is the freedom of speech: the right to express and communicate ideas, to set oneself apart from the dumb beasts of field and forest; the right to recall governments to their duties and to their obligations; above all, the right to affirm one's membership and allegiance to the body politic—to society—to the men with whom we share our land, our heritage, and our children's future.

2   Hand in hand with freedom of speech goes the power to be heard, to share in the decisions of government which shape men's lives. Everything that makes man's life worthwhile— family, work, education, a place to rear one's children and a place to rest one's head— all this depends on the decisions of government; all can be swept away by a government which does not heed the demands of its people, and I mean all of its people. Therefore, the essential humanity of man can be protected and preserved only where government must answer—not just to the wealthy, not just to those of a particular religion, not just to those of a particular race, but to all of the people.

3   These are the sacred rights of Western society. These were the essential differences between us and Nazi Germany, as they were between Athens and Persia.

4   They are the essence of our differences with communism today. I am unalterably opposed to communism because it exalts the State over the individual and over the family and because its system contains a lack of freedom of speech, of protest, of religion, and of the press, which is characteristic of a totalitarian regime. The way of opposition to communism, however, is not to imitate its dictatorship, but to enlarge individual human freedoms. There are those in every land who would label as Communist every threat to their privilege. But may I say to you as I have seen on my travels in all sections of the world, reform is not communism. And the denial of freedom, in whatever name, only strengthens the very communism it claims to oppose.

5   For two centuries, my own country has struggled to overcome the self-imposed handicap of prejudice and discrimination based on nationality, on social class or race—discrimination profoundly repugnant to the theory and to the command of our Constitution. Even as my father grew up in Boston, Massachusetts, signs told him: "No Irish Need Apply." Two

generations later President Kennedy became the first Irish Catholic, and the first Catholic, to head the nation, but how many men of ability had, before 1961, been denied the opportunity to contribute to the nation's progress because they were Catholic or because they were of Irish extraction? How many sons of Italian or Jewish or Polish parents slumbered in the slums—untaught, unlearned, their potential lost forever to our nation and to the human race? Even today, what price will we pay before we have assured full opportunity to millions of Negro Americans?

6   In the last five years we have done more to assure equality to our Negro citizens, and to help the deprived both white and black, than in the hundred years before that time. But much, much more remains to be done. For there are millions of Negroes untrained for the simplest of jobs, and thousands every day denied their full and equal rights under the law, and the violence of the disinherited, the insulted, the injured, looms over the streets of Harlem and of Watts and of the South Side Chicago.

7   But a Negro American trains now as an astronaut, one of mankind's first explorers into outer space; another is the chief barrister of the United States government, and dozens sit on the benches of our court; and another, Dr. Martin Luther King, is the second man of African descent to win the Nobel Peace Prize for his nonviolent efforts for social justice between all of the races.

8   We have passed laws prohibiting discrimination in education, in employment, in housing, but these laws alone cannot overcome the heritage of centuries—of broken families and stunted children, and poverty and degradation and pain.

9   So the road toward equality of freedom is not easy, and great cost and danger march alongside all of us. We are committed to peaceful and nonviolent change, and that is important to all to understand—though change is unsettling. Still, even in the turbulence of protest and struggle is greater hope for the future, as men learn to claim and achieve for themselves the rights formerly petitioned from others.

Write an essay in which you explain how Robert F. Kennedy builds an argument to persuade his audience that democratic societies have made limited yet still valuable progress. In your essay, analyze how Kennedy uses one or more of the features listed in the box above (or features of your own choice) to strengthen the logic and persuasiveness of his argument. Be sure that your essay focuses on the most relevant features of the passage.

Your essay should not explain whether you agree with Kennedy's claims, but rather explain how Kennedy builds an argument to persuade his audience.

ESSAY 1

I understand that my essay (without my name) may be reproduced in other IES Test Prep and IES Publications materials. If I mark this box, I grant permission to produce my essay for purposes beyond score reporting and assessment of my writing skills, including (but not limited to) publication without payment or royalties in an IES Publications book. Marking this box will have no effect on my score, nor will it prevent my essay from being made available for viewing at an IES campus.

IMPORTANT: **USE A NO. 2 PENCIL. DO NOT WRITE OUTSIDE THE BORDER!**
Words written outside the essay book or written in ink **WILL NOT APPEAR** in the copy sent to be scored, and your score will be affected.

PLANNING PAGE You may plan your essay in the unlined planning space below, but only use the lined pages following this one to write your essay. Any work on the planning page will not be scored.

Use pages 5 through 8 for your ESSAY ⟶

FOR PLANNING ONLY

Use pages 5 through 8 for your ESSAY ⟶

BEGIN YOUR ESSAY HERE.

You may continue on the next page.

You may continue on the next page.

You may continue on the next page.

STOP.

SAT® Practice Essay #17

ESSAY BOOK

DIRECTIONS

The essay gives you an opportunity to show how effectively you can read and comprehend a passage and write an essay analyzing the passage. In your essay, you should demonstrate that you have read the passage carefully, present a clear and logical analysis, and use language precisely

Your essay must be written on the lines provided in your answer booklet; except for the Planning Page of your answer booklet, you will receive no other paper on which to write. You will have enough space if you write on every line, avoid wide margins, and keep your handwriting to a reasonable size. Remember that people who are not familiar with your handwriting will read what you write. Try to write or print so that what you are writing is legible to those readers.

You have 50 minutes to read the passage and write an essay in response to the prompt provided in this booklet.

REMINDERS

— Do not write your essay in this booklet. Only what you write on the lined pages of your answer booklet will be evaluated.

— An off-topic essay will not be evaluated.

Learn more about IES Test Prep's Essay offerings at **iestestprep.com**

This cover is representative of what you'll see on test day.

THIS TEST BOOKLET MUST NOT BE TAKEN FROM THE ROOM. UNAUTHORIZED REPRODUCTION OR USE OF ANY PART OF THIS BOOKLET IS PROHIBITED.

As you read the passage below, consider how Sonia Sotomayor uses

◇ evidence, such as facts or examples, to support claims.

◇ reasoning to develop ideas and connect claims and evidence.

◇ stylistic or persuasive elements, such as word choice or appeals to emotion, to add power to the ideas expressed.

Adapted from Supreme Court Justice Sonia Sotomayor, "Dissenting Opinion: Utah v. Strieff" (2016).

1   The Court today holds that the discovery of a warrant for an unpaid parking ticket will forgive a police officer's violation of your Fourth Amendment rights. Do not be soothed by the opinion's technical language: This case allows the police to stop you on the street, demand your identification, and check it for outstanding traffic warrants—even if you are doing nothing wrong. If the officer discovers a warrant for a fine you forgot to pay, courts will now excuse his illegal stop and will admit into evidence anything he happens to find by searching you after arresting you on the warrant. Because the Fourth Amendment should prohibit, not permit, such misconduct, I dissent.

2   Minutes after Edward Strieff walked out of a South Salt Lake City home, an officer stopped him, questioned him, and took his identification to run it through a police database. The officer did not suspect that Strieff had done anything wrong. Strieff just happened to be the first person to leave a house that the officer thought might contain "drug activity." As the State of Utah concedes, this stop was illegal.

3   The Fourth Amendment protects people from "unreasonable searches and seizures." An officer breaches protection when he detains a pedestrian to check his license without any evidence that the person is engaged in a crime. The officer deepens the breach when he prolongs the detention just to fish further for evidence of wrongdoing. In his search for lawbreaking, the officer in this case himself broke the law. The officer learned that Strieff had a "small traffic warrant." Pursuant to that warrant, he arrested Strieff and, conducting a search incident to the arrest, discovered methamphetamine in Strieff's pockets. Utah charged Strieff with illegal drug possession.

4   Before trial, Strieff argued that admitting the drugs into evidence would condone the officer's misbehavior. The methamphetamine, he reasoned, was the product of the officer's illegal stop. Admitting it would tell officers that unlawfully discovering even a "small traffic warrant" would give them license to search for evidence of unrelated offenses. The Utah Supreme Court unanimously agreed with Strieff. A majority of this Court now reverses.

5   It is tempting in a case like this, where illegal conduct by an officer uncovers illegal conduct by a civilian, to forgive the officer. After all, his instincts, although unconstitutional, were

correct. But a basic principle lies at the heart of the Fourth Amendment: Two wrongs don't make a right. When "lawless police conduct" uncovers evidence of lawless civilian conduct, this Court has long required later criminal trials to exclude the illegally obtained evidence.

6   For example, if an officer breaks into a home and finds a forged check lying around, that check may not be used to prosecute the homeowner for bank fraud. We would describe the check as "fruit of the poisonous tree." Fruit that must be cast aside includes not only evidence directly found by an illegal search but also evidence "come at by exploitation of that illegality." This "exclusionary rule" removes an incentive for officers to search us without proper justification. It also keeps courts from being "made party to lawless invasions of the constitutional rights of citizens by permitting unhindered governmental use of the fruits of such invasions." When courts admit only lawfully obtained evidence, they encourage "those who formulate law enforcement polices, and the officers who implement them, to incorporate Fourth Amendment ideals into their value system."

7   By legitimizing the conduct that produces this double consciousness, this case tells everyone, white and black, guilty and innocent, that an officer can verify your legal status at any time. It says that your body is subject to invasion while courts excuse the violation of your rights. It implies that you are not a citizen of a democracy but the subject of a carceral state, just waiting to be cataloged.

8   We must not pretend that the countless people who are routinely targeted by police are "isolated." They are the canaries in the coal mine whose deaths, civil and literal, warn us that no one can breathe in this atmosphere. They are the ones who recognize that unlawful police stops corrode all our civil liberties and threaten all our lives. Until their voices matter too, our justice system will continue to be anything but.

Write an essay in which you explain how Sonia Sotomayor builds an argument to persuade her audience that police searches that contradict the Fourth Amendment are unacceptable. In your essay, analyze how Sotomayor uses one or more of the features listed in the box above (or features of your own choice) to strengthen the logic and persuasiveness of her argument. Be sure that your essay focuses on the most relevant features of the passage.

Your essay should not explain whether you agree with Sotomayor's claims, but rather explain how Sotomayor builds an argument to persuade her audience.

ESSAY 1

I understand that my essay (without my name) may be reproduced in other IES Test Prep and IES Publications materials. If I mark this box, I grant permission to produce my essay for purposes beyond score reporting and assessment of my writing skills, including (but not limited to) publication without payment or royalties in an IES Publications book. Marking this box will have no effect on my score, nor will it prevent my essay from being made available for viewing at an IES campus.

IMPORTANT: **USE A NO. 2 PENCIL. DO NOT WRITE OUTSIDE THE BORDER!**
Words written outside the essay book or written in ink **WILL NOT APPEAR** in the copy
sent to be scored, and your score will be affected.

PLANNING PAGE   You may plan your essay in the unlined planning space below, but only use the lined pages
following this one to write your essay. Any work on the planning page will not be scored.

Use pages 5 through 8 for your ESSAY ⟶

FOR PLANNING ONLY

Use pages 5 through 8 for your ESSAY ⟶

BEGIN YOUR ESSAY HERE.

You may continue on the next page.

You may continue on the next page.

STOP.

SAT® Practice Essay #18

ESSAY BOOK

DIRECTIONS

The essay gives you an opportunity to show how effectively you can read and comprehend a passage and write an essay analyzing the passage. In your essay, you should demonstrate that you have read the passage carefully, present a clear and logical analysis, and use language precisely

Your essay must be written on the lines provided in your answer booklet; except for the Planning Page of your answer booklet, you will receive no other paper on which to write. You will have enough space if you write on every line, avoid wide margins, and keep your handwriting to a reasonable size. Remember that people who are not familiar with your handwriting will read what you write. Try to write or print so that what you are writing is legible to those readers.

You have 50 minutes to read the passage and write an essay in response to the prompt provided in this booklet.

REMINDERS

— Do not write your essay in this booklet. Only what you write on the lined pages of your answer booklet will be evaluated.

— An off-topic essay will not be evaluated.

Learn more about IES Test Prep's Essay offerings at **iestestprep.com**

This cover is representative of what you'll see on test day.

THIS TEST BOOKLET MUST NOT BE TAKEN FROM THE ROOM. UNAUTHORIZED REPRODUCTION OR USE OF ANY PART OF THIS BOOKLET IS PROHIBITED.

As you read the passage below, consider how Henry Paulson uses

◇ evidence, such as facts or examples, to support claims.

◇ reasoning to develop ideas and connect claims and evidence.

◇ stylistic or persuasive elements, such as word choice or appeals to emotion, to add power to the ideas expressed.

Adapted from Henry Paulson, Statement on Actions to Protect the U.S. Economy (2008). Paulson was Secretary of the Treasury during the 2008 Financial Crisis.

1 Today, there is a lack of confidence in our financial system—a lack of confidence that must be conquered because it poses an enormous threat to our economy. Investors are unwilling to lend to banks, and healthy banks are unwilling to lend to each other and to consumers and businesses.

2 In recent weeks, the American people have felt the effects of a frozen financial system. They have seen reduced values in their retirement and investment accounts. They have worried about meeting payrolls and they have worried about losing their jobs. Families all across our Nation have gone through long days and long nights of concern about their financial situations today, and their financial situations tomorrow. Without confidence that their most basic financial needs will be met, Americans lose confidence in our economy, and this is unacceptable.

3 President Bush has directed me to consider all necessary steps to restore confidence and stability to our financial markets and get credit flowing again. Ten days ago Congress gave important new tools to the Treasury, the Federal Reserve, and the FDIC to meet the challenges posed to our economy. My colleagues and I are working creatively and collaboratively to deploy these tools and direct our powers at this disruption to our economy.

4 Today we are taking decisive actions to protect the US economy. We regret having to take these actions. Today's actions are not what we ever wanted to do—but today's actions are what we must do to restore confidence to our financial system.

5 Today I am announcing that the Treasury will purchase equity stakes in a wide array of banks and thrifts. Government owning a stake in any private U.S. company is objectionable to most Americans—me included. Yet the alternative of leaving businesses and consumers without access to financing is totally unacceptable. When financing isn't available, consumers and businesses shrink their spending, which leads to businesses cutting jobs and even closing up shop.

6 To avoid that outcome, we must restore confidence in our financial system. The first step in that effort is a plan to make capital available on attractive terms to a broad array of banks and thrifts, so they can provide credit to our economy. From the $700 billion financial rescue

package, the Treasury will make $250 billion in capital available to U.S. financial institutions in the form of preferred stock. Institutions that sell shares to the government will accept restrictions on executive compensation, including a clawback provision and a ban on golden parachutes during the period that the Treasury holds equity issued through this program. In addition, taxpayers will not only own shares that should be paid back with a reasonable return, but also will receive warrants for common shares in participating institutions. We expect all participating banks to continue and to strengthen their efforts to help struggling homeowners who can afford their homes avoid foreclosure. Foreclosures not only hurt the families who lose their homes; they hurt neighborhoods, communities, and our economy as a whole.

7   While many banks have suffered significant losses during this period of market turmoil, many others have plenty of capital to get through this period, but are not positioned to lend as widely as is necessary to support our economy. Our goal is to see a wide array of healthy institutions sell preferred shares to the Treasury, and raise additional private capital, so that they can make more loans to businesses and consumers across the nation. At a time when events naturally make even the most daring investors more risk-averse, the needs of our economy require that our financial institutions not take this new capital to hoard it, but to deploy it.

8   Nine large financial institutions have already agreed to participate in this program. They have agreed to sell preferred shares to the U.S. government, on the same terms that will be available to a broad array of small and medium-sized banks and thrifts across the nation. These are healthy institutions, and they have taken this step for the good of the U.S. economy. As these healthy institutions increase their capital base, they will be able to increase their funding to U.S. consumers and businesses.

9   I am joined here this morning by Chairman Bernanke and Chairman Bair, who have also taken extraordinary actions to support investor confidence in our financial system, so that funds will again flow through our banks to the U.S. economy.

10   We are acting with unprecedented speed taking unprecedented measures that we never thought would be necessary. But they are necessary to get our economy back on an even keel, and secure the confidence and future of our markets, our economy, and the economic well-being of all Americans.

Write an essay in which you explain how Henry Paulson builds an argument to persuade his audience that measures to protect the U.S. economy are urgently needed. In your essay, analyze how Paulson uses one or more of the features listed in the box above (or features of your own choice) to strengthen the logic and persuasiveness of his argument. Be sure that your essay focuses on the most relevant features of the passage.

Your essay should not explain whether you agree with Paulson's claims, but rather explain how Paulson builds an argument to persuade his audience.

IMPORTANT: **USE A NO. 2 PENCIL. DO NOT WRITE OUTSIDE THE BORDER!**
Words written outside the essay book or written in ink **WILL NOT APPEAR** in the copy sent to be scored, and your score will be affected.

PLANNING PAGE   You may plan your essay in the unlined planning space below, but only use the lined pages following this one to write your essay. Any work on the planning page will not be scored.

Use pages 5 through 8 for your ESSAY ⟶

FOR PLANNING ONLY

Use pages 5 through 8 for your ESSAY ⟶

BEGIN YOUR ESSAY HERE.

You may continue on the next page.

You may continue on the next page.

STOP.

SAT® Practice Essay #19

ESSAY BOOK

DIRECTIONS

The essay gives you an opportunity to show how effectively you can read and comprehend a passage and write an essay analyzing the passage. In your essay, you should demonstrate that you have read the passage carefully, present a clear and logical analysis, and use language precisely

Your essay must be written on the lines provided in your answer booklet; except for the Planning Page of your answer booklet, you will receive no other paper on which to write. You will have enough space if you write on every line, avoid wide margins, and keep your handwriting to a reasonable size. Remember that people who are not familiar with your handwriting will read what you write. Try to write or print so that what you are writing is legible to those readers.

You have 50 minutes to read the passage and write an essay in response to the prompt provided in this booklet.

REMINDERS

— Do not write your essay in this booklet. Only what you write on the lined pages of your answer booklet will be evaluated.

— An off-topic essay will not be evaluated.

Learn more about IES Test Prep's Essay offerings at **iestestprep.com**

This cover is representative of what you'll see on test day.

THIS TEST BOOKLET MUST NOT BE TAKEN FROM THE ROOM. UNAUTHORIZED REPRODUCTION OR USE OF ANY PART OF THIS BOOKLET IS PROHIBITED.

As you read the passage below, consider how Crystal Eastman uses

◇ evidence, such as facts or examples, to support claims.

◇ reasoning to develop ideas and connect claims and evidence.

◇ stylistic or persuasive elements, such as word choice or appeals to emotion, to add power to the ideas expressed.

Adapted from Crystal Eastman, "Now We Can Begin" (1920).

1 Most women will agree that August 23, the day when the Tennessee legislature finally enacted the Federal Suffrage Amendment, is a day to begin with, not a day to end with. Men are saying perhaps, "Thank God, this everlasting woman's fight is over!" But women, if I know them, are saying, "Now at last we can begin." In fighting for the right to vote, most women have tried to be either non-committal or thoroughly respectable on every other subject. Now they can say what they are really after, and what they are after, in common with all the rest of the struggling world, is freedom.

2 Freedom is a large word.

3 The true feminist, no matter how far to the left she may be in the revolutionary movement, sees the woman's battle as distinct in its objects and different in its methods from the workers' battle for industrial freedom. She knows, of course, that the vast majority of women as well as men are without property, and are of necessity bread and butter slaves under a system of society which allows the very sources of life to be privately owned by a few, and she counts herself a loyal soldier in the working-class army that is marching to overthrow that system. But as a feminist she also knows that the whole of woman's slavery is not summed up in the profit system, nor her complete emancipation assured by the downfall of capitalism.

4 Woman's freedom, in the feminist sense, can be fought for and conceivably won before the gates open into industrial democracy. On the other hand, woman's freedom, in the feminist sense, is not inherent in the communist ideal. All feminists are familiar with the revolutionary leader who "can't see" the woman's movement. "What's the matter with the women? My wife's all right," he says. And his wife, one usually finds, is raising his children in a Bronx flat or a dreary suburb, to which he returns occasionally for food and sleep when all possible excitement and stimulus have been wrung from the fight. If we should graduate into communism tomorrow, this man's attitude to his wife would not be changed. The proletarian dictatorship may or may not free women. We must begin now to enlighten the future dictators.

5 What, then, is "the matter with women?" What is the problem of women's freedom? It seems to me to be this: how to arrange the world so that women can be human beings, with a chance to exercise their infinitely varied gifts in infinitely varied ways, instead of being destined by

the accident of their sex to one field of activity—housework and child-raising. And second, if and when they choose housework and child-raising, to have that occupation recognized by the world as work, requiring a definite economic reward and not merely entitling the performer to be dependent on some man.

6   This is not the whole of feminism, of course, but it is enough to begin with. "Oh, don't begin with economics," my friends often protest, "Woman does not live by bread alone. What she needs first of all is a free soul." And I can agree that women will never be great until they achieve a certain emotional freedom, a strong healthy egotism, and some un-personal sources of joy—that in this inner sense we cannot make woman free by changing her economic status. What we can do, however, is to create conditions of outward freedom in which a free woman's soul can be born and grow. It is these outward conditions with which an organized feminist movement must concern itself.

7   We must institute a revolution in the early training and education of both boys and girls. It must be womanly as well as manly to earn your own living, to stand on your own feet. And it must be manly as well as womanly to know how to cook and sew and clean and take care of yourself in the ordinary exigencies of life. I need not add that the second part of this revolution will be more passionately resisted than the first. Men will not give up their privilege of helplessness without a struggle. The average man has a carefully cultivated ignorance about household matters—from what to do with the crumbs to the grocer's telephone number—a sort of cheerful inefficiency which protects him better than the reputation for having a violent temper. It was his mother's fault in the beginning, but even as a boy he was quick to see how a general reputation for being "no good around the house" would serve him throughout life, and half-consciously he began to cultivate that helplessness until today it is the despair of feminist wives.

8   How can we change the nature of man so that he will honorably share that work and responsibility and thus make the homemaking enterprise a song instead of a burden? Most assuredly not by laws or revolutionary decrees. Perhaps we must cultivate or simulate a little of that highly prized helplessness ourselves. But fundamentally it is a problem of education, of early training—we must bring up feminist sons.

Write an essay in which you explain how Crystal Eastman builds an argument to persuade her audience that social and economic attitudes towards women must be reinvented. In your essay, analyze how Eastman uses one or more of the features listed in the box above (or features of your own choice) to strengthen the logic and persuasiveness of her argument. Be sure that your essay focuses on the most relevant features of the passage.

Your essay should not explain whether you agree with Eastman's claims, but rather explain how Eastman builds an argument to persuade her audience.

ESSAY 1

☐ I understand that my essay (without my name) may be reproduced in other IES Test Prep and IES Publications materials. If I mark this box, I grant permission to produce my essay for purposes beyond score reporting and assessment of my writing skills, including (but not limited to) publication without payment or royalties in an IES Publications book. Marking this box will have no effect on my score, nor will it prevent my essay from being made available for viewing at an IES campus.

IMPORTANT: **USE A NO. 2 PENCIL. DO NOT WRITE OUTSIDE THE BORDER!**
Words written outside the essay book or written in ink **WILL NOT APPEAR** in the copy sent to be scored, and your score will be affected.

PLANNING PAGE You may plan your essay in the unlined planning space below, but only use the lined pages following this one to write your essay. Any work on the planning page will not be scored.

Use pages 5 through 8 for your ESSAY ⟶

FOR PLANNING ONLY

Use pages 5 through 8 for your ESSAY ⟶

You may continue on the next page.

You may continue on the next page.

BEGIN YOUR ESSAY HERE.

You may continue on the next page.

You may continue on the next page.

You may continue on the next page.

STOP.

SAT® Practice Essay #20

ESSAY BOOK

DIRECTIONS

The essay gives you an opportunity to show how effectively you can read and comprehend a passage and write an essay analyzing the passage. In your essay, you should demonstrate that you have read the passage carefully, present a clear and logical analysis, and use language precisely

Your essay must be written on the lines provided in your answer booklet; except for the Planning Page of your answer booklet, you will receive no other paper on which to write. You will have enough space if you write on every line, avoid wide margins, and keep your handwriting to a reasonable size. Remember that people who are not familiar with your handwriting will read what you write. Try to write or print so that what you are writing is legible to those readers.

You have 50 minutes to read the passage and write an essay in response to the prompt provided in this booklet.

As you read the passage below, consider how Loretta Lynch uses

◇ evidence, such as facts or examples, to support claims.

◇ reasoning to develop ideas and connect claims and evidence.

◇ stylistic or persuasive elements, such as word choice or appeals to emotion, to add power to the ideas expressed.

Adapted from U.S. Attorney General Loretta Lynch, "Remarks at the National Summit on Youth Violence Prevention" (2016).

1 As each of you knows all too well, a shadow clouds the lives of far too many young people throughout our country. While national crime rates remain at historic lows, a number of cities have experienced increases in homicides and violent crime—including crimes involving young people. In the United States, homicide is the third leading cause of death for youths between the ages of 10 and 24. Every day—every day—13 young people are murdered in our country. This means that every day, 13 young people are robbed of their chance to live a full and rich life. Every day, 13 families lose a child and are left to grapple with devastating loss and unimaginable pain. And every day, the country loses 13 people who might have grown up to defend the vulnerable or heal the sick; to inspire a community or lead a city; to raise a family or chart a future. Today, in America, this reality is simply unacceptable.

2 And as awful as these numbers are, they do not tell the whole story—because the dead are far from the only victims of violence. Its effects are felt far beyond a crime scene, inflicting invisible wounds on all who live in its presence. There are the families—whose existence is forever punctuated by the world before their loss and the darkness after. And there are the young people—our children still with us. Children who grow up accustomed to the sound of gunshots; who go to schools where disputes are resolved with fists instead of words; who are raised in homes filled with conflict, not comfort; who attend the funerals of relatives, friends and neighbors with tragic regularity—these children, too, are victims of violence.

3 We know that exposure to violence at a young age is associated with long-term physical, mental, and emotional harm. It puts youths at greater risk of failing in school and struggling to find and hold a job. And it makes it more likely that they will become involved with the juvenile and criminal justice system. Well, of course—how can you hold life dear when you have seen it go for almost nothing?

4 At the Department of Justice, we are determined to use every tool at our disposal to prevent, reduce, and end this violence—especially against young people—and to make that founding promise real. That is why we are working with partners across the federal government as part of the National Forum on Youth Violence Prevention, which President Obama established in 2010 to raise awareness about this critical issue—an issue of both public safety and public health—and to support communities' efforts to address it. As one of the agencies leading the forum, we are engaged with our federal partners across the administration and with diverse

stakeholders around the country to learn about and promote what works to prevent youth and gang violence; to support innovative solutions; and to create durable progress. We have provided funding and support to help reduce violence in Boston; to help increase school attendance in Long Beach; and to help promote safe communities in New Orleans—where I'm proud to say that we have realized a more than 30 percent drop in homicides over the last year. We are joining with faith and community-based organizations, youth and family groups, and business and philanthropic leaders in neighborhoods from coast to coast. And our U.S. Attorneys' Offices are working closely with local enforcement and elected leaders in their districts to reduce violent crime, to build capacity and to promote holistic responses to violence and its consequences. The Justice Department is proud to play a key role in this groundbreaking administration-wide effort—one of the many ways we are responding to milestone number six of My Brother's Keeper: keeping kids on the right track and giving them second chances. We will continue to contribute to the forum going forward.

5   Now, I know that the pace of that progress can seem painfully slow. I know, as you do, that we will not build that society overnight. But as I look out over this gathering of advocates and academics, volunteers and students, pastors and police officers and public servants, I am confident about the direction in which we are headed. I am excited about all that we can achieve. And I am inspired by your tireless work, your exceptional courage, your unbreakable faith and your extraordinary determination to meet the greatest tests of our time. You have already taken the most important step. Faced with daunting challenges, you joined the struggle. Encountering persistent problems, you rose above the easy temptations of cynicism and despair. And confronted by the darkest impulses of mankind, you have responded with light, with compassion and with love. People like you have made this country what it is today. People like you have brought us through the darkest hours of our past. And people like you point the way to a brighter future for us all.

Write an essay in which you explain how Loretta Lynch builds an argument to persuade her audience that America must be proactive in addressing violence among youth. In your essay, analyze how Lynch uses one or more of the features listed in the box above (or features of your own choice) to strengthen the logic and persuasiveness of her argument. Be sure that your essay focuses on the most relevant features of the passage.

Your essay should not explain whether you agree with Lynch's claims, but rather explain how Lynch builds an argument to persuade her audience.

ESSAY 1

IMPORTANT: **USE A NO. 2 PENCIL. DO NOT WRITE OUTSIDE THE BORDER!**
Words written outside the essay book or written in ink **WILL NOT APPEAR** in the copy sent to be scored, and your score will be affected.

PLANNING PAGE You may plan your essay in the unlined planning space below, but only use the lined pages following this one to write your essay. Any work on the planning page will not be scored.

Use pages 5 through 8 for your ESSAY ⟶

FOR PLANNING ONLY

Use pages 5 through 8 for your ESSAY ⟶

BEGIN YOUR ESSAY HERE.

You may continue on the next page.

You may continue on the next page.

STOP.

SAT® Practice Essay #21

ESSAY BOOK

DIRECTIONS

The essay gives you an opportunity to show how effectively you can read and comprehend a passage and write an essay analyzing the passage. In your essay, you should demonstrate that you have read the passage carefully, present a clear and logical analysis, and use language precisely

Your essay must be written on the lines provided in your answer booklet; except for the Planning Page of your answer booklet, you will receive no other paper on which to write. You will have enough space if you write on every line, avoid wide margins, and keep your handwriting to a reasonable size. Remember that people who are not familiar with your handwriting will read what you write. Try to write or print so that what you are writing is legible to those readers.

You have 50 minutes to read the passage and write an essay in response to the prompt provided in this booklet.

REMINDERS

— Do not write your essay in this booklet. Only what you write on the lined pages of your answer booklet will be evaluated.

— An off-topic essay will not be evaluated.

Learn more about IES Test Prep's Essay offerings at **iestestprep.com**

This cover is representative of what you'll see on test day.

THIS TEST BOOKLET MUST NOT BE TAKEN FROM THE ROOM. UNAUTHORIZED REPRODUCTION OR USE OF ANY PART OF THIS BOOKLET IS PROHIBITED.

As you read the passage below, consider how the author uses

◇ evidence, such as facts or examples, to support claims.

◇ reasoning to develop ideas and connect claims and evidence.

◇ stylistic or persuasive elements, such as word choice or appeals to emotion, to add power to the ideas expressed.

Adapted from Mariel Zachs, "Serve or Learn?" The author of this passage has taught for several years as a professor of anthropology.

1 Allow me to start with a question that may appear cruel and unusual: Is it possible that high school and college students do more harm than good when they do community service?

2 The first thought some of you probably had is, "No. No, no, no! Every community service hour counts!" And in some cases, that sentiment is prohibitively hard to argue against. What, for instance, would happen to Habitat for Humanity without a small army of volunteers to work on its construction projects? Decent housing for low-income families doesn't build itself. . .

3 . . . But the truth is more complicated than that. To understand why, we must set to the side an international success story like Habitat for Humanity and look, instead, at a closer-to-home story of failure—one, in fact, from my own college years.

4 I attended a university that had a few distinctions. It had a renowned biomedical engineering department and a championship-winning lacrosse team. It was also perpetually at war with the local community over noise pollution: elderly residents, young parents, and the city councilwoman who represented them would periodically rise up in arms over the college whoops and college shouts and college boomboxes that made their lives that much worse. They would send angry letters to the local paper; they would call campus security or the cops, often to no avail. The stand-off went on until a group of undergraduates, seeing the problem, decided to form a community service organization called the Housing Undergraduate Community Action Community (or HUCAC, quite possibly the worst acronym imaginable, but there it was). HUCAC was energetic, involved. It organized a street fair and a clothing drive, to help the students and their community neighbors bond. It had a sit-down with the councilwoman, to address noise pollution. It had flyers all over campus.

5 It lasted exactly six months. This was in my sophomore year. In my senior year, I wrote a school newspaper story called "Whatever Happened to HUCAC?" and invited the original HUCACers to comment. None of them did. They had all been long graduated.

6 Also, the noise complaints came back.

7   The easy interpretation of the HUCAC saga is that it was all a case of cynical resume-padding by students soon to face graduate school applications or the job market. Frankly, this interpretation is probably part true. But let's assume that there was no cynicism whatsoever motivating what happened. Why did HUCAC, which clearly served a necessary purpose at my alma matter, fall apart?

8   Why? Because our educational system does a pitiful job of teaching high school and college students how to think about community service. Part of this deficiency has been well documented by *New York Times* commentator and education specialist Frank Bruni. In the searing column "To Get to Harvard, Go to Haiti?" Bruni criticized two tendencies: first, students prefer service involving travel (supposedly more adventurous) to service involving their own communities; second, students prefer starting charities (supposedly more assertive) to helping along existing charities. As Bruni noted on the last point, there is a current proliferation of "teenagers trying to demonstrate their leadership skills in addition to their compassion by starting their own fledgling nonprofit groups rather than contributing to ones that already exist—and that might be more practiced and efficient at what they do."

9   As right as Bruni is—and as suspicious as admissions committees now are of travel-oriented token service—the trends have not been broken, because a badly-conceived values system has not been broken. Take a second look at Bruni's vocabulary: "fledgling nonprofit," "leadership skills." The idea is that community service is a means of demonstrating not cooperation but independence. Think of it as community service minus the community. . .

10   Of course, the point of high school and college is to foster independence, but community service is the one area that needs to be exempted from that purpose. The worst thing that teachers and administrators can continue to do is to take a hands-off, green-light everything approach. (Another true story: two or three years ago, a student asked me to serve as faculty mentor to a newly-formed Socialist Discussion and Awareness Club. When I explained that I wasn't a socialist, the young man responded, "That's fine. We just need you to sign some papers so we can register with the Dean.") We need to be more selective in guiding students towards opportunities that inspire lifetimes of service, less willing to allow social problems and young adult trial-and-error to mix. So trust the students, but within the framework of Habitat for Humanity, or an established peer tutoring program, or the local animal shelter. Independence isn't all they need to learn.

Write an essay in which you explain how Mariel Zachs builds an argument to persuade her audience that current ideas about college community service should be modified. In your essay, analyze how the author uses one or more of the features listed in the box above (or features of your own choice) to strengthen the logic and persuasiveness of her argument. Be sure that your essay focuses on the most relevant features of the passage.

Your essay should not explain whether you agree with the author's claims, but rather explain how the author builds an argument to persuade the audience.

ESSAY 1

IMPORTANT: **USE A NO. 2 PENCIL. DO NOT WRITE OUTSIDE THE BORDER!**
Words written outside the essay book or written in ink **WILL NOT APPEAR** in the copy sent to be scored, and your score will be affected.

PLANNING PAGE You may plan your essay in the unlined planning space below, but only use the lined pages following this one to write your essay. Any work on the planning page will not be scored.

Use pages 5 through 8 for your ESSAY ➞

FOR PLANNING ONLY

Use pages 5 through 8 for your ESSAY ➞

BEGIN YOUR ESSAY HERE.

You may continue on the next page.

You may continue on the next page.

You may continue on the next page.

STOP.

SAT® Practice Essay #22

ESSAY BOOK

DIRECTIONS

The essay gives you an opportunity to show how effectively you can read and comprehend a passage and write an essay analyzing the passage. In your essay, you should demonstrate that you have read the passage carefully, present a clear and logical analysis, and use language precisely

Your essay must be written on the lines provided in your answer booklet; except for the Planning Page of your answer booklet, you will receive no other paper on which to write. You will have enough space if you write on every line, avoid wide margins, and keep your handwriting to a reasonable size. Remember that people who are not familiar with your handwriting will read what you write. Try to write or print so that what you are writing is legible to those readers.

You have 50 minutes to read the passage and write an essay in response to the prompt provided in this booklet.

REMINDERS

— Do not write your essay in this booklet. Only what you write on the lined pages of your answer booklet will be evaluated.

— An off-topic essay will not be evaluated.

Learn more about IES Test Prep's Essay offerings at **iestestprep.com**

This cover is representative of what you'll see on test day.

THIS TEST BOOKLET MUST NOT BE TAKEN FROM THE ROOM. UNAUTHORIZED REPRODUCTION OR USE OF ANY PART OF THIS BOOKLET IS PROHIBITED.

As you read the passage below, consider how the author uses

◇ evidence, such as facts or examples, to support claims.

◇ reasoning to develop ideas and connect claims and evidence.

◇ stylistic or persuasive elements, such as word choice or appeals to emotion, to add power to the ideas expressed.

Adapted from Patrick Kennedy "But Is It Art? But Does That Question Even Matter?" © 2016, IES Publications.

1   Recently, visitors to the San Francisco Museum of Art were captivated by an unassuming "found object" display. The artwork in question consisted simply of a pair of minimalistic black Burberry eyeglasses, placed on a gallery floor, unaccompanied by any sort of explanation or identification. What was the artist's intent? Was it a silent protest against the unholy alliance of over-priced fashion (Burberry) and the increasingly corporatized art world? Was it a metaphor for the anonymity and nearsightedness of modern man? Was it an attempt to bring renewed appreciation to the formal elegance of everyday objects, a silent ode to a pair of sleekly functional, subtly beautiful black spectacles?

2   It was none of the above. It was, in fact, a prank drummed up by a Kevin Nguyen and TJ Khayatan, a couple of teenagers who were unimpressed with the art exhibits. All of this was done in good fun—with the museum staff even joking about the incident on Twitter— and that fact itself says a lot about where we are in the world of contemporary art. Fun matters. Quirkiness matters. Poking plenty of holes in art-historical seriousness (see the first paragraph) matters. Bringing artists, museums, and museumgoers together (even if you lob a few jovial insults while doing so) matters.

3   Art was not always this way. In the 19th century, intellectual crusades were waged over standards of truth and beauty: sometimes (as in the case of painter Paul Cézanne and novelist Emile Zola) a novel, painting, or piece of music could rupture a once-firm friendship. The aesthetic wars might have continued well into the 20th century, except that, somewhere in the 1910s, an artist named Marcel Duchamp abandoned sophisticated shape and color for deadpan ridiculousness. Among Duchamp's works were a flipped-over urinal, a coat rack lying on the floor, a snow shovel hanging from the ceiling, and a kitchen stool with the front wheel of a bicycle jammed through the seat. Duchamp called these works "readymades." Ever since then, it has been game-on for "artists" such as Nguyen and Khayatan.

4   What passes as "art" today may strike some novice museum-goers as completely absurd. Japanese-American artist Yoko Ono once walked into the premises of the Museum of Modern Art in New York, released a few insects sprinkled in perfume, and declared her act art. American postmodernist Jeff Koons makes huge aluminum sculptures that look exactly like balloon animals and mounds of Play-Doh, and calls these art.

5   Of course, you could try to point out that none of this is really art, and you would be in good company; critics such as Hilton Kramer and Michael Fried have staked their legacies on condemning legions of recent artists for intellectual dishonesty and empty posturing. But even these well-known critics have run into problems trying to dismiss the Duchamps and Koonses and Nguyens and Khayatans of this world.

6   Prime among the critical dilemmas here is that "art," as a category, is hopelessly hard to define. Attempts to do so run into all sorts of logical inconsistencies. Kramer or Fried or a critic of their nature would, for instance, probably reject the idea that those San Francisco glasses are legitimate art. The same critics, however, have accepted single-color canvases, out-of-focus photographs, and occasionally Duchamp's objects as legitimate art. Attempts to separate art from non-art, in light of how similar those two "categories" really can become, are at best over-ambitious and at worst, indeed, intellectually dishonest.

7   The other dilemma is that you'll automatically come off as a killjoy or a doomsday theorist if you rail against the state of the art world. Whatever else you think of Jeff Koons, it's hard to deny that his art has a sense of humor. And humor is hard to fight. Artists themselves have learned this the hard way: Jackson Pollock, who is now revered for his giant, abstract "drip" paintings, was roundly mocked when his style first appeared in the 1950s. Anybody, the news magazines laughingly said, could create a drip painting, from a third-grader to a monkey in a zoo—a critique that badly stung the moody Pollock.

8   He should have laughed along and accepted that museums threw out everything the world thought it knew about defining art when they invited in the first Duchamp readymades. The art wars are over. Openness and silliness have won.

Write an essay in which you explain how Patrick Kennedy builds an argument to persuade his audience that art has become progressively more difficult to define and critique. In your essay, analyze how the author uses one or more of the features listed in the box above (or features of your own choice) to strengthen the logic and persuasiveness of his argument. Be sure that your essay focuses on the most relevant features of the passage.

Your essay should not explain whether you agree with the author's claims, but rather explain how the author builds an argument to persuade the audience.

ESSAY 1

☐ I understand that my essay (without my name) may be reproduced in other IES Test Prep and IES Publications materials. If I mark this box, I grant permission to produce my essay for purposes beyond score reporting and assessment of my writing skills, including (but not limited to) publication without payment or royalties in an IES Publications book. Marking this box will have no effect on my score, nor will it prevent my essay from being made available for viewing at an IES campus.

IMPORTANT: **USE A NO. 2 PENCIL. DO NOT WRITE OUTSIDE THE BORDER!**
Words written outside the essay book or written in ink **WILL NOT APPEAR** in the copy sent to be scored, and your score will be affected.

PLANNING PAGE You may plan your essay in the unlined planning space below, but only use the lined pages following this one to write your essay. Any work on the planning page will not be scored.

Use pages 5 through 8 for your ESSAY ➡️

FOR PLANNING ONLY

Use pages 5 through 8 for your ESSAY ➡️

BEGIN YOUR ESSAY HERE.

You may continue on the next page.

You may continue on the next page.

You may continue on the next page.

SAT® Practice Essay #23

ESSAY BOOK

DIRECTIONS

The essay gives you an opportunity to show how effectively you can read and comprehend a passage and write an essay analyzing the passage. In your essay, you should demonstrate that you have read the passage carefully, present a clear and logical analysis, and use language precisely

Your essay must be written on the lines provided in your answer booklet; except for the Planning Page of your answer booklet, you will receive no other paper on which to write. You will have enough space if you write on every line, avoid wide margins, and keep your handwriting to a reasonable size. Remember that people who are not familiar with your handwriting will read what you write. Try to write or print so that what you are writing is legible to those readers.

You have 50 minutes to read the passage and write an essay in response to the prompt provided in this booklet.

As you read the passage below, consider how the author uses

◇ evidence, such as facts or examples, to support claims.

◇ reasoning to develop ideas and connect claims and evidence.

◇ stylistic or persuasive elements, such as word choice or appeals to emotion, to add power to the ideas expressed.

Adapted from Danielle Barkley, "Yes, You Can Spell 'Diet' without 'Denial': The Complicated Case of Restrictive Dieting." IES Publications, Copyright 2016.

1   Today, individuals in developed countries are faced with a dizzying array of food options: ethnic cuisines are increasingly available, and commercial food manufacturers experiment with innovative combinations of ingredients. Moreover, a highly visual culture nurtured by blogging and social media ensures that images of mouth-watering meals are never more than a click away. So why, in a culture where at least some individuals can eat almost anything they want, is the conversation so often turning to what people are not eating?

2   Suggestions about how one's diet can be used to achieve maximum health and vitality date back to the writings of ancient Greek philosophers. Recommendations about dietary practices will essentially always be either prescriptive (eat this) or prohibitive (don't eat that). Increasingly, popular diets are driven by prohibitive rhetoric. These diets tend to be misrepresented as offering health benefits, resulting in crucial misunderstandings about how best to eat healthfully.

3   Gluten-free, vegan, and Paleo diets have all recently sky-rocketed in popularity. "Paleo" ranked as one of the most frequently deployed online search terms in 2013. In the same year, a market-research poll indicated that 30 percent of adults wanted to "cut down or be free of gluten." That figure represents the highest percentage of people to report having this goal since the poll began asking the question in 2009. While these diets differ and even oppose one another in terms of the foods they urge adherents to embrace or reject, all three rely on eliminating the consumption of certain kinds of foods. Vegan diets resemble vegetarian diets in that they reject the consumption of meat and seafood products, but they go a step further, rejecting all animal by-products: eggs, dairy, even honey. The Paleo diet, on the other hand, takes the opposite approach and tends to be meat-heavy. Based on notions of what the human body supposedly evolved to eat during the Paleolithic era, this diet requires individuals to shun foods associated with modern agriculture such as dairy, processed grains, peanuts, lentils, beans, peas, and other legumes. Following a gluten-free diet, originally a treatment for celiac disease, involves eliminating all foods containing a specific protein called gluten, which is found in grains such as wheat, barley, and rye.

4   Individuals following diets that operate according to models of restriction and prohibition do often report weight loss and perceptions of improved well-being, at least in the short

term. However, two major problems exist with these perceptions. First, apparent health improvements in the short term may mask health risks in the long-term. The health risks associated with following a prohibitive diet may stem from either the absence of the foods one is discouraged from eating, or from an excess of the foods one consumes as a result of these restrictions. For example, individuals who stop eating grain and cereal products to meet the requirements of a Paleo or gluten free diet may become deficient in B vitamins, while vegans may lack calcium due to the absence of dairy; on the other hand, because the Paleo diet places a premium on consuming meat-based protein, it may lead to elevated consumption of fat and cholesterol.

5   Second, even if following a restrictive diet does lead to positive changes, the source of those changes can be misunderstood. It is more often a shift in eating practices rather than the elimination of specific foods that results in health improvements. Registered dietician Vincci Tsui suggests that "when people do switch over to a gluten-free diet, a lot of times it means eliminating fast foods, processed foods, refined grains, or it means cooking at home more often, eating more vegetables and fruits." As a result, "they feel better and they think it is the [avoidance of] gluten when really it may be the fact that they are eating better in general." This same pattern holds true for other prohibitive diets: both Paleo and vegan diets require the consumption of food that is largely unprocessed, and often ends up being prepared at home rather than purchased. In effect, what people perceive as a change in diet ends up being a change in lifestyle.

6   Acknowledging that prohibitive diets are not always beneficial, and that perceived benefits may be the result of correlation rather than causation, is important because it has the potential to shift the conversation about healthy eating away from focusing strictly on what should be avoided. Recognizing what eating behaviours to encourage rather than discourage tends to be empowering and often a more viable long term strategy. Moderation, rather than prohibition, should be the most important principle in determining how we eat.

Write an essay in which you explain how Danielle Barkley builds an argument to persuade her audience that restrictive diets are not necessarily beneficial or advisable. In your essay, analyze how the author uses one or more of the features listed in the box above (or features of your own choice) to strengthen the logic and persuasiveness of her argument. Be sure that your essay focuses on the most relevant features of the passage.

Your essay should not explain whether you agree with the author's claims, but rather explain how the author builds an argument to persuade the audience.

ESSAY 1

☐ I understand that my essay (without my name) may be reproduced in other IES Test Prep and IES Publications materials. If I mark this box, I grant permission to produce my essay for purposes beyond score reporting and assessment of my writing skills, including (but not limited to) publication without payment or royalties in an IES Publications book. Marking this box will have no effect on my score, nor will it prevent my essay from being made available for viewing at an IES campus.

IMPORTANT: **USE A NO. 2 PENCIL. DO NOT WRITE OUTSIDE THE BORDER!**
Words written outside the essay book or written in ink **WILL NOT APPEAR** in the copy sent to be scored, and your score will be affected.

PLANNING PAGE   You may plan your essay in the unlined planning space below, but only use the lined pages following this one to write your essay. Any work on the planning page will not be scored.

Use pages 5 through 8 for your ESSAY ⟶

FOR PLANNING ONLY

Use pages 5 through 8 for your ESSAY ⟶

You may continue on the next page.

You may continue on the next page.

You may continue on the next page.

STOP.

ies TEST PREP

SAT® Practice Essay #24

ESSAY BOOK

DIRECTIONS

The essay gives you an opportunity to show how effectively you can read and comprehend a passage and write an essay analyzing the passage. In your essay, you should demonstrate that you have read the passage carefully, present a clear and logical analysis, and use language precisely

Your essay must be written on the lines provided in your answer booklet; except for the Planning Page of your answer booklet, you will receive no other paper on which to write. You will have enough space if you write on every line, avoid wide margins, and keep your handwriting to a reasonable size. Remember that people who are not familiar with your handwriting will read what you write. Try to write or print so that what you are writing is legible to those readers.

You have 50 minutes to read the passage and write an essay in response to the prompt provided in this booklet.

REMINDERS

— Do not write your essay in this booklet. Only what you write on the lined pages of your answer booklet will be evaluated.

— An off-topic essay will not be evaluated.

Learn more about IES Test Prep's Essay offerings at **iestestprep.com**

This cover is representative of what you'll see on test day.

THIS TEST BOOKLET MUST NOT BE TAKEN FROM THE ROOM. UNAUTHORIZED REPRODUCTION OR USE OF ANY PART OF THIS BOOKLET IS PROHIBITED.

As you read the passage below, consider how the author uses

◇ evidence, such as facts or examples, to support claims.

◇ reasoning to develop ideas and connect claims and evidence.

◇ stylistic or persuasive elements, such as word choice or appeals to emotion, to add power to the ideas expressed.

Adapted from Philip Kowalski, "The Life of the Mind, and the Death of Reading?" © 2015 IES Publications.

1 The convenience of reading an e-book on the computer or other electronic device diminishes the traditional and historical pastime of curling up with a book in a cozy chair. In such a scenario, readers retreated into an individual and psychological space that provided an edifying experience not normally available elsewhere. Of course, it could be argued that readers can also isolate themselves with laptops or tablets and achieve the same result, but reading e-books perpetuates a dependency on technology that keeps readers plugged-in, as opposed to engaging with the book itself as a cultural artifact that can teach much more than a computer screen.

2 There is a long and valued history to reading as a private pleasure. The rise of literacy rates in the eighteenth century in England and America contributed to the development of the novel, and these early books provided tantalizingly "true" stories of adventure, as in Daniel Defoe's *Robinson Crusoe*, or epistolary novels written in the form of a series of letters among characters, such as Samuel Richardson's *Pamela*. These formats thus permitted readers a kind of voyeuristic pleasure at looking in on other people's lives and sharing experiences heretofore unavailable to most. Because of a latent distrust of fiction given the Anglo-American Puritan heritage, authors assured their readers that the novels they wrote were based on true stories and, above all, that they were didactic or meant to teach a lesson. These writers repeatedly emphasized this point, since critics argued that novel reading was not only a frivolous waste of time, but also dangerous, since these fictional accounts could stir up the imagination and blur the division between reality and fiction. Despite these perceived risks, the popularity of the novel in the eighteenth century also contributed to a growing sense of individuality. By retreating into silence with a book, readers separated themselves from others not only to be entertained, but also to think, reflect, and learn about the culture in which they were enmeshed, and, most importantly, to learn about who they were as beings in the world. As J. Paul Hunter explains in *Before Novels*, "the novel involves not just a raised status for the individual self but an intensified consciousness, individual by individual, of what selfhood means."

3 One can certainly find electronic editions of *Robinson Crusoe* or *Pamela*, but most online content is written at a fourth-grade level, and given the ease and ability with which anyone can publish a book online, many of these e-books are hastily and poorly composed; they

haven't stood the test of time or been weeded out by publishers seeking quality fiction. Of course, this critique could be levied at many bestsellers available in hardcover or paperback; still, being able to hold a book and encounter it as a physical artifact also brings with it the comforting thrill of the smell of ink in a brand new paperback, or the imposing mustiness of a rare book that attests to its travels through time and history.

4   So why can't e-books accomplish the same things as traditional books? As Michael Angier, a self-described "avid reader and author" of traditional print books, enumerates, e-books are "quicker and easier to obtain," "are more easily updated and upgraded," "you usually get far more than just the book," and e-books "take up less space." Certainly the wide variety of texts available is a benefit, since if readers don't like their latest download they can quickly move on to something else with little cost and effort. But this objection really underscores why reading a physical book is a superior exercise. Moving quickly from one e-book to another only perpetuates the frazzled nature of reading online. Distractions such as texting, posting comments, and following friends' activities (as well as the overwhelming abundance of stimuli that the internet offers with pop-ups, banners, and involuntary rerouting to web pages) only contribute to the fragmented nature of being online in the first place.

5   Yet reading an actual book, whether classic or popular, reinforces a kind of quiet sense of self, since stepping away from the computer allows readers to focus on themselves, on one task at a time, and promotes concentration. This arrangement also encourages the decision to finish the book one literally has in hand. Naturally, not all paperbacks or hardcovers will be finished—many will be tossed aside just as one jumps from one e-book to the next—but carving out a space for individual reflection puts readers in touch with the unique personal experience that has been available for centuries, and still proves worthwhile to those looking to escape, if only momentarily, from the demands of the noisy digital world.

Write an essay in which you explain how Philip Kowalski builds an argument to persuade his audience that physical printed books are not similar to books in electronic form. In your essay, analyze how the author uses one or more of the features listed in the box above (or features of your own choice) to strengthen the logic and persuasiveness of his argument. Be sure that your essay focuses on the most relevant features of the passage.

Your essay should not explain whether you agree with the author's claims, but rather explain how the author builds an argument to persuade the audience.

IMPORTANT: **USE A NO. 2 PENCIL. DO NOT WRITE OUTSIDE THE BORDER!**
Words written outside the essay book or written in ink **WILL NOT APPEAR** in the copy sent to be scored, and your score will be affected.

PLANNING PAGE You may plan your essay in the unlined planning space below, but only use the lined pages following this one to write your essay. Any work on the planning page will not be scored.

Use pages 5 through 8 for your ESSAY ⟶

FOR PLANNING ONLY

Use pages 5 through 8 for your ESSAY ⟶

You may continue on the next page.

You may continue on the next page.

STOP.

SAT® Practice Essay #25

ESSAY BOOK

DIRECTIONS

The essay gives you an opportunity to show how effectively you can read and comprehend a passage and write an essay analyzing the passage. In your essay, you should demonstrate that you have read the passage carefully, present a clear and logical analysis, and use language precisely

Your essay must be written on the lines provided in your answer booklet; except for the Planning Page of your answer booklet, you will receive no other paper on which to write. You will have enough space if you write on every line, avoid wide margins, and keep your handwriting to a reasonable size. Remember that people who are not familiar with your handwriting will read what you write. Try to write or print so that what you are writing is legible to those readers.

You have 50 minutes to read the passage and write an essay in response to the prompt provided in this booklet.

REMINDERS

— Do not write your essay in this booklet. Only what you write on the lined pages of your answer booklet will be evaluated.

— An off-topic essay will not be evaluated.

Learn more about IES Test Prep's Essay offerings at **iestestprep.com**

This cover is representative of what you'll see on test day.

As you read the passage below, consider how the author uses

◇ evidence, such as facts or examples, to support claims.

◇ reasoning to develop ideas and connect claims and evidence.

◇ stylistic or persuasive elements, such as word choice or appeals to emotion, to add power to the ideas expressed.

Adapted from Joy McGillian, "The Entrepreneur's Creed." © 2016, IES Publications.

1   . . . To do well in business, think about the present. You see two groups that need to connect and can't: create the social media platform that could connect them tomorrow. You see a storefront up for sale, in a good location, at a discount: create the restaurant that you, your friends, and your town have always wanted. In pursuits such as these, there will be gratifications that arrive quickly, in tangible form. You will have something concrete that gives you the immediate opportunity to make more and do more, day-to-day.

2   But to do something extraordinary in business, think about the future. Think about the needs that consumers, institutions, companies, anybody and perhaps everybody will have years from now. Thinking like this isn't easy, either intellectually or psychologically. Even if you are developing and financing an idea that definitively is the future, you will (unless you're stampeded by investors) need to bear short-term expenditures that will feel like a steady march of losses, not a determined march towards success, on most days. You will feel directionless, even if you have a business plan that could fill two IKEA bookshelves. You will feel alone, and possibly insane.

3   Imagine, for instance, how Apple's Steve Jobs must have been regarded in the 1980s for insisting that a computer should be a closed system: few add-ons, little or no ability for users to open up the computer itself and tinker around. Computer hobbyists wanted to do just these things—get inside the hardware, modify the system—and RadioShack was making a fortune selling parts for repairs and upgrades. Today, RadioShack is still around but is universally regarded as a textbook-example corporate disaster, Jobs is dead but is universally regarded as a visionary, and nobody is opening up computers. For the record, I typed this paragraph on an Apple computer that looks like you couldn't open it with a chainsaw.

4   This sort of thinking has outlived Jobs, too. I recently moderated a university-sponsored panel of entrepreneurs under 30 and, as you can imagine in the post-Jobs era, many of the participants had grand ideas about where technology could go next. Yet the truly innovative ideas were only marginally related to software and devices; the truly exceptional concepts involved the fields of publishing and education.

5 For those of you who follow the broader workings of the economy, what I have just said may seem strange, even absurd. Traditional publishing has been decimated by the rise of Amazon.com, the reactionary and self-defeating mentality of the oldest publishing houses, and the false starts that print newspapers have made in adapting to the Internet. Education may be in even worse shape: it is an industry that in no way possesses a market-leading innovator on the level of Amazon or Apple and that has enormous trouble luring top talent away from technology, finance, and even publishing. And then there is the bad press, most recently the revelation that ITT Educational Services, a for-profit provider of higher education, was being forced by the Federal Government to shut down its campuses. Roughly 35,000 students and 8,000 staff members suddenly found themselves, respectively, without degrees and jobs.

6 But the bet that those young entrepreneurs I talked with are making is that present failure does not align with future failure. Instead, one of those entrepreneurs envisioned a boom in local news coverage that would happen somewhere around 2020. Another envisioned a similar boom in English as a Second Language education that would happen somewhere around 2025, give or take. . . .

7 I am convinced that those booms will come to pass. (Disclosure: I own equity in the ESL business, LanguageOwl Learning, described just above.) Yet maybe the real value is not in being proven right or wrong by the course the market takes. The value I see in thinking towards the business future is that, when you do so, business stops being mere business and becomes an act of the imagination. After all, it's not net worth but totalizing, overpowering vision that regularly lands CEOs like Elon Musk and Marc Benioff on the covers of newsmagazines. We celebrate such creativity because we know, with some deep instinct, that creativity is the real legacy. Business stops being about the next dollar and starts being about the next surge of inspiration that transforms technology, or education, or the any field you want—no matter how long that inspiration takes to translate itself into reality.

Write an essay in which you explain how Joy McGillian builds an argument to persuade her audience that excellence in business requires foresight and strength of character. In your essay, analyze how the author uses one or more of the features listed in the box above (or features of your own choice) to strengthen the logic and persuasiveness of her argument. Be sure that your essay focuses on the most relevant features of the passage.

Your essay should not explain whether you agree with the author's claims, but rather explain how the author builds an argument to persuade the audience.

ESSAY 1

☐ I understand that my essay (without my name) may be reproduced in other IES Test Prep and IES Publications materials. If I mark this box, I grant permission to produce my essay for purposes beyond score reporting and assessment of my writing skills, including (but not limited to) publication without payment or royalties in an IES Publications book. Marking this box will have no effect on my score, nor will it prevent my essay from being made available for viewing at an IES campus.

IMPORTANT: **USE A NO. 2 PENCIL. DO NOT WRITE OUTSIDE THE BORDER!**
Words written outside the essay book or written in ink **WILL NOT APPEAR** in the copy sent to be scored, and your score will be affected.

PLANNING PAGE You may plan your essay in the unlined planning space below, but only use the lined pages following this one to write your essay. Any work on the planning page will not be scored.

Use pages 5 through 8 for your ESSAY ⟶

FOR PLANNING ONLY

Use pages 5 through 8 for your ESSAY ⟶

BEGIN YOUR ESSAY HERE.

You may continue on the next page.

You may continue on the next page.

STOP.

PRACTICE ESSAYS

MAIN IDEAS AND CONCEPTS

The following outlines include some of the main points of each passage text. However, you may come across some ideas during your annotation that are not listed here. This section is primarily designed to provide you with a general understanding of the key points in each passage text.

Main Points: SAT Essay Passages

Essay 1: Gabrielle Lenhard, "Stepping Towards a Better Balance"
Logos

- Systematic and logical discussion of the negative health effects of constant sitting (including extended reference to the James Levine study)
- Use of Gina Trapani's activities as a case study in the pros and cons of abandoning a sitting posture in the workplace
- Explanation of how incentives can be used in a thoughtful and efficient manner to encourage improved health and posture in the workplace

Pathos

- References to universal concepts (fundamental "tools") and popular companies and industries to create an intuitive connection between the reader and the topic
- Composed and balanced tone that creates a levelheaded persona for the author, but stark explanation of drawbacks that may surprise or agitate the reader
- Use of imagery ("Band-Aid on a bullet wound") that highlights the drama and urgency of a seemingly everyday issue

Ethos

- Discussion of the author's status as "the head of a human resources department," and thus as an individual deeply involved in the main dilemma considered in the essay
- Appeal to a firm set of values and principles in envisioning workplaces premised on activity, productivity, and personal happiness

Essay 2: Nelson Randall, "How to Make Money and Not Do Anything Stupid"
Logos

- Quotations from Warren Buffett and explanation of a strategy (holding stocks over a long period of time) that demonstrates the soundness of this advice
- Statistics that indicate the unlikelihood of turning a profit by rapidly buying and trading stocks, as opposed to holding stocks over time
- Examples suggesting the pitfalls of "day trading" and indicating that success stories related to this strategy are relatively rare

Pathos

- Conversational tone and brief anecdotes that make a potentially difficult financial topic more accessible and approachable
- Direct address to the reader ("you") to make the writing more engaging
- Moments of dry humor and irony that both make the writing more entertaining and challenge typical expectations

Ethos

- Discussion of the author's own background as an investor in order to show that he is a direct, active participant in the stock market
- Formulation of a clear and decisive approach to investing, with a principled emphasis on wise investment over exciting investment

Essay 3: Tallis Moore, "Brain Drain: The Dangers of Pop-Psych"
Logos

- Clear definitions and explanations of major concepts ("left brain" and "right brain"), along with criticism of the ambiguities present in such absolute ideas
- Refutation of absolute and simplistic ideas, with the goal of presenting ideas on how the brain works that are both more flexible and more logical
- Discussion of studies and empirical data that undermine the "myth" of left and right brains

Pathos

- Use of questions and short sentences to enliven the writing style, and to indicate the writer's energetic opposition to the left brain/right brain dichotomy
- Inclusion of pop culture references and appeals to innate humanity and creativity, to help the reader to connect to a difficult scientific issue

Ethos

- Explanation of the author's own status as "a professor of psychology," with a related description of one of the author's classroom exercises
- Rigorous and direct opposition of the author (and other credible experts, such as Jeff Anderson and Karen Federmeier) to proponents of the flawed left/right dichotomy

Essay 4: Patrick Kennedy, "The Adjunct Future"
Logos

- Use of a single extended example (Margaret Mary Vojtko) to represent the broader problems that adjuncts face
- Demonstration that the wages earned by adjuncts are problematic on the basis of apparent earnings versus actual hourly earnings
- Explanation of the practices that can make adjunct teaching a time-efficient practice, and discussion of why teachers are unaware of this strategy and other subtle aspects of the adjunct situation

Pathos

- Language that calls attention to poverty and misfortune to create a sense of shock and disbelief in the reader
- Sarcastic, critical tone applied to "superstar" professors and other aspects of academia that fail to address the adjunct dilemma

344

- Recurring sentence structure (used for emphasis) when offering recommendations in the final paragraphs

Ethos

- Statistics and quotations (coupled with the author's claim that he has performed his own research) to show that the author has cultivated a background on the issues
- Use of practical recommendations that oppose the current approach of not giving adjuncts sufficient on-the-job information about their role
- Reference to the background of the author and of his own father to show firsthand experience, and to show that the author's recommendations are viable

Essay 5: Danielle Barkley, "The Sharing Economy Myth"
Logos

- Rigorous definitions of terms such as "sharing economy" and "collaborative consumption," with the goal of eliminating inaccurate terminology
- Discussion of how the sharing economy actually functions, with quotations, statistics, and examples drawn from specific companies
- Precise explanation of individual "sharing economy" exchanges and consideration of the motives behind them

Pathos

- Initial example of childhood sharing that makes a potentially complex economic topic more approachable
- Focus on the economic liabilities involved in the sharing economy in order to show how compassionate standards of "sharing" have been contradicted
- Authorial voice that convincingly balances careful investigation of the evidence with strong opinions (the idea that "'Sharing economy' is a misnomer," for instance)

Ethos

- Strong set of personal principles, including empathy as part of reasonable and productive human interactions
- Willingness to admit the efficiency and popularity of the sharing economy, but confidence that such admissions will not undermine the essay's thesis

Essay 6: Larry Bernstein, "Sleep No More: Unrested and Restless in the American Economy"

Logos

- Clear and quantity-oriented explanation of the current sleep patterns (versus optimal sleep patterns) among Americans
- Statistics to call attention to the negative consequences of sleep loss, and to show the true, empirical

significance of a problem that may be easy to underestimate

- Connections between sleep loss and repercussions in a variety of areas (medicine, business, the environment) to explain the breadth of the issue

Pathos

- Use of questions to engage the reader and encourage reflection on the issue of sleep loss
- Dramatic phrasing ("sleep-deprived zombies") to lend urgency and emphasis to the discussion
- References to catastrophic events to cause fear and anxiety in the reader

Ethos

- Consistent inclusion of authoritative studies and scientific sources, in a manner that establishes the author as a rigorous and informed source himself
- Discussion of how "everyone has suffered through a bad night of sleep" to show that the author (like the reader) should have a very personal and direct investment in the topic of the essay

Essay 7: Chris Holliday, "Everything Goes: How the 1960s Made the World Modern"
Logos

- Specific examples of the music, fashion, and celebrities who shaped life in the 1960s
- Explanation of a broad historical trend involving a shift away from the stoic wartime mentality and towards a new spirit of experimentation and openness
- Argument that seemingly lighthearted changes in popular culture were bound up with momentous political events

Pathos

- Consistent use of humor and an approachable, conversational voice to appeal to the reader
- Scenes in which the author discovers new ideas (camping and music, the play performance) in a manner that conveys energy and excitement
- Short and impactful final paragraph to convey a darker tone and reinforce the idea that the 1960s involved sharp, dramatic change

Ethos

- Reliance on the author's firsthand observations and anecdotes, which offer authoritative personal responses to somewhat distant history
- Emphasis on the author's coming-of-age perspective to show that the author was profoundly impacted and transformed by the 1960s

Essay 8: Raphael Cael, "The Founding Fathers v. the Climate Change Skeptics"
Logos

- Creation of an extended analogy between past and present responses to climate change, with reference to specific past researchers and theorists

- Presentation of a detailed history of early American society and its responses to a specific, well-defined branch of scientific thought

Pathos

- Emphatic language ("advocates," "grievances," "problematic") that calls attention to the importance of the issues at hand and injects passion into a scientific examination of facts
- Direct address ("it might surprise you", "one should") in order to engage the reader and encourage an intensely thoughtful response to the issues

Ethos

- Demonstration of the author's own knowledge through quick references to complex historical events, thus showing the author's comfort with a wealth of material
- Recommendations of the best approaches for both activists and skeptics in the climate change debate, indicating that the author's own position is simultaneously balanced and constructive

Essay 9: Sheila Chode, "Water, Water, Everywhere"
Logos

- Use of studies and statistics to support the author's overarching claims about the individual-level benefits of drinking water
- Distinction between drinking water and drinking presumably healthy beverages (such as juices) with the goal of lending clarity and order to the entire discussion
- Analysis of the financial cost of obesity-related heath liabilities to add an empirical measure to an issue with a strong human and emotional element

Pathos

- Focus on the emotional side of malnutrition (aggression in children) with the intention of inspiring concern and creating a humane connection in the reader
- Use of an anecdote that shows the human cost of drinking beverages other than water, along with loaded questions and candid explanations of the niece's poor health

Ethos

- Strong background (personal experience and technical knowledge) that allows the author to credibly explain the situation of both parents and children
- Awareness of common, prevalent health principles ("make sure your child drinks plenty of water") and engagement with the ethical issues that they raise

Essay 10: Gabrielle Lenhard, "An America Hungry for Change"
Logos

- Presentation of studies that indicate the effects and outcomes (mostly positive, but with some reservations) of introducing new commercial choice in food deserts

- Use of statistics to explain the severity of the food desert crisis and the consequent need for a proportionally large response

Pathos

- Emphatic and purposeful language ("initiate change", "hankering for healthy options") to lend passion to the author's style and call attention to the urgency of main topic
- Direct address ("Imagine") and images of children who lack healthy options in order engage the reader, and to generate shock and pity

Ethos

- Reference to the author's own "research and consulting company" to indicate her expertise in the sociological issues discussed in the text
- Specialized information (Steven Cummins, The People's Garden) that indicates that the author has extensive, insider knowledge of the "food desert" crisis

Essay 11: Jonathan Holt, "Morbid Hybrid: Interbreeding as a Means of Species Depletion"

Logos

- Utilization of a variety of examples (coywolf and others) to show the potent effects of hybridization as a method of animal adaptation
- Logic and systematic argument against the "common wisdom" that favors biodiversity over hybridization
- Definition of terms (biodiversity, hybridization, species) in order to make the main concepts clear and logically accessible to the reader

Pathos

- Short expressions ("This is evolution in hyper-drive", "the list goes on") that lend strong emphasis to major points and show the author's powerful engagement with a scientific issue
- Sentence structure (numerous instances of "but" and "however") that adds drama to the essay through the presentation of counterintuitive and surprising facts

Ethos

- Reference to the author's own "various field studies," indicating the author's firsthand involvement in the essay's central issues
- Word choice ("colleagues", "we" as a reference to researchers) that shows that the author is a member of a community of experts, and that he is well aware of other biologists' perspectives

Essay 12: Cynthia Helzner, "Nepotism Now?"

Logos

- Clear definition of nepotism, with meaningful distinctions between nepotism and other types of work-related favoritism

348

- Use of statistics, examples, and expert testimony in order to indicate the extent of the nepotism problem in a specific and concrete manner
- Comparative analysis of different workplace systems (nepotism, lottery, meritocracy) with the aim of logically determining an arrangement that is effective and realistic

Pathos

- Questions and direct address ("Imagine") to engage the reader and foster a direct, emotional response to the issue of nepotism
- Inclusion of an "old adage" and other colloquial phrases ("helping your kids") to make it easier for the reader to relate to the complexities of the author's discussion

Ethos

- Appeal to a strong system of values, particularly the ideas of fairness in the workplace and rewards for individual merit
- Careful consideration of the motives behind nepotism (especially in family businesses) that shows the author's perspective to be balanced, multi-faceted, and rigorously credible

Essay 13: Derrick McQueen, "Polluter Pays"
Logos

- Logical explanation of why the "polluter pays" principle was developed as a plausible solution in environmental cleanup, with an equally logical focus on the principle's shortcomings
- Step-by-step analysis of the process of rehabilitating brownfields, with an emphasis on both the benefits and the costs of this environmental approach
- Use of statistics in discussing the Superfund effort to give the reader a concrete idea of the extent of environmental cleanup efforts and of the work that remains to be done

Pathos

- Tone of concern established through word choices ("Sadly") and pointed questions ("Where will all of the money come from?")
- Everyday examples ("Wouldn't you pay more . . .) that encourage the reader to personally connect to a momentous environmental and humanitarian issue

Ethos

- Firm and principled stand in favor of "polluter pays" as a specific course of action, despite possible and acknowledged objections to this policy
- Awareness of different variations on "polluter pays" laws (CERCLA, for instance) and thus implicit expertise on this complicated topic

Essay 14: Matthew Gaertner, "The Leaning Tower of PISA"
Logos

- Clear explanation of the reasons for panic surrounding the PISA testing, in order to set up a coherent argument that such panic is unwarranted

- Comparative analysis of the United States and Hong Kong, with careful reasoning that explains why Hong Kong outperforms the United States in STEM topics
- Consideration of STEM education and workforce earning power for the purpose of showing that PISA results do not easily correlate to success in one's career

Pathos

- Emphatic word choice in the first few paragraphs ("alarmed", "crippling", "shockingly") to communicate to the reader the high emotional stakes that surround the PISA testing
- Use of sharp contrasts, imperative sentences, and one-sentence paragraphs ("But largely stagnant wages . . .") to add verbal drama and engagement to a topic that might otherwise seem technical and alienating

Ethos

- Command of the history and guidelines of PISA testing (third paragraph) in a manner that indicates the author's expert knowledge of this aspect of modern education
- Commitment to a meaningful solution (final paragraph), but tempered with an awareness of the usefulness and importance of STEM education

Essay 15: Gabrielle Lenhard, "Trash Talk"
Logos

- Discussion of the Single-Use Plastic Carryout Bag Ordnance in order to establish the viability of productive measures and demonstrate how environment-friendly incentives operate
- Examples involving large entities (Dell, Walmart, the city of Seattle) that have developed logical systems for guiding consumer and citizen behavior for desirable results
- Abundant statistics to underscore the magnitude of the problems discussed in the essay and to provide specific measures of success

Pathos

- Modes of address ("you might say", "I implore you") that directly engage the reader and encourage a sense of urgency and responsibility
- Appeal to optimism in the belief that American consumers and corporations can take action to combat vast environmental problems

Ethos

- Direct reference to the author's position as a "Senior Environmental Planner" who has a direct stake in the problems of waste reduction discussed throughout the essay
- Close awareness of recent initiatives, and of how they guide and affect behavior on the level of individual consumers (small fees and fines)

Essay 16: Robert F. Kennedy, Day of Affirmation Address

Logos

- Discussion of broad principles such as freedom of speech, which provide the logical basis for functional democratic societies when observed and respected
- Comparative analysis of free and oppressive societies with the intention of arguing that free societies are imperfect but clearly more desirable
- Observation of a broad trend involving progress away from discrimination to prominence for religious and ethnic groups, particularly Catholics and African Americans

Pathos

- Reliance on strong emotions surrounding government activities, including the fear that government will eradicate rights and the hope that government will create a harmonious society
- Emphatic style (anaphora, dashes, and stark vocabulary choices related to oppression and poverty) that convey Kennedy's passion and can inspire the reader to feel similar concern and engagement

Ethos

- Strong and well-articulated set of moral principles premised on Kennedy's opposition to communism and on providing opportunity to groups that face disadvantages and discrimination
- Language ("We have passed . . .", "We are committed . . .") that indicates Kennedy's active involvement in initiatives to protect and promote democratic values

Essay 17: Sonia Sotomayor, "Dissenting Opinion: Utah vs. Strieff"

Logos

- Clear and precise definition of the Fourth Amendment, and elucidation of some of the legal complexities and qualifications that surround it
- Extended reference to the actions of Edward Strieff in order to demonstrate the legal and rational weaknesses of random searches by the police
- Consideration of possible arguments against the main position and of hypothetical examples that could render the main position problematic, all of which are logically and purposefully refuted

Pathos

- Language that directly addresses the reader ("you") and encourages the reader to relate the Strieff case (and related life-or-death issues) to his or her own life and emotions
- Dramatic short sentences to conclude paragraphs, and to keep the reader engaged by creating a sense of drama and anticipation

Ethos

- Direct and principled stance ("I dissent") against a decision that Sotomayor deems unwise and lacking in sufficient justification
- Citation of expert authorities (the "Utah Supreme Court") whose own judgment aligns with and validates Sotomayor's support for Strieff

- Practical argument that random police stops can and should be curtailed to protect citizens

Essay 18: Henry Paulson, Statement on Actions to Protect the U.S. Economy
Logos

- Identification of a fundamental problem in terms of U.S. economics—namely, lack of confidence in the financial system—and description of logical and practical steps to correct the problem
- Explanation of how "U.S. financial institutions" can be assisted in a time of crisis, with statistics and cause-and-effect analysis to explain how such assistance is meant to function

Pathos

- Strong language ("threat", "disruption", "objectionable") that is designed to alert the reader to the high-stakes nature of the issues that Paulson is describing
- Overview of how economic problems play out on an individual or family level (second paragraph) to activate the emotions of sympathy, concern, and perhaps fear in the reader

Ethos

- Discussion of the initiatives that Paulson himself has promoted, and of how they are designed to promote meaningful values such as "the economic well-being of all Americans"
- Appeal to other respected sources (nine large financial institutions, Chairman Bernake, Chairman Bair) whose willingness to work with Paulson reflects positively on Paulson's reliability and credibility

Essay 19: Crystal Eastman, "Now We Can Begin"
Logos

- Acknowledgment of recent progress ("Federal suffrage amendment") tempered by a logical and rational awareness that more problems remain to be solved
- Analysis of how women's freedom relates to economic issues, with a careful distinction between such concepts as inward (psychological) and outward (economic) freedom
- Cause-and-effect analysis that traces the potential for change in the situation of women overall to the measure of changing child-raising methods ("feminist sons")

Pathos

- Questions that encourage the reader to think critically, and that purposefully and emphatically lead into later stages of Eastman's discussion
- Dramatic and ideologically charged word choices ("slavery", "soul", "revolutionary") and emotionally powerful examples (the wife in the fourth paragraph) to show the high emotional and human stakes involved in Eastman's chosen issue

Ethos

- Direct discussion of the perspectives of women and feminists, with the aim of showing Eastman as a conscientious and thoughtful representative of these groups

- Consideration of the perspective of "friends" (sixth paragraph) and "Men" (seventh paragraph) with the intention of respectfully but firmly presenting Eastman's opposing viewpoint

Essay 20: Loretta Lynch, "Remarks at the National Summit on Youth Violence Prevention"

Logos

- Explanation of the negative repercussions of violent crime, with a focus on how such crime affects the psychology and development of children
- Argument that violent crime (rather than being an unsolvable crisis) is a problem that can be assertively addressed in a manner that logically justifies new initiatives and solutions
- Distinction between national and urban crime rates, with the intention of clarifying the true dangers of urban crime

Pathos

- Word and address choices ("you", "we") that form a direct connection to the audience and encourage awareness of the important issues at hand
- Diction that is designed to activate emotions such as fear and distress ("unacceptable", "awful", "darkness", "victims") and show the emotional urgency of Lynch's discussion
- Appeal to optimism and collective willpower in the final stages of the essay

Ethos

- References to Lynch's activities within the Justice Department and discussion of initiatives in which Lynch herself is involved
- Principled acknowledgment of the difficulties and drawbacks that are involved in preventing youth violence

Essay 21: Mariel Zachs, "Serve or Learn?"

Logos

- Use of an extended example (HUCAC) that ties into broader trends that involve how students structure and think about community service
- Definition of two different systems of values, and a clear argument as to why one of these systems is superior in conception
- Rigorous account of the drawbacks in current approaches, with the end goal of presenting a solution that will avoid these drawbacks

Pathos

- Creation of a colloquial style that will appeal to a reader, especially through the use of questions, short sentences, and short paragraphs
- Use of humor and irony in presenting evidence, along with short narratives that the reader will find memorable and readily accessible
- Overall, sense of seriousness about the subject and optimism about student initiatives, despite the

often whimsical and critical tone

Ethos

- Position as a member of a college faculty (and earlier position as an engaged student) to demonstrate a firsthand stake in the issues at hand
- Determination to face unpleasant or discouraging examples in order to arrive at a strong set of values and a better approach
- Awareness of other education experts (Frank Bruni) and nuanced engagement with their work

Essay 22: Patrick Kennedy, "But Is It Art? But Does That Question Even Matter?"
Logos

- Attempt to meaningfully define the concept of "art," combined with a clear sense of the logical inconsistencies in standard definitions
- Systematic survey of the status of art and museums, with the end goal of determining an optimal attitude in the reception of contemporary art

Pathos

- Presentation of a humorous yet on-topic anecdote to introduce a topic that readers, otherwise, might have trouble readily engaging
- Use of questions, short sentences, dashes, quotation marks, and other writing features to create a tone that is impressively fluid and conversational
- References to the strong emotions felt by artists (Pollock) and art critics (Kramer and Fried), with the end goal of conveying the emotional intensity of art history to the reader

Ethos

- Demonstration of a rigorous and detailed understanding of the history of art, from the nineteenth century to the present day
- Consideration of diverse perspectives, with the end goal of decisively and straightforwardly stating which perspective is optimal for museum-goers and art historians

Essay 23: Danielle Barkley, "Yes, You Can Spell 'Diet' Without 'Denial': The Complicated Case of Restrictive Dieting"
Logos

- Use of statistics and of technical definitions (Paleo diet, vegan diet) to clarify ideas and premises central to the argument
- Orderly movement away from considering the popularity of restrictive diets to examining, in detail, the drawbacks that these diets entail
- Consideration of logical principles ("correlation rather than causation") to arrive at a meaningful course of action ("moderation") that is superior to restrictive dieting

Pathos

- Appeal to the reader's desire for comfort and pleasure, and discussion of how dieting can enhance or inhibit the pursuit of these desires
- Adoption of a calm tone that wins the reader's respect and admiration, even when the author is discussing potentially upsetting topics (such as the health risks and misunderstandings that accompany restrictive diets)

Ethos

- References to both the past (Greeks) and present (Vincci Tsui) to establish the breadth of the author's knowledge of her subject
- Balanced understanding of the motives behind restrictive dieting, combined with a strong and evenhanded conviction that a better approach is possible

Essay 24: Philip Kowalski, "The Life of the Mind, and the Death of Reading?"
Logos

- Systematic comparison of the relative merits of reading a print book and reading an online document
- Discussion of the history of modern reading habits as a means of setting the context for the author's later argument in favor of reading physical print
- Analysis of different perspectives to establish the different sides of the debate, and to show that the author has settled on his viewpoint in a measured and meticulous fashion

Pathos

- Connection to the reader through references to the everyday nuisances that may attend reading electronic sources
- Language later in the passage ("quiet" versus "noisy") that quickly and effectively casts print reading as strongly positive and digital reading as strongly negative
- Tone of formality and equanimity that is designed to inspire admiration

Ethos

- References to other writers on the topic, showing the extent of the author's conscientious research
- Adoption of a strong conviction about reading, but a sense of understanding and respect directed towards those with different viewpoints

Essay 25: Joy McGillian, "The Entrepreneur's Creed"
Logos

- Strong emphasis on a central principle (planning with the future of business in mind) that leads into clear and practical recommendations
- Acknowledgement of temporary drawbacks (publishing and education) paired against a coherent final argument for long-term advantages
- Past results from CEOs and business world trends to validate ideas about the costs and benefits of long-term thinking

Pathos

- Consistent direct address to the reader ("you") to encourage the audience to think deeply and dynamically about the qualities of modern enterprise
- Descriptions of dramatically different business results to inspire emotions such as admiration (for successes) and surprise (at stark failures)
- Instances of everyday references and comparisons (IKEA bookshelves, newsmagazines) that make a potentially difficult subject easier to absorb and understand

Ethos

- Explicit acknowledgment of the author's activities within the world of business (participation in a specific panel, investment in an education company)
- Use of a confident tone when delivering specific advice; honest acknowledgment of risks, but faith that her own recommendations are ultimately sound

STUDENT RESPONSES

SAMPLES AND ANALYSES

Pick and Choose What to Analyze

Student responses can vary from student to student, but the following samples for Practice Essays 1-4 should give you an idea of the differences between an average, satisfactory, and excellent response.

Pay close attention to how similar ideas are discussed in each response and the ways in which those ideas are analyzed. You will notice that although some responses present and/or discuss the same key points, the ways in which they are analyzed can be the difference between a satisfactory and an excellent response.

In other cases, the student chose to be more selective with the information he or she analyzed, proving how particular passage features contribute to the effectiveness of the author's persuasion.

Remember: The goal is to prove HOW the author is EFFECTIVE in proving his or her argument, NOT to summarize the essay.

Each of these sample responses was handwritten by actual students who have taken IES courses and transcribed into type for reading purposes. The type represents the ACTUAL response without alteration. This includes spelling, punctuation, and other grammatical errors—if such are present. Followed by each response is an IES teacher analysis that indicates how and why each response received its score.

Note: Each score is from a single grader. Because student responses are evaluated by two graders, it is reasonable to assume that the full score for the essay would be double what is given.

PRACTICE ESSAY #1
STEPPING TOWARDS A BETTER BALANCE BY GABRIELLE LENHARD

Student Response A

"The average American spends 13 hours a day in his chair, with only a remaining few moving or standing." Here, Gabrielle Lenhard states an important fact on the lack of physical activity of Americans, which she will then go on to explain how truly dangerous and unhealthy it is. In the passage "Stepping towards a better balance", Gabrielle Lenhard effectively creates a strong argument that more balanced work environments are helpful to both the employee and the employer. She achieves this by using facts and statistics, noting drawbacks to proposed solutions, use of purposeful language and rhetoric, and all while maintaining a credible account.

In the passage, Gabrielle Lenhard effectively uses facts and statistics while noting drawbacks to proposed solutions. She states that she has received "many complaints from employees about their backs aching after sitting in an uncomfortable chair." Thus allowing her to introduce the premise of her argument to the reader. This makes the reader contemplate her argument from the beginning, which allows for the author to draw the reader in to her argument since they have already been primed with the central thesis. Lenhard continues to use facts and stats as she states that official research has concluded that "sitting most directly slows down metabolism" and "causes weight gain with the myriad of cardiovascular problems, diabetes, cancers and arthritis." This inclusion of factual statistics definitively shows the reader that sitting is bad for health and well being, causing them to believe in and support Lehnard's thesis that chairs need to be made. However, not all solutions have positive effects, as the reader finds out when Lenhard explains the "standing desk" and how aulthough those whom have used it lost 3 to 5 pounds in weeks, she also explains that it would not fit well in a "sea of sitters" where "odd man out" syndrome would have a negative effect on office health. Additionally, Lenhard explains that aulthough solutions such as company gyms are beneficial, "The onsite attraction is unattractive, as individuals favor gym time as an escape from the workplace and are too embarrassed by their physique to use the priveledge". This causes the reader to contemplate other solutions that may be possible, and to pay closer attention to see if Lenhard finds a win-all solution.

Lenhards use of purposeful language and rhetoric captures the mind of the reader, forcing them to read the passage, and to be persuaded by the author. This can be seen as in the first paragraph, Lenhard makes comparisons between homo sapien harpoons and the Samsung galaxy" later noting how both are tools and technological advances. This use of language sets the readers mind in the right state to think about and listen to Lenhards argument. Once this has occurred, Lenhard uses important numbers such as "over 11,000 trackers to 4,000 employees" to force the reader into agreeing with her, that her solution works.

Lenhards credible account within her passage makes her not only a believable source but also, a persuasive one. In the beginning of the second paragraph Lenhard tells the reader that she is "head of the human resources department" for her company which not only puts her in the perfect position to make her argument, but also makes the reader know that Lenhard knows what she is talking about, as she is the expert in that area of study. This greatly attributes to the likeliness of the reader agreeing with Lenhard and her argument. This is not all of it, however, as Lenhard goes on to include studies and definitive research done by "Dr. James Levine, an endocrinologist and co-founder of the Mayo Clinic program obesity solutions." As well as "Dr. Ron Geotzel, a senior scientist of the institute for health program studies." These inclusions cause the readers belief in the research conducted, and the conclusions of it as law, and that Lenhards argument is absolutely legitimate. In conclusion, Gabrielle Lenhard creates an effective argument for her cause. The reader, by the end of the passage, is completely persuaded by Lenhard and may even be compelled to go buy a fit-Bit by themselves. Lenhards passage success fully confirms that "The same components that make up a balanced community must be present in a workplace to sustain successful employees."

Student Response A: Score and Analysis

Reading: 3

This response begins with an accurate indication of Lenhard's main argument regarding "balanced work environments". However, as the writing progresses, the writer does not always succeed in maintaining a strong focus on this main idea; the final body paragraphs fail to make meaningful references to Lenhard's thesis, and the concluding idea that the reader "may even be compelled to go buy a fit-Bit by themselves" is rather irrelevant. These drawbacks justify the Reading score of 3.

Analysis: 2

This response features a promising and often effective first body paragraph, though here some additional streamlining and a more intensive analysis of the final quotation would be assets. The weaknesses of the two other body paragraphs are much more pronounced. While the second seldom makes effective use of quotations, the third lines up too many pieces of evidence without sufficiently insightful analysis of how they work together. These limitations justify the Analysis score of 2, though the relatively strong first body paragraph may prompt some readers to grant a score of 3.

Writing: 2

This response exhibits noticeable flaws in punctuation ("Lenhards" for the possessive "Lenhard's) and spelling ("aulthough", "privelege"). Some sentences use awkward phrasing or try to present too much information at once, the vocabulary could be much more impressive, and the body paragraphs could be much better organized. These shortcomings, taken together, justify the Writing score of 2.

Student Response B

"From homo sapien harpoons to the Samsung Galaxy, Mankind has created tools to help himself complete tasks more efficiently." Author Gabrielle Lenhard persuades her audience that more balanced work environments are helpful to both the employee and the employers in her essay "Stepping Towards a better balance." She convinces her readers of the importance of being healthy while working by using reasoning and real-life examples, and vivid language, and evidence to maintain a credible account.

Lenhard begins her essay by introducing her topic and perspective. She tells how "an economy dominated by desk jobs" causes employees to be seated in "rather uncomfortable" chairs for over "8 hours a day." She uses these statistics to show the reader from the beginning how not having a healthy office lifestyle is bad. Then, she goes even further and explains that sitting for so long can cause "cardiovascular problems, diabetes, cancer, and arthritis." Sitting for so long can lead to serious health conditions, and Lenhard uses this to her advantage to show why work environments need to be balanced. Leonard then proceeds to show that "James Levine and his associates" proved people who use "greater amounts of energy" end up heather and "leaner." This proves that exercising is a good way to boost office health, and it works. Leonard provides a real-world example of online blogger Gina Trapani and how she had lost "3 to 5 pounds" just from "pacing and fidgeting." This proves to the audience that such a physical method works. However, Lenhard then shows that just one person isn't enough. There need to be more "creative workplace health initiatives" to motivate everyone to get active and be healthier. She then explains that "Fitbit" has indeed distributed "over 11,000 trackers" to its "4000 employees." By using logic and reasoning, Lenhard has already convinced her readers that being more physical in the office will improve health standards for everyone.

The author uses vivid language to provoke emotion in her audience. She sees phrases like "putting a Band-Aid on a bullet wound" in paragraph two to show the severity of the situation. It is meant to overwhelm the readers and make them feel they need to take this issue seriously. She also quotes how Gina Trapani feels surrounded by a "sea of sitters" to show the huge contrast between the majority of inactive co-workers and Gina. This gives an incredulous tone to the paragraph and creates a sense of how big this problem really is. Lenhard's use of imagery and vidid language appeals to her audience on an emotional level, further convincing him or her of her perspective.

Lenhard maintains a credible and honest profile throughout the essay. She tells that she is "the head of the human resources department," proving that she is both trustworthy and knowledgeable in this area, This makes Lenhard's audience more inclined to believe her, considering she is probably more well-versed on this topic than he or she is, The reader is more likely to be convinced due to Lenhard's credibility and trustworthiness.

Lenhard uses a combination of logic and reasoning, emotional appeal, and credibility to persuade her audience that work environments need to be improved to benefit everyone. She wraps up her essay by giving results its success She explains that less people miss work due to "illness or injury" and produces a "higher productivity." This recognition of the "relationship between wellness and performance" shows the reader that, indeed, physical remedy is effective and yields positive results. At the end of the essay, Lenhard's readers are thoroughly convinced of more balanced work environments.

Student Response B: Score and Analysis

Reading: 4

This response is informed by a clear sense of Lenhard's main argument (which is summed up quickly though quite effectively in the first paragraph) and of the major devices (logic, emotion, credibility) that work together within Lenhard's essay. Such comprehension of how the prompt discusses the benefits of balanced workplaces justifies the Reading score of 4.

Analysis: 3

This response features a first body paragraph that effectively responds to the overall logical structure of the prompt, and also presents a few insightful points in the two body paragraphs that follow. However, the first body paragraph requires improved coordination (since it is more about various pieces of evidence than about the "perspective" referenced in the topic sentence). The two that follow, for their part, would benefit from analysis of a few pieces of evidence that are full sentences, not simply short phrases picked from the article. Despite the essay's apparent strengths, these clear weaknesses justify the Analysis score of 3.

Writing: 3

This response demonstrates a fairly good command of grammar and correct (though not especially advanced) diction throughout. Yet the response would benefit overall from stronger pacing: the final two body paragraphs seem to have been rushed, and the conclusion tries to juggle both interesting new ideas and content from earlier in the essay. These deficiencies justify the Writing score of 3.

Student Response C

"American companies must develop more balanced work environments for their employees [because of] the major health risks posed by deskbound positions." Gabrielle Lenhard calls for American business to build more health-conscious work environments in her essay "Stepping Towards a Better Balance," arguing that such environments are beneficial to both employee and employer. Leonard supports this thesis with a series of facts and examples, clear pictures and analogies, and demonstrated credible knowledge of this topic.

Lenhard provides a series of examples and facts to give her argument a logical foundation. She begins this essay with an explanation of the proliferation of desk jobs as a logical continuation of technology development "from homo sapient harpoons to the Samsung Galaxy," showing this issue is imminent and important. She follows by citing "Dr. James Levine" in the third paragraph, whose study concluded that "those who used a greater amount of energy going about their daily lives remained leaner, demonstrating that promoting fitness is easy and companies have the power to improve their employees' health. She follows with examples of companies and employees attempting exactly this, such as the "online blogger Gina Trapani . . . switch[ing] to a standing desk," "company gyms, like those at Verizon," and "Houston Methodist [partnering] with Fitbit Wellness." These examples conclusively prove the feasibility of such changes, which with Lenhard's other facts logically supports her argument.

In addition to a logical foundation, Lenhard provides her readers clear images which persuade on a deeper level. In an example where she considers more ergonomic seating, Lenhard compares this to "simply putting a Band-Aid on a bullet wound" and explains "the problem isn't the chair, it's sitting in it." This clear analogy and concise description lucidly explains to Lenhard's audience the nature of this problem (sedentary desk jobs) and its solution (making employees sit less), making her argument clear and therefore more persuasive.

Lenhard additionally demonstrates her own credibility in order to support the conclusions which she argues for. With a personal anecdote, she writes "As head of the human resources department, I have received many complaints from employees about their backs aching after sitting . . . for over 8 hours a day." She demonstrates her familiarity with exactly the type of corporation plagued by this problem, which lends authority to her claim that balanced work environments are helpful to employees and employers.

Lenhard concludes her essay with a quote from D. Ron Goetzel, who says that "companies are a microcosm of society." She determines that "the same components that make up a balanced community must be present in a workplace," implying the significance of the corporate problem as a reflection on larger communities. At this point in the essay, we are not surprised by Lenhard's claim because we have already been persuaded by Lenhard's use of example solutions, clear imagery, and her own experience.

Student Response C: Score and Analysis

Reading: 4

This response accurately presents the author's main idea and notes Lehnard's emphasis on "health-conscious work environments" in the introduction. There are also a few more subtle responses to the central ideas of the prompt, such as the idea that a workplace problem is "a reflection on larger communities," which the writer presents in the conclusion. These insights justify the Reading score of 4.

Analysis: 4

This response uses well-focused body paragraphs to address the major elements of the essay prompt. While the first body paragraph effectively draws together related "examples and facts," the second and third excel by presenting substantial sentences from Lehnard's essay and subjecting them to concise yet rigorous analysis. This sophisticated and varied approach justifies the Analysis score of 4; note, however, that the body paragraphs are somewhat short, and that a reader who works mostly from first impressions of an essay may be inclined to grant a score of 3.

Writing: 4

This response is distinguished by variety in sentence structure, effective coordination of different topics, and especially its advanced but always appropriate vocabulary ("proliferation", "feasibility", "anecdote", "plagued"). This elegant and efficient writing style justifies the Writing score of 4.

PRACTICE ESSAY #2
HOW TO MAKE MONEY AND NOT DO ANYTHING STUPID
BY NELSON RANDALL

Student Response D

"Investing in the stock market can be described as the art of making money by doing nothing—and the less you do, the more money you make." Nelson Randall tells the reader there is no need to work in order to earn money. By mentioning the phrase "making money by doing nothing" he immediately grabs the attention of his whole audience because he is confident that everyone is interested in money. Nelson Randall goes on to explain about successful investors, risks in investing, and facts and statistics to persuade the reader to start gaining interest in the stock market. By doing this he still remains as a credible source.

Nelson Randall introduces the argument with compelling facts and statistics. He uses quotes such as "The stock market is designed to transfer money from the active to the patient." Nelson Randall uses Warren Buffett because he is one of the most successful investment businessmen in the world. Nelson Randall also quotes "It's far better to buy a wonderful company at a fair price than a fair company at a wonderful price." This is also another quote from former businessman Warner Buffett. By referring to quotes of a successful businessman, Nelson Randall is gaining the reader's trust because Nelson Randall uses information from a very accurate source. By giving out information from Warren Buffett, Nelson Randall is getting his audience more eager to start investing their money on the stock market.

Nelson Randall also attracts the audience by providing personal experience in his argument. He first states every investor's dream "All investors dream of putting money on a stock and watching it double, triple, or skyrocket in a few days." By saying this he show the outline of every investor's goal. But then Nelson Randall talks about reality "The truth is that this seldom happens; in forty years of investing it never once happened to me." The audience can now trust Nelson Randall with his honesty and can learn that investing in the stock market is not an easy task and involves high risk. Nelson Randall never mentions it's easy to make money in the stock market. He then provides his personal experience in investing on a biomedical company "Late in 2014 I bought shares of the biomedical company Incyte, which doubled in value roughly five months after I made my purchase. That was the closest I ever came." By saying this Nelson Randall gives an overview of how the stock market feels like when making a long term investment.

Nelson Randall also provides some information about himself and his experience with this issue. Nelson Randall states in the fourth paragraph "All investors (myself included) dream of putting money on a stock . . ." The reader now knows that the author has invested in stocks and has experience to know what is going on in the stock market. Therefore the information stated in his argument is trustworthy and reliable. Nelson Randall goes on about his personal experience about stock marketing and in the seventh paragraph he writes ". . . put some money on them, and stick around—which is what I have done, buying stock in telecommunications companies . . ." Nelson Randall has experience with stocks of telecommunication companies which gives the reader some experience with telecommunications.

In conclusion Nelson Randall states "The principle of approaching investments as an exclusively long-term game is nothing new." Nelson Randall gives a lot of information which is more than enough for the reader to start investing in stocks. Nelson Randall explains about long term and short term stocks and gains more support from the audience in doing so. By stating all of this information it is straightforward that the author is not any layperson when it comes to this sort of issue. Nelson Randall knows more than the average person about stock marketing therefore he is able to convince people to start investing to gain money without doing anything. The author concludes his argument with a quote he has stated in the beginning but uses repetition to make sure the reader remembers "from the active to the patient."

Student Response D: Score and Analysis

Reading: 2

This response demonstrates some grasp of the basic topic and of the author's main strategies (quotations from authorities) but does not actually exhibit strong comprehension of Randall's main argument. Randall's point is that long-term investments are optimal, not that individuals do not "need to work in order to earn money." This major lapse in comprehension explains the Reading score of 2.

Analysis: 2

This response incorporates some important quotations from the essay prompt; however, the author seldom analyzes these in much depth, and often provides only a single sentence in response to a major quotation. The second and third body paragraphs also both address the topic of "experience," creating a sense of repetition and disorganization in the essay. These deficiencies in treatment explain the Analysis score of 2.

Writing: 2

This response features several stylistic flaws, including weak or awkward transitions ("In conclusion") and a lack of variety in vocabulary and sentence structure. The writer also re-states the author's full name ("Nelson Randall") in a manner that becomes distracting. Such shortcomings justify the Writing score of 2.

Student Response E

"Investing in the stock market can be described as the art of making money by doing nothing—and the less you do, the more money you make." Here, Nelson Randall defines investments in stock markets as more valuable when left alone. In his essay "How to Make Money and Not Do Anything Stupid," Randall persuades his audience that long-term stock investments are worthwhile. He proves this through the use of effective examples and purposeful language, all the while maintaining a credible account.

The logical structure of Randall's essay helps persuade the reader of his claim. The bulk of his essay contains effective examples of investors who made money by waiting on their investments. In his second paragraph, he describes the stock market ventures of a "successful investment businessman of the twentieth century" who gained his fortune by investing in "noted brands and well-structured companies and watch them gain strength over time. The reader may aspire to be as successful as such an investor, and therefore will be more likely to believe the author. He does, however, introduce the story of Tim Grittani, who was one of the few investors who made a huge profit from short-term investments in "small, volatile companies." He uses this example as an opportunity to tell the audience that not all short-term investors are as successful, and people often "lose money on penny stocks and day trading." This acts as a reminder to the reader of the potential dangers of short-term investments, therefore making long-term investments seem like the more practical option. Since the audience yearns for a stable investing option, Randall's strategy of telling the stories of different investors was effective.

The language Randall uses also helps convince the reader of his argument. He begins his first paragraph by assuring the reader that he is "actually giving you a sound piece of advice" to show camaraderie towards the audience. This makes the reader regard the rhetor as a friend who genuinely wants to be helpful. He maintain use of personal pronouns and a friendly tone throughout the passage, insisting to the reader that "the alternative [to long-term investments] . . . will probably lose you money anyway." This was done purposefully to comfort the reader and to show the reader and the writer as on the same level. Moreover, Randall's use of strong diction strengthen his argument; he uses words with negative connotations to describe short-term investments, charging that they are "pitfalls" which have success or failure based on "market volatility." This can engrave the idea that these "day-trading" tactics are simply not as reasonable and much more dangerous than long-term investments in the stock market. By posing himself as a companion of the reader and using purposeful language, Randall effectively pulls the reader to his side.

Randall's personal experience further strengthens his argument. He presents his argument as a person who has participated in "forty years of investing" himself. He elaborates on this by . . . This assures the audience that Randall is familiar with the stock market industry and therefore adds merit to his claim. Furthermore, his use of technical language to explain stock market investments demonstrates his aptitude in this field. He defined several investment terms in order to guide the reader, such as day-trading, which is "investing based on . . . making daily buys and sells in the hopes of accumulating a profit." This ensures that Randall has stock-market expertise that the reader can rely on. The writer's background and use of technical language lend credibility to his argument.

Ultimately, Randall concludes that the reader should invest in a company that "[he or she] likes and trusts, put some money on them, [and] stick around" for optimal profit. He includes that though the detriments of "day-to-day financial posturing are evident to many," investors are affected by "media-driven fantasies" and urges the reader to make more worthwhile investment decisions, even if they don't seem as exciting. He adds a statistic to show the rate of failure, which is an immense "over 80%" of hedge funds, which rely on short-term day trading to show the reader it's true danger to investors. If Randall's examples, emotional language, and merit fail to persuade the reader, his last defense of the "quiet thrill" of long-term stock investments surely does the trick.

Student Response E: Score and Analysis

Reading: 4

This response features a brief but generally effective synopsis of Randall's main argument (investments are "more valuable when left alone") along with a firm grasp of the major rhetorical tactics that Randall uses to make his case. These strengths justify the Reading score of 4.

Analysis: 3

This response's body paragraphs are effectively distinguished from one another, since each one addresses a different major feature of Randall's writing. However, the analysis itself is open to refinement. For instance, the first paragraph signals the topic of people who "made money waiting on their investments" but then mostly discusses the pitfalls of day trading. The second paragraph, for its part, is devoted to the topic of "language," but moves from one language choice to the next without addressing any one tactic in depth. These flaws justify the Analysis score of 3.

Writing: 3

This response features a writing style that is generally clear and precise, but is not as impressive as it could be in terms of vocabulary or grammar. The writer seems to rely too much on short declarative sentences beginning with "The" or "This"; careful readers may also notice a few instances of subject-verb disagreement. These shortcomings, along with the disorganization of some of the body paragraphs, justify the Writing score of 3.

Student Response F

"All investors dream of putting money on a stock and watching it double, triple, or skyrocket in a few days." Here, Randall describes the common mindset of investors. In his essay, "How to Make Money and Not Do Anything Stupid," Nelson Randall convinces his audiences that long-term stock investments are worthwhile. He proves this by appealing to the audience through the use of compelling facts and statistics, citing reliable sources, and using purposeful language, all while maintaining a credible account.

Randall builds a convincing, logical argument through the use of facts and statistics. In the second paragraph, he writes, "the idea is to find sound investments that may not do much day to day, but will excel decade to decade." Randall uses this paragraph to explain how Warren Buffet, one of the most successful investors was able to make his fortune. By citing Buffet, Randall proves to the audience that investing in companies that make tons of money in the long term has made some people extremely wealthy. Later, Randall writes, "hedge funds, which rely on professional day trading as a fundamental business strategy, have underperformed the stock market at large." In addition, he writes "late in 2011, over 80% of hedge funds were operating at a loss." Randall uses this shocking statistic to alert the reader that even the biggest trading companies have lost money using the day to day trading strategy. All of this information can be used to bring the audience to the climax of is argument: people should take the path of long term investment instead of day trading.

The author also tells the stories of a few successful traders. For example, he writes about "Tim Grittani, who began trading a few thousand dollars worth of penny stocks in 2011 and had amassed $1 million by 2014." Grittani's story strengthens

Randall's argument that even people who start with very little can amass huge fortunes using long term investments. Continuing along the same line of though, Randall also informs the reader that the news does not accurately portray the success of penny stocks. While some have become successful through day trading, the majority of people "lose money on penny stocks and day trading" and "they may lose their entire investment." Randall purposefully uses these quotes to make the reader cautious of the dangers of day trading and skillfully encourages them to pursue long term investing instead.

Randall's background further adds to how convincing his argument is. The reader learns early on in the essay that Randall is not simply a layperson when it comes to this issue. He tells us that he has firsthand knowledge. As Randall writes in the fourth paragraph, "Late in 2014 I bought shares of the biomedical company Incyte, which doubled in value roughly five months after I made my purchase." Here, the author describes the time when he made a lot of money in a short amount of time. However, he tells the audience that this only happened once. This shows that he as an engaged writer is an active investor himself. The reader is more likely to believe him because he knows more than the average person does about this issue. The fact that he is knowledgeable helps lend credibility to his argument.

Ultimately, Randall concludes that "seeing firsthand how the stock market transfers money 'from the active to the patient' has its own quiet thrill." And the reason we, as readers, accept his solution is that by the time he gives, it, he has already convinced us of his argument that being patient and using long term investment strategies will come with far greater benefits than being impatient and using short term investment strategies. If his logic, language, and credibility do not win over the reader, surely his final maneuver of assuring the readers and telling the audience to be patient does the trick.

Student Response F: Score and Analysis

Reading: 4

This response efficiently establishes early on that "long-term stock investments are worthwhile." While this statement is helpful, the high reading score can be better explained by the author's firm awareness of the strengths of "decade to decade" stock investments and the weaknesses of alternate approaches. This clear understanding justifies the Reading score of 4.

Analysis: 4

This response includes important quotations from throughout the passage and divides up its Analysis topics efficiently (logic of long-term investments; flaws of other approaches; Randall's background). The writer also excels at explaining the significance of the included evidence: for instance, the writer notes that Randall's stories are designed to make the reader "cautious of the dangers of day trading." Such insightful responses justify an Analysis score of 4.

Writing: 4

This response demonstrates an excellent variety in sentence length, sentence structure, and word choice. The phrasing is error-free and the vocabulary is vivid and precise ("patient," "maneuver") but not overly complex. Along with excellent paragraph structure, these strengths justify the Writing score of 4.

PRACTICE ESSAY #3
BRAIN DRAIN: THE DANGERS OF POP-PSYCH BY TALLIS MOORE

Student Response G

"Are you right brained or left brained?" According to Tallis Moore, a proffessor of psychology, there's no difference. This notion is repeatedly proven by Moore, as her use of paragraph structure, credible sources, and dynamic chose of working all prove that the pop-psych theory about "left brain and right brain" is ultimately inaccurate. By the end of the passage, the reader will also believe this, as methods and information used by the author leave no loose ends.

In the passage, Tallis Moore persuades the reader through her effective use of paragraph structure which, leaves no questions unanswered and solves all problems. She repeated states the claim which she then proves through the use of evidence, whether it be explaining how math and creativity fit into a "mixed bag" of both brain hemispheres, or how although the halves of the brain behave differently when separated, they both do the same thing in a regular full-brained human being. The effective deployment of this structure in her passage allows Moore to deny any counter argument that arises while further improving her own, causing the reader to stay attached to the passage and keep reading.

Additionally, Tallis Moore keeps her audience engaged and somewhat entertained, by appealing to their emotions through the use of rhetoric and mild humor. This can be seen as she poses the question "who says I can't be a trilingual CPA who paints watercolor landscapes on the weekends." In an attempt to chastise the popular belief of left sided brains and personalities versus right side personalities. The effect of rhetoric such as this keeps the reader entertained and amused, while still conveying and supporting the argument. This is akin to the multiple credible sources and evidence given by the author throughout the passage. She, herself being a proffessor of psychology, knows a great deal about the subject at hand. And the repetitive use of studies from institutions like the "university of Utah" where "1,000 brains" were subject to care full experiment, leaves no room whatsoever for the reader to deny or mistrust her claims.

Student Response G: Score and Analysis

Reading: 3

This response does mention the author's basic main idea (that the right brain and left brain theory is "ultimately inaccurate"), but creates confusion at other points. It is not clear, for instance, how the writer's idea that the "halves of the brain behave differently when separated" relates to Moore's basic thesis. Such moments of imprecision justify the Reading score of 3, and may even lower the Reading score to a solid 2 from some readers.

Analysis: 2

This response quotes important evidence from the passage, primarily in its second body paragraph, and attempts to explain how such evidence strengthens Moore's main point. However, the writer's own sentences of analysis tend to jumble important-sounding ideas together, rather than referring to the passage's information and carefully explaining the significance of such information to the reader. These deficiencies in handling justify the Analysis score of 2.

Writing: 1

This response exhibits considerable flaws in writing technique, including awkward and grammatically flawed sentences and abundant misspellings. Even a rushed or somewhat superficial reader will notice that the response lacks an effective conclusion and refers to author Tallis Moore by the wrong gender. These noticeable problems justify the Writing score of 1.

Student Response H

"Who says I can't be a passionate trilingual CPA who paints watercolor landscapes on the weekend?" Author Tallis Moore persuades his audience that the pop-psych theory about the "left brain and right brain" is ultimately inaccurate. The author convinces his audience in "Brain Drain, The Dangers of Pop-Psych" by incorporating statistics and facts, providing legit. examples, and choosing vivid language, all the while maintaining a credible profile.

Moore structures and organizes his essay in a logical and reasonable fashion. He starts by introducing his topic, explaining how "Internet" and "print media" has been predisposed to the idea that "there are two types of people in this world": the ones that are "right-brained" and the ones that are "left-brained." Moore introduces his topic so his audience has a sound understanding on the subject matter. He then poses a real life situation that he categorizes as a stereotype, before delving into the history of this stigma. The writer takes the readers back to "the 1960s" and how Roger Sperry found how "the two hemispheres had different levels of involvement in a variety of tasks." Moore incorporated this historical context to show where such information had risen from. He then continues to show how such information has been "undermined" and "directly contradicted" by modern research. This goes to show that the stereotype is flawed, but the idea has "caught on like wildfire." Moore continues to give examples of how both hemispheres of the brain are connected and both are needed to function, talking about how even math required "a number of discrete skills." The author acknowledges that there are "striking differences" in the two hemispheres, but activity is still "widely distributed." This further disproves the stigma of left and right. The logical reasoning of the essay leaves the reader agreeing with Moore's statement.

The author maintains credibility during his essay. He himself is a "professor of psychology," indicating that he is well educated in this topic and a reliable source. The author also uses real life examples like the classroom situation to show his experience in the matter. Moore is well-versed in this subject and is trustworthy about his information.

Moore uses vivid language carefully to simulate a feeling inside the reader. He questions the ridiculous "amorphous terms" such as "creative" and "rational." Moore uses such terms to show the unreasonable categorizing of each individual aspect, reminding readers that "art is . . . subjective." This goes to evoke emotions of how such arbitrary terms can be defined by such straightforward way of thinking. He created a sense of disbelief and an incredulous attitude toward the left and right brained pop-psych theory. Emotion is another aspect that will sway the reader to believe in Moore's ideas.

Author Tallis Moore uses logical reasoning, vivid language, and examples in his essay to convince his readers on the blasphemous left and right brained psychology. In his conclusion, he showed that not only was it wrong and contradictory, it also "[risks] ignoring the human being underneath." Moore adds this final tidbit of information to really drive home his argument. It was the one last push of his essay that combines all aspects of his writing piece. By the end of reading Tallis Moore's "Brain Drain: The Dangers of Pop-Psych," the reader is thoroughly convinced of the inaccuracy and flaws of the left-brained and right brained stigma.

Student Response H: Score and Analysis

Reading: 4

This response both addresses the basic argument of Moore's essay (the inaccuracy of the right brain and left brain theory) and makes a few other important points about Moore's overall position. For instance, Moore focuses on the topic of human individuality; the writer effectively accounts for this theme by referring to "the human being underneath" in the response's conclusion. Such firm yet subtle understanding justifies the Reading score of 4.

Analysis: 3

This response features a very strong first body paragraph, which effectively discusses the issues of logic and structure by incorporating key quotations from the essay prompt. However, the two that follow exhibit clear flaws, especially in comparison to the first. The second body paragraph only features a single quotation, while the third is imprecise about how Moore uses emotion, at least until the writer begins explaining the "sense of disbelief" that Moore aims to inspire. The presence of these too-brief discussions justifies the Analysis score of 3.

Writing: 3

This response is generally free of errors and displays a variety in terms of sentence length and sentence structure. It is likely, though, that readers will react poorly to the underdeveloped later paragraphs, the occasionally repetitive statements, and especially the presence of colloquial language ("legit.", "tidbit", "really drive home"). These shortcomings are not catastrophic, but they do justify the Writing score of 3.

Student Response I

"Are you right-brained or left-brained?" Tallis Moore asks the readers of his essay Brain Drain: The Dangers of Pop-Psych" this question to introduce the popular left- and right-brain personality dichotomy. He ultimately argues against this theory, which divides all personalities into creative ("right-brained") and rational/analytic ("left-brained"). Moore uses quotations from relevant scientific experts, carefully chosen wording, and demonstrated credibility and personal involvement to support his argument in this essay.

Moore quotes relevant psychologists and their studies to logically show that the modern theory differs from its original form and is inaccurate. He paraphrases the study from the 1960s, that "a team of researches under Roger Sperry" studied individuals whose left and right brains had been separated and found "notable differences." We see that Moore introduces the study show the modern incarnation of this theory has drastically altered: taking "the complex differences . . . enumerated [and] distill[ing]" them into something less accurate. Moore follows with quotations from modern experts who elaborate on the complicated inter-brain relationship, such as "Dr. Jeff Anderson," who found "it is not the case the left hemisphere is more associated with logic or reasoning more than the right." More uses all of this information to reach his conclusion that the pop-psych left/right brain concept is ultimately incorrect.

In addition to a logical structure. Moore also uses creatively chosen wording to imply this concept really is preposterous. He introduces the concept as one which "both Internet and print media have long been smitten" with. By using a word connected with irrational and spontaneous love, Moore implies the foolishness of the idea and reinforces the argument that it's not scientifically based. Similarly, Moore directly draws the readers into the argument with his sentences, including "Before you conclude that [the left/right brain concept] is true, keep in mind that. . . other activities are more widely distributed," forcing his audience to consider his argument actively. While this word choice's persuasive power is not obvious, it effectively convinces the reader of the argument.

Moore also demonstrates personal engagement in this topic, showing that he is a credible speaker. He writes how "I begin every first day of [psychology] class by asking my students who is right-brained" and still "hopes for" the student who "challenges the question." By showing his active participation in this topic's development, he demonstrates that his argument is coming from a credible speaker and is worth listening to.

Moore finishes his essay with the conclusion that "no personality test . . . can truly capture the fascinating complexity of the mind." The universal acceptance of such a statement—no one would say the human mind is simple—adds additional power to his argument that the pop-psych left/right brain concept is simplistic and inaccurate. Moore uses relevant expert quotations, careful word choices, and demonstrated credibility to persuasively argue and prove this conclusion.

Student Response I: Score and Analysis

Reading: 4

This response begins with a nuanced discussion of the Moore's overall objections to the theory of left and right brains, then presents lucid information about Moore's major tactics (expert testimony, logical structure, strong wording, personal engagement). Along with the intelligent analysis of "complexity" (another of Moore's main ideas) in the conclusion, these strengths justify the Reading score of 4.

Analysis: 4

This response features an extremely well structured first body paragraph. The writer uses this portion of the response to lay out the essence of Moore's logic, but the shorter second and third body paragraphs contain their own strong insights. The observation that Moore's word choices are designed to make the reader "consider his argument actively" is one instance of the writer's firm grasp of the significance of Moore's statements. Such efficient yet thoughtful work justifies the Analysis score of 4.

Writing: 4

This response is informed by a strong command of sentence structure, a lucid division of topics, and a clear ability to coordinate and integrate small, important pieces of evidence. Some rather uncommon essay elements (ellipses, brackets, dashes) are used in a correct and sophisticated manner. Together, these manifestations of writing aptitude justify the Writing score of 4.

PRACTICE ESSAY #4
THE ADJUNCT FUTURE BY PATRICK KENNEDY

Student Response J

"Anyone who enters adjunct teaching should be aware of the basic economics of the profession." Here, Patrick Kennedy is cautioning those considering adjunct teaching to understand that that profession can be deceiving. In his essay "The Adjunct Future," Kennedy proves that college student considering educational careers should be better informed to the realities of that career choice. He does so through the use of facts and statistics and purposeful language, all while maintaining a credible account.

Kennedy builds a convincing argument using facts and statistics. He opens up the essay with a testimonial from an adjunct professor who was "not even clearing $25,000 per year" even during the best of her working time. A salary as low as this during the "best of times" shows there is something wrong with the education industry. Kennedy then proves several statistics that are also alarming: An adjunct's salary comes out to roughly $2500 for a fifteen-week course, equally about $48 per hour. While that may seem like a lot, once factors such as travel, lesson-planning, conferences with faculty and students are added in, they can "turn what looks like a $48 per hour salary on paper to a barely-minimum wage salary in reality." Kennedy then acknowledges that using adjuncts is a brilliant idea, but only in theory, which brings us back to his main point that students thinking about educational careers should be better informed about them.

Kennedy's background further adds to how convincing his argument is. The reader learns early on that Kennedy has firsthand knowledge of this issue, being an adjunct professor himself. In the fifth paragraph, he warns that "if you haven't crunched the salary numbers . . . if you don't have good time management skills," don't even think about being an adjunct professor. Kennedy says this with such confidence because he understands the consequences of entering the field without being prepared. A reader is more likely to believe him because he knows more than the average person does about this issue, and has actually "learned . . . mostly through my own research that the economics of college and university teaching are mostly awful on the teacher's end." Being knowledgeable and thorough in his research helps lend credibility to his argument.

Ultimately, Kennedy concludes that adjunct teaching "pays off only if you can lecture largely from memory and streamline your grading and administrative work to a few hours a week." However, he doesn't leave the reader hanging at this point; he still provides hope for those interested in the educational field. And the reason we, as readers, buy his solution is because it comes at a time when we are receptive to it. If his facts, language, and credibility don't convince the reader, then surely his final maneuver of a call-to-arms does the trick.

Student Response J: Score and Analysis

Reading: 3

This response accurately indicates that Kennedy's main argument concerns career choices related to college teaching. However, the writer frequently resorts to repeating Kennedy's thesis verbatim (rather than noting any of its subtleties) and offers a muddled conclusion paragraph. These points of weakness justify the Reading score of 3.

Analysis: 2

This response includes important quotations, but subjects them to analysis that is mostly quick and superficial. Major pieces of evidence are too often followed by only a single sentence of examination, while the ideas in the first and second body paragraphs (facts and background, respectively) need to be related much more aggressively to Kennedy's negative outlook on the education industry. A third body paragraph is also necessary for full development, and together these noticeable flaws justify the Analysis score of 2.

Writing: 2

This response exhibits a writing style that is mostly free of errors but that does not include any especially impressive turns of vocabulary or sentence structure. The absence of a strong third body paragraph also hurts the quality of the response as a whole; after all, the writer mentions "purposeful language" in the introduction but never actually analyzes this feature of the passage. Shortcomings such as these justify the Writing score of 2.

"Today, a basic Google search of 'adjunct professors on food stamps' can yield hours . . . of reading," writes Patrick Kennedy as he argues that college students considering educational carriers should be better informed to the realities of that career choice. In "The Adjunct Future," Kennedy unveils the harsh reality of the education industry. He does so through the use of facts and statistics, including sound reasoning, and subtle purposeful language, all the while maintaining a credible account.

Kennedy includes a myriad of facts and statistics to build his argument. In paragraph one, he presents the tragic story of Margaret Mary Vojtko, "an adjunct professor of French" who "died underpaid and underappreciated." The author's purpose for presenting Margaret's death was to immediately provide the reader an example of an educator who lived a difficult life due to the realities of her profession, He then proceeds to explain how the education industry went "horribly wrong" by presenting the "time consuming" aspect of the job. The hours put into "travel, grading, lesson planning," and more trickles down a possible "$48 per hour salary" on paper to a barely-minimum-wage salary. Furthermore, he also shares the unfortunate reasoning that "using adjuncts, in theory, is a brilliant idea" as Universities benefit from paying "superstar" professors who have "no real commitment" six figure salaries at the expense of "resourceful" adjuncts. As the harsh reality of adjuncts emerges in the numbers, Kennedy's use of facts, statistics, and reasoning strengthens his argument.

The author's use of a subtle purposeful language and tactics further builds his argument. His initial story, although intended to introduce his prompt, managed to leave an emotional impact on the reader. Margaret's unfortunate story evokes sympathy and even shock at the fact that this woman who devoted her life to educating struggled "to afford cancer treatment and basic upkeep" due to her low salary as an adjunct professor. Although Kennedy uses some emotion-jarring words, his lack of overt emotional appeal is what enhances his argument. His stacato, factual, and direct tone resonates with the reader as they feel his urgency. Kennedy uses subtle language tactics to jar the readers emotions and pull them onto his side. The author enhances his credibility by showing he is knowledgeable about the issue as well as telling the audience a personal experience. Kennedy's factual tone and abundance of statistics shows the reader that he has a breadth of knowledge regarding the issue, which builds trust. Also, Kennedy shares the first-hand experience of actually being an adjunct professor along with his father, which only

[incomplete]

Student Response K: Score and Analysis

Reading: 3

This response effectively uses its first paragraph to present Kennedy's argument that students aiming to enter the education industry "should be better informed to the realities of that career choice." While the body paragraphs outline Kennedy's major devices, the response does not directly say much more about Kennedy's main ideas; perhaps this response simply cannot, since it does not have a firm conclusion. This incomplete discussion justifies a Reading score of 3.

Analysis: 4

This response demonstrates the writer's firm ability to present quotations and explain their significance, sometimes in subtle yet effective ways. The first body paragraph moves efficiently from discussing Margaret Mary Vojtko to discussing the larger mass of adjuncts who face similar predicaments, while the second succinctly explains the emotions at play in Kennedy's essay. These aptitudes justify the Analysis score of 4, though the quick and sketchy final paragraph would probably incline some readers to grant a score of 3.

Writing: 3

This response is mostly free of errors, is clear and precise in its phrasing, and is informed by considerable variety in sentence length and sentence structure. However, the writer's deficiencies in pacing and organization are apparent in the overly broad final body paragraph, which breaks off rather than leading into a proper conclusion. This noticeable flaw in approach justifies the Writing score of 3.

Student Response L

"Where did the education industry go horribly wrong?" Here, Patrick Kennedy laments the fact that educators are severely underpaid in spite of their efforts. In his essay, "The Adjunct Future," Kennedy argues that college students considering educational careers should be better informed to the realities of that career choice; he does so through the use of a logically structured argument, facts and statistics, purposeful language, and anecdotes, all while maintaining a credible account.

Kennedy builds a officially structured argument through the use of facts and statistics. In the third paragraph, Kennedy introduces the harsh reality that "76% of all college professors in the United States are 'adjuncts'—instructors who receive no tenure and . . . are paid primarily on a course-by-course basis." This statistic shows readers the truth about a respected profession: most educators in America are adjuncts who do not have a reliable source of income. Kennedy shows that this can be especially debilitating by citing a House of Representatives study—"most adjuncts . . . earn below the U.S. poverty line." Kennedy then explains that adjuncts earn so little because of their "time-consuming travel," turning "what looks like a $48 per hour salary . . . to a barely minimum wage salary in reality." Readers will mostly be alarmed by the fact that educators, who are teaching future generations how to improve society, are not being paid enough for their important job.

Moreover, Kennedy claims in the fourth paragraph that "the entire adjunct situation is a . . . sign of how poorly theory and practice line up." He addresses a potential counterargument about the soundness of the idea of adjunct professors, then quickly refutes it by indicating that "this is just where the theory fails, on multiple levels." All of this information brings the readers to the crux of Kennedy's argument: educational careers are laden with overlooked realities, of which interested students must be aware.

Kennedy's purposeful language and powerful anecdotes also help him convince the audience of his argument. He begins his essay with the story of Margaret Mary

Votjko, an adjunct professor who "died underpaid and under appreciated." Kennedy recounts how "the media was stunned to learn that Votjko was . . . a teacher, and further reports of the saddening conditions faced by American professors have proliferated." Kennedy includes this anecdote in order to draw sympathy from the audience, emphasizing Votjko's pitiful and "saddening" conditions. Additionally, in paragraph 5, Kennedy warns readers against participating in adjunct teaching. He writes, ". . . don't think about it if you expect adjunct to be anything more than an accompaniment to . . . primary employment." Kennedy directly addresses the audience in this paragraph in order to establish a closer connection. His assertive instructions, which order students not to "even think about [it] . . . if you don't have good time management skills," serve to directly influence their emotional resolve. Thus, tugging at the audience's heartstrings and utilizing words meant to jar the readers are effective techniques Kennedy uses to pull the audience to his side.

Kennedy's background further adds to the credibility of his argument. In paragraph 6, he mentions that he himself is an "adjunct professor in an English . . . program." The fact that Kennedy is one of the adjunct professors he writes about shows readers that he has first-hand experience in the situation. Thus, readers are more likely to believe him. He also informs the audience that he was able to avoid the horrors of college teaching because he "learned . . . that the economics of college . . . teaching . . . are mostly awful on the teacher's end," proving that he is knowledgeable enough in the issue to avoid the ghastly fate of other adjuncts. Kennedy thus demonstrates that he is not a layperson; he is, in fact, experienced and knowledgeable, which help lend credibility to his argument.

In all these ways, Kennedy uses a potent combination of logic, emotion, and personal credibility to show his audience the extent of the problems that adjuncts face, and to offer a way out of the current adjunct crisis by drawing on his own positive example.

Student Response L: Score and Analysis

Reading: 4

This response features a brief statement of Kennedy's main argument in the introduction. However, the writer's understanding of the essay prompt is by no means basic, as the well-developed body paragraphs and the insightful reference to Kennedy's "own positive example" in the conclusion show. Together, these strengths of comprehension justify the Reading score of 4.

Analysis: 4

This response demonstrates a firm command of Kennedy's most important evidence: the quotations are set up clearly and efficiently, and the writer excels at explaining the significance of Kennedy's writing tactics. In the second body paragraph, the writer firmly shows how Kennedy "quickly refutes" flawed ideas; in the third, the writer effectively explains that Kennedy addresses the reader to "establish a closer connection." Such clear yet subtle analysis of Kennedy's aims justifies the Analysis score of 4.

Writing: 4

This response is well-structured and virtually free of errors. While a few portions (such as the extremely short conclusion) may be open to improvement, the sophistication of the writing generally should be apparent to any reader. Particularly impressive is the writer's ability to use ellipses and brackets without in any way distorting the meaning of quotations. These signs of writing skill justify the Writing score of 4.

Made in the USA
Middletown, DE
23 June 2019